THE SCIENCE OF HAPPINESS

## Also by Amit Goswami

*The Self-Aware Universe*

*Science and Spirituality*

*The Visionary Window*

*Physics of the Soul*

*The Quantum Doctor*

*God Is Not Dead*

*Creative Evolution*

*How Quantum Activism Can Save Civilization*

*Quantum Creativity*

*Quantum Economics*

*The Everything Answer Book*

*Quantum Spirituality (with Valentina R. Onisor, MD)*

*Quantum Politics*

*The Quantum Brain (with Valentina R. Onisor, MD)*

*Quantum Activation: Changing Obstacles into Opportunities (with Carl David Blake and Gary Stuart)*

*See the World as a Five Layered Cake*

## Also by Sunita Pattani

*My Secret Affairs with Chocolate Cake*

*The Transcendent Mind*

# Quantum Psychology and the Science of Happiness

## LIVE QUANTUM, BE HAPPY

## Amit Goswami, PhD
## & Sunita Pattani, MSc

LUMINARE PRESS
WWW.LUMINAREPRESS.COM

First Published in March 2022
Printed in the United States of America

On the cover: *Daniely Brito* - Masters Graduate from our Educational Program in Quantum Science of Health, Prosperity and Happiness
Photo: Mayank Kukreja
Cover design: Debabrata Dey Biswas

Luminare Press
442 Charnelton St.
Eugene, OR 97401
www.luminarepress.com

LCCN: 2022906120
ISBN: 978-1-64388-958-0

*This book is dedicated to people who
are in search of happiness.*

*May everyone discover that there is a science
to guide them to the happiness they seek.*

# Table of Contents

*Preface* . . . . . . . . . . . . . . . . . . . . . . . . . . . . . . . . . . . 1

PART 1

## Introducing Quantum Psychology as A Science of Happiness . . . . . . . . . . . . . . . 5

1.  Introduction: Live Quantum, Be Happy . . . . . . . . . 7

2.  A Scale of Happiness . . . . . . . . . . . . . . . . . . . . . . . . 37

3.  Amit's Story: How A Quantum Physicist
    Found Happiness . . . . . . . . . . . . . . . . . . . . . . . . 55

4.  Sunita's Story: My Journey To Becoming
    A Quantum Psychotherapist . . . . . . . . . . . . . . . 67

5.  Can the Unconscious Be Scientific?
    Consciousness and the Two-Level Reality
    of Quantum Physics . . . . . . . . . . . . . . . . . . . . . . 79

6.  The Mystics Claim: "Experiencing"
    the Unconscious Oneness . . . . . . . . . . . . . . . . . 105

7.  The Multiplicity of Our Experiences . . . . . . . . . . 110

8.  Discovering Happiness Within the
    Mind-Brain Relationship . . . . . . . . . . . . . . . . . 124

9.  Happiness at the Chakras: Vital Energies
    and Their Relationship to the Body . . . . . . . . . . 137

10. Intuitions and Archetypes . . . . . . . . . . . . . . . . . 167

11. Regaining the Promise of Paradise . . . . . . . . . . . 177

12. The Science of Mental and Vital Creativity
    and Manifestation . . . . . . . . . . . . . . . . . . . . . . . 188

13. Reincarnation and Evolution: The Purpose
    of Human Life . . . . . . . . . . . . . . . . . . . . . . . . . . 199

PART 2

# From Neurosis to Normality to Positive Mental Health ........... 217

14.  Beginning the Journey:A Pedestrian Approach
     to Internalizing Quantum Psychology's New
     Contexts of Mental Health and Happiness ....... 219

15.  The Dichotomies:The Fundamental Clouds
     that Cover the Sun ....... 236

16.  The Brain Game: Handling Your Emotions ...... 252

17.  Emotional Trauma, the Subconscious
     and Belief Systems ....... 265

18.  The Four Fundamental Aspects of
     Emotional Healing ....... 278

19.  Keys to Unlocking Happiness for the
     Me-Centered You ....... 299

PART 3

# Happiness and Enlightenment ....... 325

20.  The Mid-Life Transition ....... 327

21.  Inner Creativity and Positive Mental Health ..... 332

22.  Balancing the Negative with Positive Emotions ... 337

23.  Exploring the Archetype of Love ....... 346

24.  The Archetype of Wholeness: A Pathway
     to Total Healing ....... 356

25.  Perfect Happiness:The Final Stage of Traditional
     Enlightenment ....... 369

26.  The Quantum Eight-Fold Way: Your Path
     to Happiness ....... 373

Recommended Reading ....... 379
Index ....... 385

# PREFACE

Ready to leave behind the many barriers that have prevented you from living life with more joy and less fear? Interested in discovering more meaning in your life, finding purpose and passion for living, along with a transformational approach to a quantum way of life and truly be happy? This book is positive psychology based on a quantum worldview-primacy of consciousness and integration of science and spirituality.

In the conventional approach based on *matter-is-everything* philosophy, the bottom line is this: a human being is a robotic zombie. In the transpersonal /spiritual approach in which consciousness is primary, the bottom line is: the human being is a disembodied spirit. Both approaches are clearly incomplete and the insights they provide a person for healing, happiness, and personal growth is quite limited.

In the materialist approach, happiness is tantamount to pleasure. You can relate to that. But what is pleasure in your experience? Pleasure is the positive feeling associated with sensing aspects of brain physiology. Yes, neuroscientists have figured out what these aspects of physiology consist of: the presence of certain neurochemicals (for example dopamine) and body hormones (for example oxytocin).

But of course, you experience happiness also in looking at a flower, hugging a child, or cuddling with your lover after sex. Why? You care, you are including the object in your consciousness; in other words, your consciousness has expanded. In this way, happiness as expansion of consciousness is distinct from pleasure. And here only conscious-based approach can help.

In this way, happiness is a subject where a scientific approach must integrate science and spirituality. This is a quantum psychology is needed based on the quantum worldview.

In this way, our extensive yet common sense approach is about a scientific integration of the material (eat, drink, and be merry) and spiritual (explore oneness and be happy) paths to happiness. The very fact that it took us a century to take psychology from its divided beginnings and mixed messages about psychological suffering and happiness to this integration of all the forces of psychology to one integrated science of happiness should speak volumes about the importance of this work. This new science's integrative power is derived from the fact that it is based on the ideas and concepts of quantum physics.

The aims of Quantum Psychology and The Science of Happiness are as follows:

- To explain how quantum physics helps us build a science of the human being with consciousness as the ground of being, and how quantum physics' integration of science and spirituality leads us to a science of happiness.

- To develop a science of your self-experience and to show how your free will and creativity works.

- To develop a science of all of your experiences of external and internal objects for you to get a grip on the ecology and hygiene of your psyche.

- To develop a genuine science of manifestation, specifically of the three I's of empowerment: Inspiration, Intention, and (creative) Insight.

- To outline why some people find it difficult to maintain psychological normalcy level of happiness (for example, due to trauma and addiction) and to explicate the healing process for them. Particular attention is given to the role of the subconscious and how quantum principles can help in healing.

- To provide an overarching framework that outlines the different facets required for wholesome emotional healing.

- To provide tools and techniques that will help you to apply quantum science to maintain normal mental health.

- To empower you to embark on a journey of personal growth and transformation towards positive mental health and emotional intelligence.

- To chart the transformational journey toward becoming an original, and to explore joy and happiness in the world in the form of what we call quantum enlightenment.

- And if you venture to seek spiritual enlightenment of perfect happiness, we dedicate a chapter to that subject also.

So then, it is with great joy and reverence for your journey, that we share our collective experiences and efforts, and urge you to live quantum and be happy!

Amit Goswami, Ph.D.
Sunita Pattani, M.Sc.

PART 1

# Introducing Quantum Psychology as A Science of Happiness

# CHAPTER 1

# Introduction: Live Quantum, Be Happy

Despite the promises of greater happiness based on buying the latest cell phone, right toothpaste, watch, brand of car or truck, hair coloring or jeans, the material world always comes up short, and yet people continue to look outward to fill the well of happiness that resides inside of them.

In May 2017, a Harris Poll surveyed 2,202 Americans ages 18 and older and found that only 33% of those surveyed said they were "happy." However, when asked if they would like to be "happier" nearly 90% responded "yes." Almost everyone wants to be happy, but how do we become happier in a world that seems at times to limit our happiness, let alone encourage and create ongoing, long-lasting, happiness no matter what life throws in our path? This book makes the case that there is a science of happiness, and if you follow the blueprint step-by step, you will experience increasing levels of happiness over unhappiness on a scientifically verifiable scale culminating in eternal happiness, a state of enlightenment.

This new science of happiness is based on quantum psychology that is emerging from the new quantum worldview that integrates science and spirituality. In 1989, I published a scientific paper proclaiming how quantum physics gets a paradox-free interpretation if the essence of spirituality—consciousness is primary-is integrated into science. Then, in 1993, I wrote the book *The Self-Aware Universe* which expanded on that concept, and now research on the quantum world-view has reached a stage that even the *Dalai Lama* is enthusiastic about it. "No model of reality is possible without quantum physics," he said.

Quantum physics, according to this correct (because it is paradox free) interpretation says, unequivocally agreeing with the spiritual traditions, consciousness is the ground of being and then adds a few novel insights. One new insight says, matter consists of waves of possibility of consciousness itself; consciousness chooses out of its possibilities the actu-ality of manifest matter in space-time reality and in the process separates itself into a subject and object(s).

Pretty powerful stuff.

That science and spirituality can be integrated still surprises a lot of people because they are used to sepa-rating the sacred (the domain of spiritual wisdom) from the mundane (the domain of scientific wisdom). But if you are familiar with psychology, this is hugely good news. Around 1900, Sigmund Freud discovered and propounded the idea of the unconscious—a domain of underlying reality—affecting our conscious behavior;

ever since psychologists have been divided into two factions: One has followed Freud to Jung, finally dividing into two separate forces: depth psychology and height psychology (aka transpersonal psychology) depending on how you want to visualize the "other" reality (the unconscious—outside space and time), underlying or up above. The other has stuck to a hard science everything-is-matter-moving in one domain of space and time view, initially as behaviorism and later as cognitive-behavioral science which is somewhat more inclusive of the nuances of our human experience.

If you are familiar with the esoteric side of the great spiritual traditions, especially some of the Eastern traditions, this discovery of an integration of science and spirituality should not surprise you. According to these traditions the sacred and the mundane are not really separate; it is all sacred. In the new quantum science we say, it is all a play of consciousness which is the ground of all being.

From this perspective, that psychology should be a science of happiness is to be expected. Heed the message of *Vedanta-Hinduism*. Vedanta defines consciousness as sat (Sanskrit for existence), chit (Sanskrit for conscious awareness), and *ānanda* (Sanskrit for joy). *Vedanta* flatly declares, the goal of life is joy, happiness, *ānanda*. *Vedanta* is not alone; Taoism has the same message. Go with the flow and be happy. And among the Judeo-Christian religions, the message of the Jewish Kabbala is the same—the goal of life is living joyfully.

Transpersonal psychology is based on the same metaphysics as *Vedanta*—consciousness is the ground of all being. Thus, it is not surprising that that this psychology is an outgrowth of Abraham Maslow's empirical discovery that classified the human health into three groups: 1) mental illness or subpar; 2) normal; and 3) positive mental health. This is the first attempt to recast psychology as a science of happiness if we allow that people who suffer from mental illness (psychosis and neurosis) are at the lowest level of happiness—very little happiness and mostly suffering; people are normal when happiness and suffering is roughly half and half; and people of positive mental health live more happiness than suffering.

On close examination, some more details follow. People who are psychotic cannot be said to experience any happiness at all. Furthermore, they are pretty much unresponsive to therapy. However, neurotics have some happy times; with help they can recover.

And then again, brain research shows that our brain is disposed to be five times more negative than positive. Consider. Your brain gives you: 1) a machine-like tendency to process information alone and no meaning, a tendency that has a "dumbing down" effect; 2) *me-centeredness*, a tendency to make all relationships transactional—what is in it for me? 3) negative emotional brain circuits with memory/software of negative emotions such as fear, anger, jealousy, competitiveness, domination, etc.; 4) pleasure circuits that can lead to addiction—trying to enhance pleasure is a major source of addiction.

In this way, what we call normal more reflects a medical point of view; those people are normal who do not need therapy on a regular basis.

Further examination also reveals that positive mental health comes to people only if they do some consciousness-expanding exercises, meditation being the principal among them. In other words, just as transition from neurosis to normal require some kind of psychological healing, reaching positive mental health from normal requires some kind of transformation.

Behavioral/cognitive approach to psychology regards human being as a mechanical machine, as an epiphenomenon of the brain. As such, although there have been claims that (read B. F. Skinner's novel *Walden II*) people live happily in a machine-like state, given the discoveries above of brain science, nobody needs to take those early claims seriously. However, the positive psychology of recent times that has emerged from Harvard without making any explicit break with establishment materialist science not only is to be taken seriously but also applauded. Hopefully, this is setting a trend.

Quantum psychology and the science of happiness that we build in this book is a natural fruition of that trend. What positive psychology recognized is that the negativity of our brain can be overruled with simple attitudinal shifts and recognition of the importance of transformation and transformative exercises. We propose in addition that the attitudinal shift is accompanied by a belief system re-visioning that puts creativity and experiences of feelings in the body in the equation of transformation. This re-visioning is demanded because quantum physics and neuroscience data are demonstrating that we are not merely a brain, we are instead made of consciousness embodied in the brain as well as in the body. We show that if you follow through the transformative exercises of positive psychology to achieve positive mental health with the newly discovered quantum principles fundamental to the quantum worldview, then there are several more peaks of happiness waiting for you in potentiality only to be redeemed.

The key to new science of happiness is quantum psychology—a tour de force integration of all the psychologies developed before often using widely different metaphysical beliefs.

To give you feel for the enormity of what we have accomplished, let's go back to the basics once more.

## Matter-Based and Consciousness-Based Psychologies of Happiness

You might be surprised to know the news above that establishment science now has a psychology of happiness or what is increasingly called a positive psychology. If you doubt why this is already big news think again. Twenty years ago, as of this writing I went to a conference on consciousness in Bangalore, India, and a yoga psychologist by the name of Uma Krishnamurthy who was a speaker, introduced the subject thus (and I paraphrase):

"When I was a graduate student in psychology, I asked my professor what mental health is. The professor said, that is a big subject for me to answer. Check the library. I went and looked and looked; but all I found were books on abnormal psychology, neurosis, and psychosis, and reading these books made me kind of depressed. And the answer to the question, what is normal mental health? was not to be found in any of those books. So, I went home, and read a book on yoga by Swami Vivekananda, and that book lifted my depression in no time. So, although I did get my degree in psychiatry for the sake of credentials, I practice only Yoga Psychology."

As this psychologist noted, even a few decades ago books on traditional academic psychology were heavily biased toward the negative although the branch of transpersonal psychology did talk about positive mental health which is another name for a condition of more happiness than unhappiness. However, the subject of positive psychology took off when a Harvard professor Martin Seligman started writing about and teaching what he called positive psychology. Seligman's psychology was not yoga psychology (a psychology developed in ancient India around 100 A.D. based on meditation and creativity) by any means; his worldview remains more or less what we call material monism—all is matter. But still a psychology that emphasizes the positive over negative, happiness over unhappiness within mainstream is a breakthrough of sorts. Some see it as a step toward the integration of materialist science and religion. The psychologist Lisa Miller's anthology, *The Oxford Handbook of Psychology and Spirituality* is an excellent resource if you want to further explore this idea.

The philosophy of material monism is built around objects; behind everything are material objects and their interactions. Scientists of this ilk state that the world is made of elementary particles, little chunks of matter. Elementary particles make bigger objects called atoms, atoms make molecules, big molecules make the living cell; cells called neurons make the brain. Its objects all the way up! If the brain produced consciousness, it would also be an object (*Figure1*).

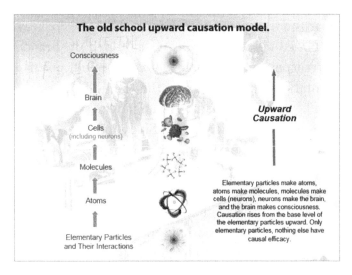

*Figure 1: Reductionist picture of the brain and consciousness*
*If consciousness were a brain product, it would be an object.*

The field of experience has two poles: subject and object. Who (or what) am "I," the subject? What is the explanation of the subject, the "I" that you experience with when you experience happiness?

So, it is tricky to talk about positive psychology within the worldview of material monism that holds humans are just a *physical body* and brain and material interactions within the brain and the body produce all phenomena including experience. Why is this tricky? Because to repeat, in that worldview, experiences cannot exist. Interactions between objects can only produce bigger and bigger conglomerates of objects; but experiences, as explained above, have two poles: a subject that experiences and objects that are experienced. So, materialists denigrate experiences and especially experiencers: they are ornamental associations of material phenomena with no causal consequence. But of course, turning the average brain dictated negative perspective of people (the brain gives us five times more negativity than positivity) to a positive one certainly would require some causal power of the experiencer who is making the shift!

Simply ask, without the "you," who is checking the validity of this statement? Without your "you, who is sorting out worldviews? And does it not have causal consequences such as changing your entire lifestyle?

Without the "you" that experiences happiness, does happiness matter anyway? Through subtle (if not deceptive reasoning), you may try to convince yourself (as majority of scientists still do), that somehow brain interactions make it appear like it is a subject experiencing an object, but if you don't have an axe to grind (like these scientists often do) this rationalization will not satisfy.

Yoga psychology of the old and transpersonal psychology (and depth psychology as well) that was developed in the 1950's and 1960's, hold a very different view of reality. As mentioned already, these psychologies have the worldview that consciousness is primary. Instead of holding matter is everything, yoga psychology or transpersonal psychology holds the worldview that consciousness, on the ground level of existence, is a "oneness" of everything. According to this worldview, the "great chain of being"—material body (the source of sensing), life (the source of vitality), mind (the source of thinking meaning), soul (the source of higher experiences), spirit (the source of oneness experiences)—all arise from one being, but that ground of being—consciousness—is inclusive. In material monism, only sensing is legit, all experiences are epiphenomena of the brain and what it gathers by sensing.

But one important question remains unanswered in the consciousness-based worldview and the psychologies based on it. How does separateness and diversity arise if oneness is all there is?

According to speculations of yoga psychology, consciousness uses a "force" (called by the Sanskrit word *maya*) to produce the illusory trick; through the action of maya, consciousness makes it appear to itself that it has divided itself into a subject experiencing objects;

in this way experience happens. Bottom line is, experiences are illusory appearances. Hence, to find ultimate happiness, we must go beyond these experiences and find oneness. That will make you enlightened and happy. But once again that confusing question, who is being happy if there is no separate you?

The immediate problem, as it relates to all the above-mentioned approaches to happiness psychology is this: Either these psychologies are entirely matter-based; consciousness, mind, happiness, love, and all that is considered "brain epiphenomena. "In this view, you are a little more than a philosophical robot, a "hu-machine," (a term coined by authors Nada R. Sanders and John D. Wood) basically a robot/machine with causally impotent experiences. This group of psychologies' discourse about happiness makes sense in a mechanical way as synonymous to pleasure.

Or the psychology that is consciousness-based, matter is ignored. In that view, consciousness is regarded as nonmaterial, that part is good. Consciousness as a form of "oneness" is also a good idea and it agrees with our experience that expansion of consciousness makes us happy. But how this nonmaterial *One Consciousness* relates to the material brain and the body is left out except to say that there are separateness producing agencies. So, now you are theorized to be a disembodied holistic spirit with a separateness producing force but you in your everyday consciousness have no idea if you can access the spirit or how to access it or if accessing it will take you beyond separateness and toward wholeness and make you happy. In this way, all the consciousness-based psychologies are mostly one-sided science, mostly empirical. Do practices and find out.

Obviously, both approaches above raise tantalizing possibilities but do not deliver much of a result; most importantly, being incomplete, they just don't satisfy. They cannot empower you with conviction for much psychological transformation for finding your way to increase your happiness level either.

The good news is, (and why you are reading this book) there is now many integrative scientific ideas, quantum physics the one among them that binds them together, on which to base an integrative science integrating science and spirit appropriate for normal people of the world looking for lasting happiness. The brain has a causal role to play in your life no doubt, but so does your consciousness and how it manifests in the brain and in the body. In this way, the book you are holding in your hand holds the potential to supply you with definitive, satisfying, scientific answers to some of the most important questions of science today. What is consciousness? What is the science behind manifest experiences in conjunction with material bodies? How do you make over this consciousness-matter duo, so that you are undoubtedly, unequivocally increasingly happy?

This both-matter-and-consciousness validating quantum psychology that we explicate here also illustrates how your free will and creativity work together to manifest new potentiality in your life. It tells you where the purpose of your life comes from or the meaning that you seek; it tells you about the scope of your individual development, even about your agenda of personal growth in increasing happiness.

One comment in passing. Today, there is an explosion of simple self-help ideas for taking you to happiness that promises, "things don't have to be hard to be good." So, for example, one idea is, you intend, and then just wait. This is all the secret of the science of manifestation that you need to know. Another one: good stuff is attracted to you; all you need to do is develop a sensitivity. Are such ideas scientific? Yes, but they are not the whole story. They are misleading. They remind me of an old-world Hungarian story.

*A man goes to a curiosity shop and is looking around, and comes across an interesting object, but does not know what it does. When he takes it to the shopkeeper, the shopkeeper looks at the label and says, "It's a barometer." The man is impatient. "Yeah, I too saw the label. But what is a barometer? What does it do?" The shopkeeper says, "With its help you can tell if it is raining." "How?" Now the shopkeeper is at a predicament; he doesn't know. But he comes up with this answer. "See, take this barometer to the window, hold it in your hand and put it outside and then pull your hand back in. If the barometer is wet, you can tell it is raining."*

*But the guy scoffs, "I can do that with my bare hands!" The shopkeeper says gravely, "But that sir, would not be scientific, would it?"*
*The shopkeeper's idea is not wrong, is it? It is just not the complete story of how a barometer really works. A fully developed science that can be verified by experimental data is needed to get the whole scoop. This is why quantum psychology, and a science of happiness is needed.*

## Quantum Physics: One or Two Domains of Reality?

A quick review of the two groups of psychology. The materialist group, positive psychology included, works on one level of reality: matter moving in space and time. The other group, including ancient yoga psychology and modern depth psychology and transpersonal psychology, holds that there are two levels of reality: 1.) Domain of Oneness reality, (call it consciousness;) and 2.) Domain of Separation, including the split between subjects and objects.

Even at a first glance, quantum physics supports the idea of a two-level reality rather than the one level reality (space-time) of scientific materialism and (also) Newtonian physics that scientific materialism is based on.

Consider. In quantum physics, objects are waves of possibility; only when they are measured, do they manifest as actuality, as particles. Where do the waves

reside before measurement? Werner Heisenberg, a
co-discoverer of quantum physics, maintained that
they reside in a domain of potentiality outside of
space and time, and he was correct. And as if this is
not enough by way of explanation, an idea from the
physicist Niels Bohr clarifies the situation. The two
realms—potentiality and space-time actuality—are
not connected in any continuous way. It takes a discontinuous transition—a quantum jump, Bohr's phrase—
for waves of possibilities to convert into particles of
actuality. And to top it off, the idea of quantum object
being waves in a transcendent domain of potentiality
outside space and time has been verified by myriad
experiments, starting with Alain Aspect and his collaborators in 1982. The notion of quantum jump has
also been verified.

Confused? How does one verify there is an "outside" space and time? How does one visualize a quantum leap? In space and time objects communicate via
signals all of which travel at the finite speed of light
or less. So, all communication takes a little time. In
contrast, in the domain outside space and time, communication can be signal-less, instantaneous. This
idea of signal-less instant communication is called
quantum nonlocality.

To visualize discontinuous quantum leaps, think
of Niels Bohr's picture of how atomic electrons jump
from one atomic orbit to another (*Figure2*).

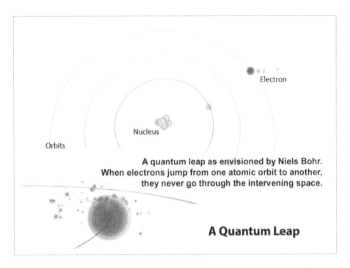

*Figure 2: A quantum leap- when an electron jumps from one atomic orbit, it never goes through the intermediate space: instead, it jumps discontinuously*

They disappear from one orbit and reappear in the other, never going through the intermediate space.

I used the word "transcendent" above to remind you that the idea of a transcendent level of reality as opposed to the immanent level where we live is as old as all our spiritual traditions that have been talking about reality in this way for at least five millennia. This is the way yoga psychology based in *Vedanta* and depth and transpersonal psychology define existence at the ground level.

Around the turn of the twentieth century, two prominent psychologists, Sigmund Freud and Carl Jung gave us the ideas of personal and collective unconscious respectively. You know from personal experience that unconscious, both kinds, is important for the functioning of your psyche. Your neurotic tendencies, impulsiveness for example comes from your personal unconscious. And your collective unconscious presents you with evocative transformative symbols in your dreams. Now ask yourself: since conscious awareness pertains to the space-time reality, where is the unconscious located? It has to be outside space and time, right? Materialists deny this, there is no outside space and time; positing unconscious gives you voodoo psychology; we don't need it, it is all in the brain, they say. It is the brain that acts mostly in the unconscious, and a little bit in the conscious. This is the materialist's position. Never mind that they cannot explain how the brain can act in two modalities when it should always be unconscious.

But never fear the materialist, quantum physics is here. The quantum concept of nonlocality is the one-word summary of the two-level reality, and it is experimental fact.

Transcendent-immanent, unconscious-conscious, unmanifest potentiality-manifest actuality, nonlocality-locality-how many times do we have to discover the wheel before it gets accepted by our mainstream scientists?

So, in this book, with quantum physics to guide us we develop a science for some of the phenomena of consciousness that baffle the researchers of psychology and cognitive neuroscience: the unconscious, the self, and the self's experiences, especially experiences of happiness as an expansion of consciousness.

## Objects of Your Experiences

Let's now deal with the question: what are the objects of your experiences? What you experience as "outer material objects" come to your awareness through your senses, no confusion about those. What you call psyche is made up of your internal experiences and here there is plenty of room for confusion. At first glance, as Rene Descartes said a long time ago, "I think, therefore I am," your internal experiences seem to consist of objects that we call thought, and we conventionally associate an entity called the "mind" with it. Thoughts are mental objects and if thoughts are the only objects of the psyche, then psyche is one and the same as the mind. But what is the mind? Is mind different from the body as it experientially seems to be? If so, how? If it is different, if mind is nonmaterial, how does nonmaterial mind interact with the material body? They have nothing in common. If you posit a mediator such as a signal, where then is the mediator? These questions have not been very easy to answer. Not for you, and not for philosophers.

And if you look carefully at your thoughts, the problem gets worse! Because all thoughts, you will notice, are not the same. There are those thoughts that we call rational thoughts; we recognize them as the product of step-by-step logical algorithmic thinking.

But then, there are some special thoughts-emotional thoughts-that come with a lot of passion, which we often call "energy"- is it however- physical energy? If this energy is nonphysical—some people call it vital energy and call the experience of it "a feeling" but then again, the same puzzle, how does the nonphysical energy interact with the physical body?

The confusion gets even worse upon further inspection. There are still other thoughts that are a little rarefied, but everybody has them all right at least on occasions; we call them intuitive thoughts. Their specialty is that they come with truth-value; something rings so true about them that even without being able to rationally back them up, you want to follow them through to find something deep about reality, about yourself. And if you become sensitive to your body while you have these intuitive thoughts, sooner or later you will recognize feelings in your body when these intuitive thoughts arise. For example, you may recall feelings that you call a "gut feeling" perhaps energy in your naval area, or tingles in your heart area, when you last intuited. Or like the poet William Wordsworth, you may feel "a presence that disturbs me with the joy of elevated thoughts." What does that mean?

A millennia old idea given by Plato is that entities called archetypes visit us in these experiences of intuition; that is the presence that Wordsworth is talking about. And intriguingly, Plato says that the archetypes-love, beauty, truth, self, abundance, power, goodness, justice, wholeness, to name the important ones-are timeless; they do not change with time or culture. We call them Platonic archetypes.

So, the ecosystem of the psyche is more complicated than first meets our eyes. Descartes made an error ignoring feeling and intuition. It seems that we have four different kinds of experiences: sensing, this one is physical; and then thinking, feeling, and intuition. Those last three make up the objects of the psyche.

Our conventional science (let's call it old science) recognizes only the experience of sensing without any challenge. Old science can deal with the experience of thinking with the added assumption that all aspects of thinking are computable and that the brain (which produces thoughts according to the old science) is a computer.

But this, too, has a discernible problem and you can readily relate to it. Thoughts have two aspects: content and meaning as a sentence of grammar has two aspects: syntax and semantics. Computers can represent meaning as software using their hardware symbols. But, if such programmed meaning was all that we were capable of processing, what accounts for creativity—the invention and discovery of new meaning?

What about our feelings? Some feelings, research shows, certainly have brain associations; there indeed are brain molecules associated with some of our feelings. For example, endorphins are related to your experiential "high." But what accounts for visceral feelings, feelings that are associated with body organs?

For example, what is the explanation that you feel love in the region of your heart that Easterners refer to as the heart chakra?

Where do intuitions come from? As you get familiar with this aspect of your experience, you will notice that what we intuit, we value greatly. There are intuitive objects we variously call truth, love, beauty, justice, goodness, power, abundance, wholeness, self, they are some of the things we value most among our experiences. There is no way the old science can explain intuition as brain phenomena; these values are not computable.

This much is clear; we need a new science that includes all of our experiences including that as the subject or self. As it stands right now, cognitive-behavioral approach assumes the brain as cognizer, talks about thinking as information processing by a computer of artificial intelligence, leaving meaning out, leaving creativity out, ignores feelings in the body. The transpersonal group has room for consciousness and self and mental and intuitive/spiritual experiences but in a dualistic ad hoc way that ignores the role of the brain and the body; in this way, they miss the objective rational part of our cognizing including the behavioral ego, and also the feeling/emotional part. They, too, leave out the nuances of the creative experiences.

Quantum science says that our primary reality is potentiality, the domain that we call unconscious. In quantum science, we assert that all our experiences, not only material but also thinking, feeling, and intuition, come from the manifestation of quantum potentialities of unmanifest consciousness or the unconscious.

Unconscious is the source of a causal force that converts potentiality into experience. Some people call this causal force a quantum field, nonlocal and nonmaterial to be sure. In *Vedanta* this causal force is called maya. In a somewhat diluted context, in Christianity this causal force is called downward causation. I choose to call this separateness-producing causal force downward causation because it is in nice contrast to material forces that can be called upward causation because cause rises upwards from the elementary particles to the brain (see *Figure1*).

It is straightforward to see what this causal force of downward causation consists of—choice—once we have identified the source as consciousness in the form of the unconscious. Notice that a wave of possibility means an entity of many facets. When we say, an electron is a wave of possibility we mean an object of many possible positions. The actualized electron of an experiment has only one of those possible positions. So downward causation consists of consciousness in the state of the unconscious choosing one facet out of the many, one position out of the many possible positions in the case of our electron.

Consciousness creates the material experience by choosing from a material many-faceted wave of possibility that one facet that we find for the object of our material experience. It is equally straightforward to see how our other experiences—feeling, thinking, intuiting—are created. Consciousness creates its other experiences the same way, choosing from their respective potentialities. A wave of possibility of the mind has many possible meanings; consciousness creates the experience of a thought by choosing one of those meanings. And so forth.

What about the experiencer, the I-subject of the experience? This is where the brain enters. Quantum science shows that in every event of choice from potentialities of objects, consciousness uses the brain to experience it with, in the process identifying with the brain.

Earlier, I mentioned the experience of spirit. In quantum science, spirit is the "I" that you can experience in the immediacy of choice from potentiality to actuality in response to a stimulus; it is called *the quantum self*. There is oneness in this experience, bringing joy. Your normal ego-experience of the same stimulus is the result of reflection in the mirror of previous memory.

Materialists miss; they get lost in matter (brain) and the behavioral ego and the pleasure they bring—"eat, drink and be merry" kind of pleasure. Spiritual traditions have always maintained that the journey to happiness consists of looking inward—exploring the experiences of the psyche. The new science agrees with both recipes: looking outward if done in moderation can give us positivity; looking inward to the experiences of the psyche of course brings you closer and closer to the spirit, the quantum self, and you experience expansion of consciousness and joy (*Figure 3*).

*Figure 3: Three views of happiness*

Behold! Before experience, consciousness is really un-consciousness—one undivided nonlocal existence without subject-object polarities that we call unconscious. But note that this unconscious is of much greater scope compared to the concept's earlier use by Freud and Jung. Freud's concept of the unconscious now can be recognized as our personal unconscious—the repository of potentialities that we have previously experienced personally, our personal memory. Jung's collective unconscious refers to humanity's collective memory; it was made when humans lived in nonlocally connected communities. But in the new usage the unconscious refers to all quantum potentiality, previously manifest as well as never before manifest. We call the unconscious of never before manifest potentiality quantum unconscious.

## Choosing Happiness

If consciousness chooses experience, then why can't everyone choose happiness? You can choose emotional well-being instead of neurosis, you can choose happiness instead of negativity, you can choose to pursue meaning and purpose and opt out of the information and pleasure-as-happiness culture that does not satisfy. All you need is congruence of your personal choice with that of the One Consciousness in the form of the unconscious. In old parlance, all you need is to get God on your side. For that, you need to know what keeps you away from establishing congruence and remove these obstacles. You also need the science and art of creativity, of transformation that takes you toward congruence.

## Breaking News: Experimental Data

The message of the spiritual traditions, yoga psychology, depth and transpersonal psychologies is conveyed by two radical assertions that are beyond ordinary experiences: 1) There is oneness in potentiality via which we are all potentially interconnected; and 2) Beyond the ego, there is an inner transpersonal self with the flavor of unity. The new science, while giving scientific basis to these assertions, makes them into predictions that can be experimentally verified: 1) There is potential oneness that interconnects our brains; 2) The brain acts in two different modalities:

a) the quantum modality and b) the ego modality. The breaking news is that both of these predictions of the new science have been verified.

The experiments by the University of Mexico neurophysiologist Jacobo Grinberg-Zylberbaum and his collaborators and some two dozen others directly support the idea of quantum nonlocal connection between human brains; these experiments are the equivalent for macroscopic brains of the Aspect experiment in submicroscopic realm.

Typically, in these experiments, two subjects are instructed to meditate together for a period of twenty minutes in order to establish a "direct communication" without exchange of signals that quantum physicists call correlation or entanglement. Afterwards, they enter separate Faraday chambers (enclosures that block all electromagnetic signals) while maintaining their meditation on direct communication for the duration of the experiment. The subjects' brains are connected to individual electroencephalogram (EEG) machines. One of the subjects is now shown a series of light flashes that produce electrical activity in his or her brain. From the brain waves detected by the EEG attached to this brain, experimenters extract a signal called an evoked potential upon computer-aided elimination of noise. But amazingly, in about one in four cases, EEG measurement of the unstimulated brain also shows electrical activity producing an EEG signal, a "transferred" potential quite similar in shape and strength to the evoked potential (*Figure4a*).

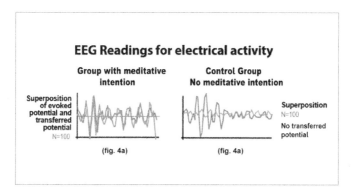

*Figure 4: The Grinberg experiment*
*a) Subjects who meditate with intention show transferred potential*
*b) control subjects: no transferred potential*

Control subjects who do not meditate together or are not able to establish and maintain direct communication never show any transferred potential (*Figure4b*). The straightforward explanation is quantum nonlocality-the two brains act as a nonlocally "correlated" or "entangled" quantum system of oneness. In response to a stimulus to only one of the correlated brains, nonlocal quantum consciousness actualizes close-to-identical states in the two brains: hence, the similarity of the brain potentials.

## Brain Evidence for the Quantum Self: Synchrony in the Brain and the 40 Hz Brain Waves

The evidence is clear, and the whole matter of the quantum self has also now been settled by neuroscience data in favor of its existence.

The evoked potential mentioned before in connection with the transferred potential experiment is related to the light flashes that the subject was shown; for that reason, it is also referred to as event-related potential (ERP). Brain wave data, for many years, have been revealing the P300 potential, recorded on the scalp 300 milliseconds after the event/stimulus. This is usually considered as an unconscious event which is however a precursor of a conscious event like a verbal report some few hundred milliseconds later. In a paper written with Jacobo Grinberg many years ago but published only recently, I had speculated that this P300 ERP has got to be associated with the primary perception of the quantum self and the later what neuroscientists call the conscious event, is associated with our conditioned ego.

More recently, neuroscientists have learned how to put microelectrodes deep inside the human brains of epileptic patients. Much to our scientific surprise, these measurements by microelectrodes reveal a sudden burst of approximately 40 hertz oscillation (called a gamma brain wave) immediately following the P300. This is the signature of conscious awareness of the primary quantum self. Why? Because apparatuses in distant areas of the brain are simultaneously communicating in synchrony suggesting quantum nonlocality.

The famous biologist Francisco Varela agrees. In a report to the Dalai Lama about recent progress of neuroscience he said:

*"When we perform a cognitive act-for example, we have a visual perception-the perception is not a simple fact of an image in the retina. There are many, many sites in the brain that become active. The big problem, Your Holiness, is how these many, many active parts become coherent to form a unity. When I see you, the rest of my experience-my posture, my emotional tone-becomes all one unit. It is not dispersed, with perception here and movement there.*

*How does that happen? Imagine that each one of the sites in the brain is like a musical note. It has a tone. Why a tone? Empirically, there is an oscillation. The neurons in the brain oscillate all over the place. Each goes whoomph and then ffhhh. The whoomph is when different places in the brain oscillate, and these become harmonized. When you have a wave here, a wave there, from different parts of the brain, several become harmonized, so they oscillate together.*

*When the brain sets into a pattern—to have a perception, or to make a movement—the phase of these oscillations become harmonized, what we call phase-locked. The waves oscillate together in synchrony....*

*Many patterns of oscillations in the brain spontaneously select each other to create the melody; that is the moment of experience. That is the whoomph. But the music is created with no orchestra conductor. This is fundamental.*

*You don't have a little man there saying, 'Now you, and you, and you.'"*
    (Quoted in *Flanagan et al, Measuring the Immeasurable*, p. 202-203)

Varela is right. You don't have a little man there sitting in the back of your brain conducting the brain's symphony. What you have is a brilliant mechanism, the quantum self-consciousness, identifying with the brain itself.

CHAPTER 2

# A Scale of Happiness

Happiness is no stranger to any of us; matter of fact, it comes as standard equipment at birth, and is our natural state of being. Beside material pleasures, happiness comes to us in many more different ways; for example: happy thoughts of positive emotions, satisfaction, and flow. If you make a conscious effort to walk those four avenues during your lifetime, a state of happiness will be the result. Even those who attach their happiness to the material side of life, can experience a different dimension of happiness, when they embrace the non-material, the seemingly esoteric options that are actually available to all of us.

I once had an interesting discussion with two notable consciousness researchers: Stan Krippner famous for his research on the paranormal and Joan Borysenko who is a transpersonal psychologist. Stan said, the pragmatic thing to do is to simply and consistently explore these four pointers of happiness. I think he was implicitly saying: why bother about a theory of happiness? Joan added from the therapy side more or less the same opinion. Clouds cover the sun of happiness, if you remove the clouds, happiness will eventually shine through, even in the most difficult of times.

Let's elaborate on their comments. The positive side first. For example, the experience of pleasurable activities, such as the joy of eating, the joy of sex etc. A staunch materialist will say what we call joy is really the product of the dopamine molecules in the brain. It is strictly mechanical, and that happiness is nothing, but the play of the brain's pleasure circuits built into us.

But the transpersonal group will say this. As mechanical as these pleasure-full activities might be, conditioned brain circuits and molecules of explosive pleasure are involved no doubt, however, we do feel expanded when we eat a fantastic meal or engage in sex, we do become a little more elated or heart-centered as an after effect of a good meal, or a satisfying sexual encounter. This can be seen as a movement toward a higher self, a transpersonal self beyond ego and this movement can in turn take us toward happiness.

So, do happy thoughts, because they are meaningful, lead to an expansion of consciousness—a movement toward the transpersonal self—and makes us happy that way? Certainly, happy thoughts are the results of activation of memories. And it is reasonable that recalling these memories expand our consciousness. But materialist will say, happy thoughts are happy because they activate brain's pleasure circuit.

When we discover new meaning or even understand somebody else's exploration of meaning such as a piece of art, have you noticed there is happiness in it although there is no previous memory?

With that point made, the materialist, if well-read will have no response, as they do not equate happiness with the experiences of meaning, but rather, the material world only. Recently there has been a lot of excitement as to why computer scientists have not yet been able to manufacture a meaning-processing computer. In the eighties and nineties, the philosopher John Searle and the mathematician Sir Roger Penrose demonstrated (I'd say "proved") that meaning is well-nigh impossible for computing machines to process. In contrast to Seligman's positive psychology which equivocates on the subject of meaning, the quantum science of happiness makes room for meaning unambiguously by introducing a nonmaterial meaning processing mind.

Now consider the second pointer of happiness—positive emotions. Yes, brain memories can evoke them. Additionally, though, feelings in the body especially in the form of higher noble emotions like love felt in the heart makes us happy even in situations for which there is no brain memory. I submit that they must be due to expansion of consciousness! Unfortunately, many men in Western culture, seem to have been taught to universally suppress these emotions, so they don't travel this avenue of happiness very often. However, if you ask women what their main source of happiness is, it is likely that many of them will say: when my heart is open. They are talking about love, a noble feeling.

The third concept in the above list is satisfaction, and specifically satisfaction of a purpose. When we accomplish something purposive, we feel happy, like the energy exchange of two businessmen shaking hands after making a deal. Or to take a less prosaic example, singing love songs in the shower. Dopamine molecules in the brain, brain memory? Maybe. In quantum science, we associate satisfaction with the exploration of the objects of our intuition that we call archetype: love, beauty, truth, wholeness, abundance, etc. Quantum science of happiness maintains that whenever we pursue these archetypes, it brings us satisfaction. For the businessmen above, the archetype is abundance; for singers in the shower, the archetype is love. Try it and see for yourself. Being good to others is another example; it evokes satisfaction via the archetype of goodness.

And finally comes the fourth point of happiness known as flow. Athletes often talk about their being "in the zone" and how their improved performance makes them happy. Psychologists have given the name "flow" to such experiences of happiness. You have plenty of flow experiences as well, from cutting the grass in your lawn to dancing to working on your favorite hobby. I once fell into a flow while playing poker. Go figure.

In the new science, it is easy to figure out what is happening. Beyond our ego, we have a higher transpersonal quantum self; when we are in flow, our identity goes back and forth between the ego and this quantum self, the spirit within us. So, the joy of flow is really spiritual joy! Even creative physical activity can lead us to flow!

In the quantum science of happiness, we have a science explaining these two self-identities in our manifest being. We call the higher self the quantum self, the self we experience spontaneously as we choose actuality from potentiality. The quantum self is nonlocal, cosmic. Our usual ego self is the result of repeated reflection of the experience in the mirror of memory. And neuroscientists agree that we experience the ego with a time lag of about half a second.

Can we reach the quantum self in a game of poker? Not ordinarily of course (unless it's your favorite hobby,) but that one time it happened to me, I was also having the uncanny experience of knowing my opponents' moves; in other words, something telepathic was taking place—instant communication, nonlocality was involved. And therefore, there was quantum self! I have no explanation of how I fell into the flow—I just did.

## View from the Psychotherapy Side

Let's consider some clouds of unhappiness that cover the sun of happiness. We can easily find many instances of clouds. For example, it is well known that we have negative emotional brain circuits: jealousy, anger, lust, competitiveness, envy, etc. When they cloud our mental/emotional sky, we become unhappy.

Another example is childhood or adult trauma, for example PTSD or post-traumatic stress disorder. Who hasn't suffered at least a little of the first and heard of the second, thanks to the rampant incidents of PTSD among war veterans?

Still another example is "me-centeredness" which is abundantly on display as "selfies" have become prevalent. Every time it has an experience, our "I" casts a shadow. You know it, we all know it. Part of the shadow is patterns of habit or traits that we call character. Part of the shadow is the "me," our persona. At the stage of the adult, our quantum self-experience ordinarily gives way to an I/me experience that I call ego/character/persona (details later). In this way, excessive me-centeredness also blocks the sun—the joy of the quantum self-experience.

Let's get back to pleasure. Have you ever noticed that pleasure involving a partner, combined with the me-centeredness produces a tendency to objectify the partner? In this way, pleasure is happiness no doubt, but it is different from the happiness that comes from the expansion of consciousness. Pleasure with excessive "me-centeredness" often leads to a contraction of consciousness; this too is a shadow our ego uses to cover the sun of happiness.

Moreover, the pleasure circuits of the brain are accompanied by addiction circuits. Soft addictions like video games, digital media, smart phones, and overuse of "social media" (which can lead to unsocial behaviors) can contribute to unhappiness in a major way. The studies on hard addictions like alcohol, drugs, pornography, and other deep diversions, are well documented and are a sure-fire way to subvert your inherent capacity for happiness.

Living with scientific materialism has created yet another cloud that covers the sun of the quantum self—information processing. Information consists of other people's meanings programmed into symbols. Your brain carries them as software if you so choose. So, if you live on information alone, never bother to understand what the information means, you are no longer using your mind, nor are you using your causal power to process meaning and understand. In this way, information processing, carried to the extreme that many kids do today, literally makes them into p-robots or hu-machines, (concepts that I introduced in Chapter 1), and it keeps them from realizing the joy of meaning and purpose. In this sense, information junkies block the sun of the quantum self from their experience.

So, the psychotherapeutic way to reconnect to happiness is to remove as many clouds as possible. Psychotherapists try to help their clients to do that with various degrees of success. Once the clouds are gone, all the experiences of happiness are available to anyone who wants to be pragmatic about it.

However, it may not be so simple. Spiritual traditions give another perspective for what constitutes the fundamental clouds that cover the sun consisting of the three fundamental dichotomies of the human nature that need to be integrated as part of the exploration of the archetype of wholeness: transcendent-immanent, outer-inner, male-female. This quote from

Jesus in the Gospel of Thomas illustrates it perfectly:

*"When you make the two one,*
*and when you make the inner as the outer*
*and the outer as the inner,*
*and the above as the below,*
*and when you make*
*the male and the female into a single one*
*so that the male will not be male*
*and the female not be female,*
*then shall you enter the Kingdom [of God]."*

Let's take a scientific look at substance addiction to understand the importance of integrating these dichotomies. People take opium and related substances that fill up the opiate receptor sites that the neurotransmitter molecules like dopamine fill which the brain itself produces. Think about it! Joy of sex best reveals itself only if you pay attention not only to your release but also your partner's pleasure. But to engage the brain that way making dopamine so you can forget your pain requires a lot of focused work. Addiction prone people use molecules of drugs like cocaine taken externally to achieve the same dopamine molecules in the brain and it is effortless with external drugs. Unfortunately, drugs are addictive. Moreover, once you start using them, your brain's ability to produce dopamine is compromised. This double whammy makes the psychological treatment of addiction very challenging.

A scientific study has shown that only 5-10% of patients find help under the present regimens of healing addiction and in those cases, it is found that the doctors involved were unusually compassionate. Obviously, it is important to give people of addiction better choices to find happiness than substance addiction. Hence the conclusion: psychotherapy is missing some things in the existing forms. One thing they are missing is quantum creativity which is a systematic scientific method of introducing new potentialities in the unconscious for the addict to choose from, so that in time, with some help from a therapist, the addict discovers the particular healing potentiality that he or she needs. The other thing they are missing is the importance of addressing the archetype of wholeness for healing; for example, the necessity for balancing the fundamental dichotomies just mentioned.

As you will see in subsequent chapters, the quantum science of happiness can explain these dichotomies and doing that can help us integrate them as well.

## The Three Fundamental Dichotomies

The first fundamental dichotomy is the unconscious-conscious dichotomy (that spiritual traditions call the transcendent-immanent or above and below or sacred-mundane dichotomy). In the unconscious, we are one; in conscious awareness, we experience the subject-object split.

But the unity is not compulsory in the quantum worldview; it is only a potentiality. Materialists can take advantage of that, choose to remain contracted, and declare, there is no transcendence. They devise an attractive philosophy—eat, drink, and be merry (have sex and of course easy access to the information superhighway) and manage to confuse people and keep them from fulfilling their potentiality. So, this additionally has augmented the already existing mundane-sacred dichotomy.

The second fundamental dichotomy is the outer-inner dichotomy. We experience material objects outside of us but experience the subtle feeling, meaning, and archetypes as internal objects. How do we explain that? Materialists say, why bother? They assume everything is matter and that's all that matters. This keeps them not only from paying attention to the psyche, but also from paying attention to purely internal experiences like dreams, intuitive nudges and the like.

Finally, the male-female dichotomy. Approximately half of our population is one sex, half the other, and the two sexes process things differently.

Materialists say the difference is all in the brain. For example, males have 4% more neurons, but females have more capacity to make synaptic connections that makes them better at multitasking necessary for motherhood.

But spiritual traditions don't see male-female difference that way. They are referring to this male-female dichotomy as head-heart dichotomy. Carl Jung has theorized about the anima and animus archetypes in the collective unconscious in the same vein. Animus is the Jungian archetype of suppressed male potentiality in females; anima is the Jungian archetype of suppressed female potentiality in males.

Spiritual traditions claim that we are designed to thrive when we balance and harmonize all three polarities.

The quantum worldview is giving us an explanation of these dichotomies maintaining justice to both poles as you will see in subsequent chapters. An understanding of this concept is leading us to the ways of balancing and harmonizing with ourselves and one another.

So, coming back to all those pragmatic means of achieving happiness—physical pleasure, meaning, satisfaction, and flow—you need to see them as part of balancing these fundamental dichotomies. When you supplement the feeling of happiness you get from your pursuits of physical pleasure along with pursuits of meaning and purpose that satisfies you are balancing the outer and the inner. When you are in flow, you are being creative which is a way of balancing the unconscious-conscious transcendent-immanent dichotomy.

In this way, in quantum science based on the dicta of the quantum worldview, we can explore happiness in all the ways previously mentioned.

Living the pleasure circuits of the brain, the physical way. But beware! This one is a blind alley because of those addiction circuits in the brain.

Living with positive feelings centered around the body's associated chakras is the vital way.

Living in a meaning centered way with under-standing rather than information processing, this is the mental style of living.

Living purposively, with one or more archetypes to guide us, creatively developing intuitive intelligence, this is the intuitive way of exploring happiness.

And finally, living in flow while dancing with the spirit (the quantum self) is what I call the way of living for a person of quantum enlightenment in the world.

Add one more:6.) Quantum science additionally points us to the way of jumping out of the bondage of the world entirely as in yoga psychology, the way of enlightened happiness out of this world.

## The Quantum Science Spectrum of Happiness

The question of what mental health or happiness is many clouds not so hard to address. If the components of the ecosystem of the psyche—the subject (self) and the objects-are in balance and harmony acting as a whole- we could call that perfect mental health. To what extent we attain this perfection gives us the scale of mental health in terms of quality. In the 1960s, the psychologist Abraham Maslow gave us the simple scale of happiness: pathological, normal, and positive.

In the 21$^{st}$ century, we can do better. Today we classify people in ascending levels of happiness, from Level 0 to Level 6. We will call this scale the Quantum Science Spectrum of Happiness (*Figure5*).

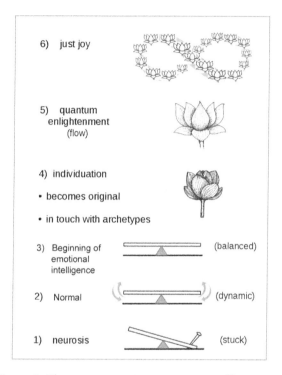

*Figure 5: The quantum science spectrum of happiness*

You can estimate your own level of happiness by its stability; roughly recognizing how much time it takes for you to return to normal from an upset or an emotion upheaval.

In more detail, the levels are as follows:

**Level 0**—are those who are susceptible to pathology of both psychosis and neurosis. There are various factors including genetic issues and childhood traumas that may lead to the experience of these lower levels.

Level 0 is the level of virtually zero self-awareness and happiness; here even pleasure is experienced in a mechanical/molecular way; consciousness remains contracted. The people of this level suffer from psychotic tendencies. But with hardly any capacity to focus or meditate, they are not much available for psychotherapy. Negative emotional upsets last for days, even months and years for these people. This is what makes the phenomenon of serial killers possible.

**Level 1** — is the level of moderate self-awareness and minimal happiness. A little happiness may come because pleasure is experienced along with some awareness of the expansion of consciousness and thereby a little bit of happiness in the aftermath. Neurosis is common. Fortunately, people of this level can pay some attention to objects and also can relax and experience relief as wholeness returns albeit momentarily with some help from teachers and therapists. So, they are accessible to therapy. When these people get upset, calming down may take a few hours to many days.

**Level 2** — is the level of maximal ego self-awareness (conscious of being conscious) but only moderate happiness. The psychologically "normal" people are happiness Level 2, but actually they fluctuate between happiness Level 2- and 2+. In quantum science we use the term 'normal' to represent people who can cope with their neurosis in most situations, with the help of some occasional therapy if the going gets tough.

People of 'normal' mental health enjoy a balanced psyche without too many ups and downs; they are able to carry out living functions appropriately. When "normal" people cope with neurosis, think of it as Level 2-. When they explore happiness, when they explore their own meaning of things rather than always follow other people's meanings (that is, information), when they explore noble feelings, they are in Level 2+.

The lowest common denominator of "normality," 2-, is a me-centered personality struggling with the pleasure-pain dynamics of the brain circuits of pleasure and negative emotions and also information addiction in more recent times.

For Level 2, happiness is still largely pleasure-based, though not necessarily mechanical but somewhat mixed with feelings in the body. Happiness of the exploration of meaning and purpose, and even the joy of flow albeit mostly physical are accessed occasionally by people of this level. People of creativity in the world—outer creativity—enjoy flow in their creative pursuit, but they too fluctuate between 2- and 2+.

Make no mistake about it: the happiness of this level of people comes largely from pleasure and accomplishments. They can hold intimate relationships but based mainly with the pleasure bond. They can engage in outer creativity, both situational and fundamental, in many cultures' men more so, and women less so. With some inspiration and prodding they can engage in even inner creativity or personal growth work, but only using other people's context. In other words,

people of this level would be better off having a therapist or a guru for 2+ optimal functioning.

These people take less time to recover from upsets
than the previous levels, but still at least some minutes
to maybe even hours and sometimes even days (for
example when recovering from a fight with an intimate
relationship) to recover from an emotional upset.

**Level 3** — is when, usually with help, people develop
positive emotional brain circuits, balance the negative
to some extent, and thus acquire some emotional intelligence. This is the beginning stage of positive mental
health. You are happier more often than not.

At this level we consciously engage in our personal growth and self-enhancement. We fully explore
our human potential and work on embodying and
expressing the archetypes although only as followers
(of gurus or traditions) using situational creativity.
We have discovered the importance of authenticity,
found some balance of our transcendent/immanent
dichotomy and even some balance between outer and
inner experience.

**Level 4** — is the level of becoming an individual with
one's own take on at least one archetype: an end result
that I call individuation coopting a concept from Carl
Jung. People of this level have mostly integrated the
three fundamental dichotomies in the way they live.
They experience substantial happiness (much more
happiness than unhappiness). The joy of flow has come

into their life in a substantive way; they thus live-in flow at least some of their time almost every day.

The telling sign about these people is that they bounce back from upsets very quickly, although less so in intimate relationships. They are on their way to complete mastery of emotional intelligence.

Aside from the three fundamental dichotomies, there are also archetypal dichotomies associated with the archetypes: good evil, true-false, beauty-ugly, etc. The fulfillment of the exploration of wholeness arrives when all the major fundamental and archetypal dichotomies are integrated which requires the creative exploration of each. You become an original in how you go with the flow with the quantum self at Level 4.

**Level 5** — is the successful exploration of the wholeness archetype. In this way, Level 5 is achieved when people have arrived at a mastery over all the common archetypes except self (eight of them: truth, love, beauty, abundance, power, justice, goodness, wholeness) and achieved the capacity of virtually living in creative flow. So, Level 5 is "enlightenment" of a sort, (but not the traditional one) and these people are living more or less in a constant state of joy, the joy of flow in a conflict-free way. Instead of "going out of the game of the ego" as in traditional enlightenment, people of this level stay in the world and serve it. In Buddhism, this is called the *bodhisattva* (a Sanskrit word meaning intellect guided by fundamental creativity) way of living.

**Level 6** — begins with traditional enlightenment where we experience the reality of who we really are (self-realization) and the attempt to live it. The adept stabilizes at Level 6 when he or she lives in Nirvikalpa Samādhi—samādhi without separateness, the most exalted state of consciousness. Traditions call this state *God-realization.*

It is important to remember that this is a spectrum of happiness, which means that we may move between the different levels. The Quantum Science Spectrum of Happiness serves as a loose guide to help us reflect upon where we are in our own personal journey. It is not intended to place people in categories as such, but rather it is a tool for self-reflection.

It is also important to note that gurus or psychotherapists are useful guides along much of this spectrum of happiness, up to Level 4 at least, although, after Level 3, the guru or therapist's role is more as a collaborator and inspiration-provider.

In order to have a consistent integrative model of psychology that works across all levels and guides people how to advance in one's level of happiness, we need a unifying science of all these levels of happiness. We will see that the new science—quantum psychology looked upon as the quantum science of happiness—is giving us such an integral science.

# CHAPTER 3

# Amit's Story: How A Quantum Physicist Found Happiness

My journey from unhappiness and scientific materialism began not with the quest for ultimate truth, not with the quest of love, but rather the quest for wholeness, in response to deep questions that must have come from my quantum self. "Why am I so unhappy?" which was followed by "Does quantum physics have anything to do with happiness?"

Initially, I just wanted to do physics in a way that it is relevant to life; the quest was for happy physics, physics that would make me happy, came as a byproduct of my efforts. What I discovered as the outcome of about ten years of research on the quantum worldview is this: consciousness is the ground of all being; all our experiences come from possibilities of consciousness that consciousness chooses from. So, consciousness can choose happiness over unhappiness. I agree with the spiritual traditions that unanimously declare that consciousness wants us to find happiness. This is expressed by the adage, "God is benevolent." But we have to be in synch with the purposive movement of consciousness. This is why your choices become so important.

*Figure 6: My wife and my mother-in-law (artist's rendition of the original cartoon by W. E. Hill)*

For example, look at the picture (*Figure6*). Some of you will see a young woman; others will see an old woman. In 1915, the late British cartoonist William Ely Hill, published the picture titled *My Wife and My Mother-in-Law*. The perspective you are looking from, determines the image you see. Try it for yourself; change the perspective a little by shifting your head; sooner or later you will see the other meaning emerge from among the same lines. The meanings are within you; and much like life, what you "see" is what you "get."

Many scientists deny that we have such a choice to make. They subscribe to the worldview of archaic Newtonian physics, believe it or not. Centuries ago, Newton said material bodies move in a deterministic way, that choice is not a factor. But Newton was talking about material bodies in the macro-world, and the question of happiness is a question for us, live sentient beings. Newton's laws are pertinent to the external movement of bodies in physical space and time. Happiness is a condition we attribute to our internal state-a state of what we call our psyche. Why attribute the properties of apples to oranges?

If you were a physicist in the 1970s, searching for happy physics would sooner or later lead you to what is called the "quantum measurement problem." Allow me to explain before you stop reading any further because the words "quantum measurement" scare you. The concept of quantum measurement is anything but scary. Quantum physics says objects are waves of possibility and a few renegade physicists in the 70s, among them a Nobel laureate, were hinting that our consciousness is involved in converting the possibilities into actual events of experience when we observe or measure them. One physicist even went as far as to proclaim, "we create our own reality," through this quantum measurement. Unfortunately, nobody in science knew at the time what consciousness is. The conventional scientific ways of thinking about consciousness as brain phenomenon prevalent at the time gave rise to seemingly unresolvable paradoxes. In this way I got bogged down into thinking about how to resolve these paradoxes, how to think about consciousness and its relation to quantum physics that will solve the paradoxes related to quantum measurement.

When it came to the question of "What is consciousness?" I did not think of spiritual traditions then; I was strictly a materialist. Etymology suggests consciousness is our vehicle of knowing. But how do we know about that which is instrumental in how we know at all? See the difficulty? In the 1970s, I was a physics professor at a university; I had access to neuroscientists and psychologists, and even philosophers. But consulting them did not help much; all these fields were bogged down with paradoxes, too, whenever consciousness in its aspect of subjectivity entered the discussion. The problem was that practitioners of these fields more or less universally wore the straight jacket of scientific materialism with which you are now familiar. Much later the problem of conscious awareness came to be known as "the hard problem;" but by then, I had already solved the problem.

What opened my mind to think of consciousness beyond the party line was first of all an experience of oneness itself. It was so special, so very illuminating, that I wrote it down, and I quote:

> *On a sunny November morning, I was sitting quietly in my chair in my office doing Japa. This was the seventh day since I had started, and I still had a lot of energy left. About an hour of Japa, and I got an urge to take a walk outside. I continued my mantra deliberately as I walked out of my office, then out of the building, across the street, and onto the grassy meadow. And then the universe opened up to me.*

"... *when m*eadow, grove and stream
The earth, and every common sight,
To me did seem
Appareled in celestial light,
The glor*y and freshness of a dream*."

> —W. Wordsworth in Hutchinson and de
> Selincourt, *Collected Poems of William
> Wordsworth* (1967)

*I seemed to be one with the cosmos, the grass, the trees, the sky. Sensations were present, in fact, intensified beyond belief. But these sensations were pale in significance compared to the feeling of love that followed, a love that engulfed everything in my consciousness-until I lost comprehension of the process. This was ānanda, bliss.*

*There was a moment or two of which I don't have any description, no thoughts, not even feeling. Afterwards, it was just bliss. It was still bliss as I walked back to my office. It was bliss when I talked to our cantankerous secretary, but she was beautiful in the bliss, and I loved her. It was bliss when I taught my large freshman class; the noise in the back rows, even the back-row kid who threw a paper airplane was bliss. It was bliss when I came home and [my wife] Maggie hugged me, and I knew I loved her. It was bliss when we made love later.*

*It was all bliss.*

The feeling of all love and all bliss did not stay long. By the end of the second day, it started fading. When I woke the next morning, it was all gone.

Second, what helped me solve the quantum measurement problem was hobnobbing with mystics, people who claim there is a Oneness beyond all the diversity of the observed world. Religions call this Oneness "God," and their popular renditions cause much confusion and often are irrational from a scientific point of view. But this is not true of the mystical teachings. I found that what mystics say maybe non-rational, but not irrational, and they cannot be refuted by rational arguments.

So, one memorable day in 1985, while talking to a mystic I discovered that if we conclude that consciousness is the ground of all being and quantum possibilities are possibilities of consciousness itself to choose from, all the paradoxes of quantum measurement dissolve like dew in the morning sun. I will tell you the details of the story later (see Chapter 5), but soon Berkeley physicist Henry Stapp came up with a similar resolution and the Rutgers University physicist Casey Blood further elaborated on the issues involved. A new way of thinking about both quantum physics and consciousness was on the way.

Unfortunately, my solution was "unacceptable" to academic scientists, psychologists, and philosophers alike. Even within the quantum context, a metaphysics of primacy of consciousness must be classified as idealism-what is consciousness but an idea, never mind that in quantum physics matter is also an idea in the form of possibility waves. Indeed, I called the new dictum monistic idealism; consciousness is nondual, one without a second.

As I mentioned before, in 1982, a group of physicists headed by Alain Aspect had already experimentally demonstrated the existence of such oneness called quantum nonlocality. Nonlocality is signal less communication; if there is only One, who needs signals to communicate? In this way, it was clear to me that the philosophy of monistic idealism, like scientific materialism, is also scientific. You can call it scientific idealism if you wish. Scientific materialism is a philosophy that can adequately explain the affairs of the nonliving but gets bogged down with paradoxes when it is applied to the living. I was convinced that scientific idealism is the proper metaphysics for the living including human beings.

But in the early 1980's, the academic thinkers had already purged all idealist thinking from academic disciplines opting instead for scientific materialism. Never mind that that view is an exclusive dogma and excludes many empirically established phenomena of biology, medicine, and psychology let alone religion and spirituality. Such is the power of dogma on the human mind!

Fortunately, there were renegade scientists in all fields especially in psychology where the new fields of Jungian and transpersonal psychology welcomed the quantum approach. I established a new paradigm of science called science within consciousness and began the work of integrating the conventional and alternative approaches to biology, medicine, and psychology continued under its influence and concepts.

Crucial in this endeavor was my discovery of a science of all our experiences as a result of a series of coincidences (Carl Jung would call them *events of synchronicity*). They began in 1993 after my first book on the new paradigm *The Self-Aware Universe* came out; I was on my very first radio show when this old lady asked me, "What happens when we die?" I didn't know! The question took me aback, learned as I was, obviously I wasn't ready for a question of that magnitude. It is embarrassing for an academic to profess ignorance, but I recovered and soon forgot about the question.

A month or so later, an elderly Theosophist started taking a reading course on *The Self-Aware Universe*. But in truth, he only started to fill my head with Theosophical ideas such as reincarnation. At first, I did not take the subject seriously. Then as I was dreaming one night, I heard something. It was as if a voice was speaking to me. More and more the voice grew louder. Soon it became an admonition I could clearly hear, "*The Tibetan Book of the Dead* is correct; it is your job to prove it." The admonition was so loud it woke me up. *The Tibetan Book of the Dead* is a guide to the "experiences" of the surviving "soul" between death and rebirth. I started taking survival after death and reincarnation seriously after this dream.

A couple of months later, a graduate student whose boyfriend had died came to my office for help with her grieving. I told her that I was no therapist or healer, but she insisted talking with me and kept coming. Then one day, I was trying to say to her by way of consolation that maybe her boyfriend's subtle body-mind, vital, and all that essence, all nonphysical to be sure- survived his physical death, an idea I had picked up from my Hindu upbringing but never took seriously because of inherent dualism: how do physical and nonphysical interact without a mediator? Suddenly a thought came to me-suppose both the physical and the subtle essence of a person consists of quantum possibilities and consciousness mediates between them nonlocally, without exchanging signals? Could that not solve the problem of dualism as well as that of survival? Subsequently, I wrote a book titled *Physics of the Soul: The Quantum Book of Living, Dying, Reincarnation, and Immortality.*

Suffice it to say, that the idea above opened the way to treat the ecology of the psyche within science in a manner that has never been possible before. The new approach also enabled me to develop a theory of creativity, give a scientific basis for the Eastern concept of the chakras, define a quantum path for personal growth and spiritual transformation, and opened the door for developing a science of what is called spiritual enlightenment.

Obviously, I was close to developing an integral approach to happiness within science where the connections of consciousness and brain, the meaning-giving mind and the brain, the feelings of energy and the body organs, the archetypes and intuitions and the creativity and flow required to explore them, all could be treated in a well-defined scientific manner. This I thought would be welcome to any person looking for meaning and purpose in life, creativity, personal growth, and happiness and spiritual enlightenment.

There were only a couple of important things lacking-two very big questions. Ultimately, to find happiness, one has to clean up some of the chronic unhappiness that is built into the brain either at birth or via interaction with environment as we grow up. Dealing with such built-in unhappiness requires psychotherapy. So, the first big question, is there any evidence that the quantum approach has relevance for psychotherapy?

The second open question was even more daunting. In 2000, I had published a book specifically on the integration of science and spirituality where I coined the phrase "quantum yoga for integrating science and spirituality in one's own life". My life's journey had begun with the idea of integration, and I saw Quantum Yoga—the integration of the three fundamental dichotomies (see Chapter 2) as the exploration of the archetype of wholeness. Unfortunately, the sad truth was, there was no definitive evidence that one can use quantum yoga to achieve such integration. Yes, I had done some of it based on spiritual wisdom traditions with the help of a few spiritual teachers. But it was by no means complete. It was then that I realized the importance of the spiritual teacher Krishnamurthy's words, "Truth is a pathless land. "Ever since I became a serious practitioner of inner creativity with the exploration of the archetype of wholeness in mind. I have to use quantum yoga firsthand before I can ask anyone else to use it.

After all these years, I can say this: I have walked my talk enough to know that quantum yoga works. Chapters 24 &25 will supply details.

As for the first question, in 2013, I had a surprise. A young psychotherapist named Sunita Pattani had written a book discussing many case histories applying the quantum ideas to psychotherapy and proving their relevance. I was asked by her publicist to write the foreword which I happily did proclaiming her book as the "first book" on quantum psychology. Two years later, I met Sunita in London and we decided to co-write the book that you are reading this very moment.

In the early 1990s, I went to a conference on consciousness in Bangalore, India. I gave my talk, and it was well received. I was very pleased and got quite excited when the head spiritual teacher there asked to see me. I went to see him with the idea that we would have a nice intellectual discussion on quantum physics, and I can teach this fellow the wonders of the new integration of science and spirituality. Alas! After the pleasantries were over, the fellow floored me with this question: "Tell me professor, what do you do when you are by yourself?" I was totally humbled. What did I do when I was by myself in those days? Like most of you

I could not handle boredom, which is a mild form of unhappiness. And I, too, looked for something to do, at least something to think about.

After so many years, now my life is very different. Sometimes when I am by myself, I just relax, just sitting quietly doing nothing. What was boredom before has become relaxing. And every now and then, with all the activity going on around me as I am sitting in an airport waiting for the next flight, flow happens, and the world disappears in the joy that it brings. What made the change? Living the quantum way and walking my talk. So, have I found a better way to live a life of more or less unblemished happiness?

The answer is a resounding… "Yes."

A final confession.

I am not enlightened either in the quantum sense (Level 5) let alone in the traditional sense (Level 6). However unabashedly, I do consider myself having reached Level 4 of happiness and well advanced in my quest for Level 5. This qualifies me, (I hope) to contribute to this book in a meaningful way not just from theory, but also experience, and I submit to you fully, that you too can create happiness as I have.

# CHAPTER 4

# Sunita's Story: My Journey To Becoming A Quantum Psychotherapist

There are two very different voices in this book: one is that of the theoretical quantum physicist, Dr. Amit Goswami whose story you just read, and the other belongs to me, Sunita Pattani, a psychotherapist. At this point, you might be wondering what two people of such diverse disciplines might have in common? The answer quite simply is a deep desire to understand who we are at the very core of ourselves- for how can we expect humanity to achieve more of an enlightened state of happiness if we each do not first understand the depth of our own being?

If there was one thing that became apparent to me early on in my psychotherapeutic practice it was this: the client would progress only to the extent of their therapist's own experience and understanding. In other words, although there is some fairly general agreement in psychology (for example, the existence of a conscious and an unconscious psyche), the truth is that different psychologists and therapists will tell you different things in answer to your questions about pathology (way more unhappiness than happiness), "normal mental health" (a good balance between happiness and unhappiness), and positive mental health (more happiness than unhappiness) depending on the metaphysics they follow.

Consider the following three examples: Susan came to me for therapy after spending four weeks in rehab to deal with an alcohol addiction. Although she was no longer drinking, she did have other issues that she wanted to address. When I asked her how she had finally managed to stop drinking, she told me that she believed that her body was a temple that was housing her inner being—her spirit. This realization had prompted her to treat her body with the respect that it deserved. I noticed that Susan was hesitating slightly as she was telling me about her breakthrough. When I asked her why this was the case, she told me that her previous therapist had not understood what she had meant when she referred to her body as temple. The therapist had told Susan that she was a little concerned about this analogy, and this of course had made Susan feel uncomfortable and in her own words, "a little silly."

Anna, a lady who attended one of my workshops said to me, "I have been to so many therapists over the years, but most recently, I found a psychotherapist and it was so great! She helped me work through my family issues of narcissism and it was crazy how much I worked through! But! I kept feeling like I was hitting a wall. I tried to explain the need I felt in my mind to reach deeper into myself. I talked about the desire I had to meditate and to dig deep within, but it was pushed aside. I am not complaining because this therapist taught me that I need to take care of 'me' and love myself! This was something I had never thought about in my 36 years. It was so exciting, and I loved the idea of self-care and self-love. But it never went beyond that. It was always about buying a special perfume or pampering myself with some THING. This kind of reinforced my idea that I couldn't get to that deeper part of myself until I worked through everything and got to be the perfect weight and better person to start the process."

The third example that I am going to share is personal, because it's my story. A few years ago, I was suffering terribly from binge eating disorder. It was exhausting, and quite frankly was literally draining the life force out of me. My health was seriously deteriorating, and I gained nearly 60 pounds in a very short space of time. My marriage was falling apart, and to make matters worse my career was going nowhere. I was "broke" on so many levels, including financially.

Perhaps the most frustrating factor to me was the opinions of others who would come along and tell me that I needed to lose weight, have more will power, or that I just "needed to get a grip." People just didn't get it and conventional therapy just didn't seem to work. Conventional self-help books would suggest that I had unresolved emotional issues and that I had to find the roots of the issues, which of course were hidden in some corner of my childhood—that I couldn't quite ever reach. I tried all sorts of different things, including hypnotherapy, but in my case it didn't work.

Eventually, I attained healing after working on different areas of myself, recognizing that my mental, emotional, physical, and spiritual aspects all needed individual attention. I had to learn how to trust my body, work with my energy and use my intuition. First and foremost, I had to employ compassion and empathy to myself, and ultimately, I had to believe that I was designed to move towards wellness.

In many ways, conventional therapy such as cognitive behavioral therapy (CBT) had come close to this but had fallen short. There was an answer to my healing, but it required serious, spiritual creativity.

The examples above illustrate the need for psychotherapy to go further in its approach. They ask us to incorporate spirit, along with exploring our deep yearning to know more about who we are.

My mid-twenties into my early thirties was a period of 'the dark night of the soul', where everything just seemed to go wrong. My health, wealth, relationships, and career were all in trouble, and I was desperately trying to find a way to make life work. During this period, I read many books and tried many different tools, techniques, and approaches–some of which worked and some that fell short. Eventually, towards the end of this phase, I began to be trained as a psychotherapist, because the truth is, we teach that which we most have to learn ourselves.

Perhaps the most valuable insight that I gained from this experience was that I got to understand more about who I was, both from an energetic and physical perspective. But I hadn't yet managed to blend these two aspects together within my therapy practice. This meant that I had the theory, but there were gaps in my practical knowledge and application. It wasn't until I encountered a client that I couldn't help (because of my lack of practical skill), did things significantly change for me. I went on to train in a number of different modalities and learned more about psychological trauma. With time and practice, I learned how to use the quantum worldview to facilitate self-healing for clients, and today I am engaged in research to move this field forward.

## About Counseling

Before I present more information however, I would like to share some of what I have learned through my journey as a therapist.

• **Start where you are.**

In a society where we have become accustomed to instant gratification, it is important to recognize that healing for some individuals will take time. We all experience trauma and in turn healing, in different ways. I have worked with clients in the past who have endured years of abuse, with devastating consequences, and it takes time to facilitate the healing and work through these traumas. Aside from the time factor, here it becomes essential to understand both the multiplicity of experiences and how they apply to you.

- **There is no one correct method for therapy.**

Quantum science-based psychology is an inclusive psychology that recognizes the importance of the different tools and techniques required in the healing process. The process that I share with you in this book is my interpretation of how quantum-based psychology can be used to facilitate healing. I would invite therapists to use the quantum worldview to inform their practice and build their tools and skillset in a way that works for them.

- **Therapy and self-help are an amalgamation of art and science.**

Tools and techniques are important but knowing when to utilize them is equally essential. Learning how to pay attention to your gut feeling about where and at what pace you need to move at is essential. I often work with clients that need to take things slow, and that's ok.

Experiencing deep shifts in perception is when we begin to understand the underlying unitive reality of our existence. Our focus changes from self-service to serving humanity, as we begin to encounter and embody more of the fundamental archetypes, such as truth, justice, love, goodness, and wholeness. We know that a deep healing is occurring when love, compassion, kindness, and unity become natural expressions for us. We begin to recognize who we really are. We are able to view life's challenges through a fresh perspective as we begin to experience a greater level of inner peace and happiness. These deep shifts are a result of us actualizing a new meaning for life often in a new archetypal context from the unconscious.

On the other hand, it is possible for a person to experience a deep shift, (hence attaining greater wisdom) and yet still struggle with specific healing issues, such as addiction. I know from experience that this predicament can be quite challenging.

In some cases, I have found that using the tools and techniques that I learned in training are enough to help a client resolve their issues. However, I have also observed that in other cases these approaches alone are not enough to help one with emotional healing. Clients quite often intuit that there is a deeper purpose to life-something that they can feel but yet are unable to describe; an inner yearning or even an emptiness at times that they can't quite comprehend.

Through my own personal research, I have come to understand that these un-named feelings have been addressed in previous psychological theories, but in my opinion, they are not always fully understood or considered in practice because they have (what some may refer to as), a spiritual/mystical element to them.

Having made the choice to continually work on my own personal development, and to explore other areas of research in transpersonal psychology, I feel that I have gained a much broader perspective on emotional healing. I have personally experienced both shifts in consciousness and glimpses of what I consider to be the truth, and I feel that this has greatly impacted the way in which I work with clients as a psychotherapist.

My psychotherapy training alone did not equip me to fully connect with the depth of consciousness, but rather it has been my personal inquiries into who I really am that has gifted me with this experience. Furthermore, I have become aware that I can only help my clients to the extent of my own personal experience and understanding.

It's also worth mentioning, that my choice of methods is not the only way to facilitate emotional healing. Every therapist and client are different and has his or her own methods of working and responding. What am I proposing is that instead of just looking at an individual's challenges and behavior, we start to ask the all-important question of "Who Am I?"

When we start to go beyond observing and managing the ego self, we begin to realize that we are in fact not just this ego, an often-complicated mass of beliefs and experiences-but additionally we are something far greater, interconnected with everything else, forming one universal truth. The question, "Who am I?" asks that we entertain the notion that we are more than just the body and the ego. It asks that we expand our awareness about ourselves and perhaps consider the place where psychology, mysticism, and science meet.

## Quantum Science

Quantum science takes us to an approach to psychology that addresses who we are at the very core, hence attention is given to both healing specific issues as well as recognizing the importance of the deep shifts that people can and do sometimes experience in therapy.

Up until recently, my work encompassed some aspects of near-death experiences, eastern philosophy, and parapsychology. However, what was missing was the inclusion of quantum physics and energy psychology. Although I was aware that quantum physics had some connection with consciousness, the prospect of incorporating this within my work was extremely daunting because I didn't feel as if I had an adequate grasp of the topic.

Although we were somewhat familiar with one another's work, I first met Dr. Amit Goswami in May 2015 while he was visiting London to give a workshop. It was during this meeting that he shared his concept of the science-spirituality integrated approach of quantum happiness with me and told me that he had nearly finished writing this manuscript. As the hours passed, it became increasingly evident that we both shared the same vision of a multi-disciplinary approach to consciousness and happiness.

This requires a multi-disciplinary exploration of ourselves, one that includes psychology, spirituality and quantum physics-one that quantum science of happiness-developed and presented in this book-opens the door to.

Etymology suggests that disease is about fragmentation of some kind, and healing is about regaining wholeness. Followers of scientific materialism can be cynic about healing in the sense of achieving any kind of "wholeness." If determinism-the idea that we are material machines following deterministic laws of physics *ála* Newton that ultimately determine our behavior-holds, then our behavior cannot change in any fundamental way, only modified, or adapted to cope with new life situations.

Obviously, this approach adapted by cognitive/behavioral psychotherapists does not have long-term healing potential. They can equip you with ways to cope with your symptoms so you can handle them, make them tolerable. But add consciousness, free will, and creativity to your "machine" in your science, you get a lot of leverage for real change. Add unconscious as a reservoir of your potentialities, old and new-another level altogether of your being that is outside space and time and that of which you are unaware but still can causally affect you. The processing and causal power of the unconscious will add to your creative ability to change.

Add emotions and the concept of subtle energy movements to affect your emotional states in your science, you get leverage for emotional intelligence-a necessary ingredient of psychological wholeness. Add "super-unconscious" states of a higher consciousness beyond your conditioned subconscious to your repertoire in your science, you get even more leverage for making change and becoming whole. Then, add intuitions that come to you as the forerunner of these super-unconscious states and add the creative process in your toolbox as a science of manifestation, you get real empowerment. This is what quantum approach to psychology and quantum science of happiness enables you to do. It's truly a DIY building block approach to becoming happier on a more consistent basis.

The truth is that psychotherapeutic practice is changing as many therapists are beginning to recognize that traditional techniques have limited use. At the end of the day, the only question that we as therapists are concerned with is, how can I help my client to heal? The fact of the matter is, that many of us today are incorporating techniques such as hypnotherapy, emotional freedom techniques (EFT), matrix re-imprinting, past-life regression, and meditation (to name a few), into our practices because THEY WORK! These approaches not only push us beyond scientific materialism to seriously consider the role of quantum physics in the healing process, but also suggest that quantum physics, psychology, and spirituality come together to help humanity move forward in the exploration of happiness.

This integration has enabled me to bring into psychotherapy two very important missing elements that require detailed attention. One is creativity; the other is the idea of three fundamental dichotomies that create fundamental barriers to our journey toward mental health and happiness.

## The Book

By the end of the meeting in London, Amit and I had decided to write this book together. He would provide the scientific explanation for the primacy of consciousness, outlining how the unconscious could be scientific, how experiences could be explained, and the journey of transformation from mostly unhappy to mostly happy can be approached within science. Amongst other factors he would also provide evidence for the notion that consciousness is the ground of all being. In short, he would lay down the scientific theory for a quantum science of happiness and experimental data to support it. I, on the other hand, would add the practical elements—the tools required for application of this science to the lives of ordinary people experiencing neurosis. People who clearly needed therapy before they could approach the spiritual higher components of happiness. For me the most important factor is to be able to take theory and find ways to apply it to our lives for the purpose of enhancing both ourselves and our future generations; and it is my sincere hope that this book, *Quantum psychology and the science of happiness* will set the foundation for you to do just that!

# CHAPTER 5

# Can the Unconscious Be Scientific? Consciousness and the Two-Level Reality of Quantum Physics

Question: What does consciousness and quantum physics have in common? The answer is one word: transcendence. Let's explore that word and its application to this work.

Our ancestors millennia ago did not have the instrumentation we have today to study the material world, so the curious researchers of the era mostly spent their time studying their own consciousness using experiential methods such as meditation. And every once in a while, a researcher would come out with a proclamation like this:

We exist not only in this space-time immanent world where separateness reigns but also in a world that lies outside space and time where there is only oneness; call it the transcendent world. I have discovered this oneness; and I became so full of joy and happiness afterwards!

In time, these people gathered a lot of supporters for their ideas thanks to their followers who used a lot of marketing techniques (called a religion, each religion defining a brand) that a modern business would be proud of. But these followers, too lazy to meditate did not really fathom how one can experience being "outside space and time," and so misinterpreted everything and eventually these curious teachings came to be called mysticism; "nobody can understand mystics (and their mystical concepts of oneness and transcendence)" became the prevalent wisdom in more modern times. People started saying, "get real" as there is only matter moving in space and time-one realm, one world, independent separate objects, period—end of story. As mentioned before, we call this modern view material monism.

The materialist scientists have a lot of influence today. Before I started writing this chapter, I looked up the meaning of "transcendence" in the Oxford English dictionary. The dictionary defines the word as "to lie beyond experience" and to "existence beyond the normal or physical level." There is no mention of consciousness anywhere in the definition.

Of course, the mystics were talking about consciousness. The realm outside space and time is realm of unmanifest consciousness, not another dual world. If one of those ancient mystics came across one of these modern scientists, they would explain the futility of trying to understand transcendence without researching consciousness. These mystical people are a relatively rare breed today; but if you are so lucky and meet one of them, they too would say the same thing.

Interestingly, around the tail end of the nineteenth century when material monism had not quite attained the status it enjoys today in our academia and our media, there was a scientific genius named Sigmund Freud who revived the concept of two realms of reality: he called the two realms unconscious and conscious, leaving no ambiguity that he is talking about realms of consciousness. Indeed, in Freud's conceptualization, unconscious is beyond experience, beyond our subject-object awareness, much like what the mystics meant by transcendent realm of consciousness. Naturally, materialist scientists did not like it. They called Freud's psychology "voodoo psychology."

And truly, you cannot blame even spiritual people not seeing the connection between Freud's conceptualization and the mystics' conceptualization. Freud's unconscious is where our mental aberrations-neurosis and psychosis-come from; such pathology is in no way close to the mystics' experience of joy and happiness.

Freud's ideas caught a popular nerve though, and everybody today uses the word unconscious. To makes things worse for materialists, Carl Jung further generalized Freud's psychology and declared that the unconscious has not only a personal and "negative" aspect but also a collective and often "positive" aspect as well. In other words, the unconscious is not only a repository of personal memory but also a repository of humanity's collective memory!

This raises the specter: Do all of us then have a shared unconscious as well? This sounds much like the mystical concept of a transcendent consciousness of which also, ordinarily, we are unconscious. Just like Freud, Jung has quite a bit of following among psychologists and their clients even today. It works! When you live in a burning house (troubled psyche) you don't worry about metaphysical validity, you want results.

Now let's talk about quantum physics. Curiously, also in the tail end of the nineteenth century, a breed of scientists called physicists began looking into submicroscopic matter and began discovering strange things about them. If you read the history of physics, you would discover that that the word quantum means "a discrete quantity" thus, the original idea was that energy, like matter, consists of discrete building blocks. For matter, we call these building blocks elementary particles, for energy, the building blocks were called *quanta* (plural of quantum). Unfortunately, both energy and matter also show wave-like behavior. This wave-particle duality was initially seen as a paradox.

Eventually, in the hands of two physicists, Werner Heisenberg and Erwin Schrodinger, physics became down right mystical. These two physicists discovered a mathematical equation that governs the behavior of all submicroscopic objects of matter and energy. The solution of the equation gives us waves, period. This could only make sense if you flatly accept that quantum objects are waves of possibility. They then become concrete objects of our experience-particles- when we observe them (the observer effect). But where do they reside before we observe them? They reside in "potentia" which is the realm of potentiality or possibility, said Heisenberg. Where is this realm of potentiality? It has to be a world that transcends space and time.

Three physicists, Albert Einstein, Boris Podolsky, and Nathan Rosen explained (although they themselves did not approve the explanation) that if two quantum objects of possibility interact, they acquire a strange property called *correlation*. They become entangled so they can communicate instantly even though they can be galaxies away and not interacting anymore (*Figure7*).

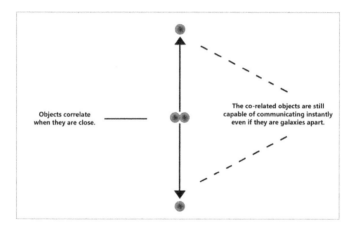

Objects correlate when they are close.

The co-related objects are still capable of communicating instantly even if they are galaxies apart.

*Figure 7: Quantum objects, when they are correlated, can communicate instantly even when at a distance, any distance*

Now, in space and time, objects communicate with signals and signals move with a speed limit (the speed of light). This is the message of Einstein's relativity theory. So, EPR thought quantum physics contradicts the theory of relativity, and this they did not approve of.

But, of course, their prejudice blinded them, and there is a simple explanation. To be sure, objects cannot communicate faster than the speed of light when they communicate with signals as they do via space and time. But suppose when quantum objects are entangled into oneness of the domain of potentiality, they communicate without signals, they are One. You don't need signals to communicate with yourself!

In Chapter 1, you will recall that I introduced the concept of *locality*—communication in space and time with the help of signals, and *nonlocality*—signal-less communication, taking place via the domain of potentiality, outside space and time. Nonlocality is observed fact and so is the domain of potentiality; and physicists have to come to terms with this reality.

But before we get too far ahead of ourselves, I suppose you might still be puzzled about one concept. What is a wave of possibility? Great question! Quantum physics should puzzle you. As the physicist Niels Bohr said, if you are not puzzled by quantum physics, you couldn't possibly understand it.

## What Is a Possibility Wave?

What does it mean when we affirm that a quantum object, say an electron, is a wave of possibility? How do we know this?

Imagine an observer has released an electron at rest in the middle of a laboratory with no forces acting on it. Imagine that there is not even the gravity force pulling the electron down; this will keep things simple. So, Newton's laws of motion tell you that the electron should stay put where the experimenter released it. Quantum physics says otherwise; the electron is a wave, and waves never stay put, they expand. So, the electron wave should be everywhere in the room in a matter of moments. To settle the matter, we observe, we measure, we do an experiment.

An observation or measurement of electron's position requires an experimental apparatus, say, a Geiger counter. You may have seen one go tick-tick-tick in the presence of radioactive material. The experimenter sets up a three-dimensional grid of Geiger counters in the room. What he finds is this: In a given measurement only one of the Geiger counters ticks, the electron will show up at one place but not necessarily in the same position that the electron was released. So, Newton's physics is wrong physics for electrons, but is quantum physics, the right physics? Yes. If the observer makes a very large number of identical experiments, the electron's measured positions will look like a bell curve (*Figure8*) in agreement with quantum physics' predictions.

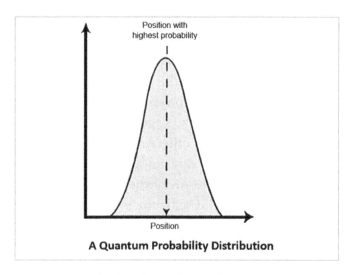

*Figure 8: The free electron's probability distribution
(the bell curve), the plot of the probability of the electron
being at a position plotted as a function of the position,
agrees with the prediction of quantum math*

So potentially, in possibility, the electron is everywhere
in the room as a wave in a nonlocal domain of reality
that is everywhere and nowhere; when we measure
or observe, the electron becomes actuality, a particle,
and manifests only at one place in a given observation.

Some instructors tell their students, "Nobody
understands quantum physics," making not understanding quantum physics a virtue that allows achieving success by moving on and using quantum physics
without understanding it. But what is there not to
understand if you are ready to give up the idea that
there is only one domain of reality, namely space
and time?

Just when you thought electrons are very friendly (since they wave at you) you find out they wave from another domain where you cannot see them; when you see them, they don't wave, they are particle. Are you disappointed? I have illustrated this via a thought experiment because it is the simplest to understand. In an actual experiment, we take known wave behavior and check if electrons exhibit the same wave behavior. For example, take the so-called double-slit experiment. If you pass water wave through a screen with two slits, one wave becomes two, and the two waves mix, do a phenomenon called interference and make a pattern called an interference pattern. The wave is augmented in some places; in-between places, no wave arrives at all. Can electrons make an interference pattern with a double slit arrangement?

Say, we throw one electron at a time from an electron shooter at a double slit arrangement. So again, the electron becomes waves, and then splits into two waves at the double slit; the two waves interfere, and we watch. Each electron arrives at the photographic plate as a particle obscuring the wave nature as before. (*Figure9*)

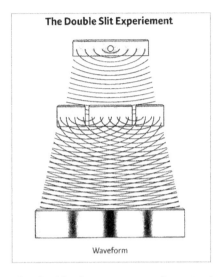

*Figure 9: The double slit experiment for a single electron
when repeated for many identical electrons show
a wave interference pattern*

But we know what to do. We repeat the experiment; as the second, the third, the umptieth electron comes through the double slit (which we do not see) and falls on the plate, we behold the pattern. And lo! Just as predicted, as is the case with water waves, the electrons have made an interference pattern leaving no doubt that each electron individually is a wave behind the scene in the domain of potentiality that becomes particle when observed.

We can then allude and confirm to another domain of reality, transcendent and all, but is it consciousness as the mystics said millennia ago and the spiritual traditions that exist even today affirm? They say this knowledge has been maintained through the ages without any break because there are always a few "mystics" who verify the truth of transcendence by direct "experience," paradoxical as that may be. In Sanskrit this idea is called *guru parampara*. Mystics are an unbroken continuous lineage of seers.

A bit more history. Some physicists (I was one of them) realized that the final message of transcendence in quantum physics has to be consciousness. Even Heisenberg anticipated this when he said that the change that takes place when we measure (observe) a wave of potentiality changing it into a particle of actuality is really a change in our knowledge about the object. And…what is the agency that we know with? It is called *consciousness*, that etymologically means *a vehicle to know with.*

I got into consciousness research via pondering the question, "What agency produces the change from possibility to actuality?" To make a long story short, the answer to the question is consciousness, but only if you define consciousness as the transcendent ground of all being that is common ground for all objects just like the mystics think of our being and Carl Jung thought about our unconscious. Consciousness, not matter is the primary foundation of reality. I call this metaphysics *monistic idealism.*

Behold! There is something very practical about this. You know, as I discussed in Chapter 1, today's materialist psychology, with the brain-oriented concept of consciousness that they entertain, is mostly a negative psychology. Our brain is wired (it is true!) via evolution for negative emotions-lust, anger, violence, competitiveness, domination, and all that. If the brain is all there is and you maintain it the way it is, negativity is part of your lot; and because many people think that their brain is all there is to them and it remains the way it is, they have become believers of negativity (which shapes their behavior and reality.) But the brain is not a static thing; neuroplasticity, brain's ability to change is now common knowledge. Suppose we are immanent consciousness in the brain, and also transcendent consciousness beyond the brain—the unconscious, what then? Then positivity comes back in a hurry. We can balance the negativity with our intuitions of positivity from the unconscious (what ancient philosophers called "the voice of angels") like love, goodness, and beauty. And then room is made for a genuine positive psychology.

Indeed, historically, the message of spiritual psychology has always been positive which Carl Jung brought back in modern psychology. And now quantum physics and experimental data of nonlocality are making it all scientific.

## How Consciousness Creates the World

So, this is what we know: Consciousness changes waves of possibility into particles of actuality when we measure them with a Geiger counter. That is not so puzzling, you think, "I can buy that. "But, wait,...

there is puzzle here for people who believe that consciousness is simply a brain phenomenon. A Geiger counter is made of electrons and quarks, all possibility waves; so, the Geiger counter itself must also consist of possibility. Possibility coupled to possibility only gives you bigger possibility, never actuality. In fact, even the human observer, the experimenter's brain, is made of possible elementary particles according to materialist scientists. When coupled with the electron and the Geiger counter, it will generate even bigger waves of possibility, but no actuality. However, we must accept that in the presence of a human observer observing an electron with a bunch of Geiger counters, a Geiger counter always ticks. What is the explanation of this observer effect?

Puzzling? Perhaps…especially if you believe that a human observer is a material machine, it can become quite the puzzle. This measurement paradox kept many quantum physicists awake through many nights for decades. The paradox and your puzzling over it, gets even thicker when you learn that it is a mathematical theorem attributed to the mathematician John von Neumann that no material interaction can ever convert possibility into actuality. Go figure!

If you are a scientific materialist, you will go down the proverbial rabbit hole even further, when you realize that this one paradox is fatal to the whole metaphysics of scientific materialism since the validity and durability of quantum physics is beyond reproach. Is it time to change the worldview?

Absolutely.

Von Neumann himself did some of the requisite figuring: a human observer is not made of only elementary particles; additionally, an observer has individual nonmaterial consciousness—his or her facility for knowing, he argued. Being nonmaterial, the observer's consciousness is outside of the possibility calculus of quantum physics. This nonmaterial consciousness chooses one facet out of a many facetted waves of possibility and collapses it to the actuality of that one facet: for the electron in our thought experiment, a particular position.

But the physicist Eugene Wigner pointed out a paradox with von Neumann's thinking. Suppose two observers are simultaneously looking at the same electron choosing two different Geiger counters at two different positions for its manifestation. Who gets to choose? Whose choice counts? If both choices count, two Geiger counters at two different places will simultaneously tick; experience contradicts that. If one gets to choose overruling the other because, he is the "head honcho," the problem shifts to who gets to be the head honcho? The paradox remains intact.

The paradox is resolved if it is nobody's individual consciousness that chooses, but some bigger everybody's One nonlocal consciousness (God) that chooses. Sound familiar? This is how spiritual/religious pundits think.

One of these thinkers was Bishop Berkeley of the 18th century. He was an idealist—a believer of a philosophy that material things are not really real; it is our ideas of the consciousness about them that are real because without these ideas how would we get the information about material things?

But of course, there is a problem of that assertion too. You may have puzzled over this riddle that causes quite a stir in our minds even today: if a tree falls in the forest making a sound but nobody is there to hear it, is there a sound, or not? Berkeley seems to be saying, there should be no sound because there is no person there in the forest with consciousness. But of course, this contradicts Newton's laws of cause-effect: if a tree falls, there got to be a sound. So, Berkeley explained: there is always the consciousness of God that is ever present; so, there is always a sound.

So, does a quantum collapse happen because of the causal action of an omnipresent God? But this too is paradoxical; if, as Berkeley argued, "God is always in the quad," then the quantum possibilities would always collapse leaving no room for the possibility waves to expand and do their experimentally demonstrated magical waving.

As it happens, in May 1985, I was talking about all this with the mystic and author, Joel Morwood. I was ranting that if consciousness is brain phenomenon, it is paradoxical; if consciousness is individual nonmaterial consciousness, it is paradoxical; if consciousness is dual omnipresent God consciousness, it is paradoxical! What does a quantum physicist have to do to resolve the paradox?

The rest is history. We had a heated dialog. At some point, Joel asked, "Is consciousness prior to the brain or is the brain prior to consciousness?"

To this, I responded smugly (I am the physicist, he is just a filmmaker!) "I know all about that. You are talking about nonlocality." Indeed, as I discussed before nonlocality defines the domain of quantum potentiality where waves of possibility reside; in this domain communication is without signal, is instantaneous. Naturally this domain is outside space and time; what is prior to what cannot be asked.

Joel was acerbic, "You have scientific blinders on your head," he said. Then he shouted, "There is nothing but God!"

Mind you, I have heard those words many times before; they are from Sufism, but all mystics talk like that. As Jesus similarly said, "The kingdom of God is everywhere." And the Vedanta says, *Sarvam Khalydam Brahman* (Sanskrit for "all is consciousness"). But this time my internal response was unexpected, a total surprise to myself. Suddenly I am thinking, suppose consciousness is the ground of being in the domain of potentiality and matter (including the observer's brain) are possibilities of consciousness itself, what then? A 180- degree turn in my thinking? Yes, but who cares? I have solved the measurement problem. If the nonlocal domain of reality that we call potentiality is consciousness—the one and only, inseparable from its possibilities—consciousness is choosing from itself, no signal, no energy exchange is needed, as the word nonlocality already suggests. All that is needed to start a new paradigm is to identify the nonlocal domain of potentiality with consciousness itself, the way mystics think, especially in the East and when consciousness chooses not only is the object actualized but also the brain and the observer—the subject. Consciousness has then identified with the brain in the measurement process.

## The Importance of the Observer

So, the answer to the paradox that Berkeley's idea of God being omnipresent creates is to assert the observer effect: not only God or unity-consciousness but also the presence of the observer is needed for every event of quantum collapse. Berkeley was wrong to assert that God consciousness is separate from the human consciousness; I realized that somehow, God-consciousness works through the human consciousness.

Thus, there is no sound of a tree falling, no actualization, unless there is some observer to hear the sound. But then, according to quantum physics, observer—his or her brain—is potentiality before the actualization; so, there is no manifest observer without actualization. There is a circularity in this logic. A paradox unless you realize, as stated above that quantum measurement consists of a "dependent co-arising" of subject and object. And you know what? The phrase dependent co-arising comes from Buddhism enunciated millennia ago.

Many scientists today take it for granted that today's people are smarter than people of the olden days! Really? Scientific materialists still conveniently miss the import of the observer effect. They continue to think that quantum actualization is the actualization of the object alone. If it were, they can make ad hoc assumptions to distract and confuse the poor layperson.

The most well-known of these distractions is called the Many-Worlds Interpretation of Quantum Measurement (MWI). Suppose at the moment of measurement, the universe splits up into many different parallel universes each containing the actualization of one of the facets of potentiality; in other words, instead of an event of "actualization," all potentialities are actualized in one or another of the many worlds. No need to invoke an agent of actualization. In some later version of this theory, even the observer's brain is included; each of the universes contains the appropriate brain-state of the observer.

According to my insight, the scientific materialists are missing the point. They are missing the question of the subject. The real question is, how does the brain become the self or subject of the experience of the object, which is what distinguishes a measurement from a mere interaction? Once again that hard question arises.

After actualization, consciousness is found to have identified with the brain and become the manifest observer who hears the tick of the electron at the Geiger counter and reports in the first person, "I hear the tick." So, the brain must be special to capture consciousness in this way. This special thing in the brain I call a tangled hierarchy, a tangle of two brain apparatuses that is able to capture consciousness when it enters the brain to look through it so that the brain acquires a self, a representation of consciousness.

In a simple hierarchy, one level causes the other in a linear relationship. A tangled hierarchy is a circular relationship, each level creates the other, so you cannot tell which is at the top. The chicken or egg question: which comes first? is akin to a tangled hierarchy. You may have seen the Charlie Brown's cartoon in which Charlie Brown says to his psychiatrist friend Lucy, "How can I correct some of my faults?" Lucy says, "You know why you have faults, Charlie Brown? It is because of your weaknesses! It's all your weaknesses that cause your faults." "Well, how can I cure my weaknesses?" asks Charlie Brown. "You've got to get rid of those failings." You can see the causal circularity in this humorous exchange.

The idea that a tangled hierarchy in our brain is crucial for solving the quantum measurement problem came to me while I was reading Doug Hofstadter's book, *Gödel, Escher, Bach: An Eternal Golden Braid*, in 1981. Hofstadter's idea was about building a self-conscious computer program of artificial intelligence and in that field the idea did not pan out. My intuition was that the idea was right for thinking about the brain, for solving the quantum measurement problem.

I've stated above, that even after recognizing that consciousness, not matter is the ground of being, there is still a paradox with the observer effect that smacks of circularity: No manifest observer, no actualization; no actualization, no manifest observer! The answer is that the reason collapse occurs in the presence of an observer's brain but not a Geiger counter is that the brain has a tangled hierarchy built into it.

How does a tangled hierarchy give self-identity? Following Hofstadter, consider the liar's sentence, I am a liar. In an ordinary sentence, which is called a simple hierarchy, a sentence such as I am an author, the predicate "author" qualifies the subject "I" once and for all. But notice the circularity of the liar's sentence: the predicate at the end qualifies the subject, but then a contradiction occurs drawing our attention back to the beginning. *If I am a liar, then I am telling the truth*, a contradiction; and this contradiction goes on and on: *if I am telling the truth then I am a liar, then I am telling the truth,* ad infinitum.

Here is the thing. If you enter the circularity of the sentence and identify with the circularity, you tend to get caught. Try it; you will think you are embodied in the sentence. Of course, in this case, it is easy for you to get out of that eternal loop. After all, it is your learned, universal acceptance of the rules of the English grammar that got you in. Technically speaking, you belong to the "inviolate" level of the implicit English grammar where the sentence cannot go, but you can.

So, the idea that came to me was this: If the brain has a tangled hierarchical system within it, then when consciousness enters it with the idea of looking through it, and tries to choose from its possible facets, it gets caught; the choice actualizes the brain state, but consciousness identifies with it and considers itself separate from the other actualized objects the observer is looking at such as the Geiger counter and the electron. The observing subject/self and the observed objects co-arise in awareness via quantum actualization.

It works. In all events of perception, the perceiver's brain is always one of the objects involved, but the observer never experiences the brain separate from self. The experiencing brain and the self are like painting and canvas. You cannot peel one away from the other.

In the case of the liar's sentence, we really belong to the inviolate level, so the identification with the sentence is a pretend identification; we can get off from identifying with the sentence at will. In the case of the brain, the inviolate level is our unconscious, we cannot go there and retain our separateness and awareness and therefore our identification with the brain in manifest experience is total; we cannot get out of the identification by wishing it or by virtue of this knowledge of the mechanism behind our identification. We gain something, a self, that's huge. But we also lose something; we develop the beginning of an ignorance of who we are, a kind of forgetfulness.

The liar's sentence has two levels to make the tangle—the subject and the predicate; what are the two levels of the tangled hierarchy of the brain? One day I was reading an article by the neuro-philosopher Susan Blackmore, and she points out that perception and memory are a circularly connected pair: perception requires memory to operate, and memory requires perception. Blackmore's remark helped me identify the two levels of tangled hierarchy in the brain as the perception and memory apparatuses.

Perception and memory are the dual partners of the brain's tangled hierarchy: there is no memory without perception; there is no perception without memory. Pretend that you are consciousness. Enter the tangle with the idea of choosing and actualizing. Where do you start? Let's say you start with the perception apparatus. But that won't do; manifest perception requires manifest memory to be operational. So, you shift attention to memory and try actualizing that. But that does not work either, there is no manifest perception to memorize. So, you get caught in the brain going back and forth between the two apparatuses. The brain, because of its tangled hierarchy has acquired a self that sees itself separate from any other objects of perception.

Obviously, the answer to the puzzle of what to actualize to begin the process of actualizing a circular hierarchy is: 1.) That consciousness in charge of the unconscious domain of potentiality actualizes both; 2.) That unconscious is the inviolate level and 3.) That actualization is nonlocal. And "you" can go there but so does the brain with you and both become potentiality.

Therefore, in the final reckoning, perception and memory are made manifest both in the same fell-swoop by the act of downward causation causing the appearance of memory creating perception and perception creating memory!

Thus, the experience of the self of the tangled hierarchical processing in the brain, the subject of a subject-object split experience in its immediacy is always fresh; there is no prior memory of it. It has no individuality, it is cosmic. This is why I call it *the quantum self* (for which the Sanskrit word is atman; the Sanskrit word for the immediacy experience of the quantum self is called Samadhi). The response of the quantum self to a stimulus is always spontaneous. The transpersonal psychologists call the quantum self-transpersonal self.

A note in passing for the connoisseur: if you are wondering how the brain, a macroscopic object at room temperature, can have macroscopically distinguished states for consciousness to choose from, in other words, how can the brain be quantum, no worries. I have solved this problem while researching quantum neuroscience; read my book with physician Valentina R. Onisor, *The Quantum Brain*. Succinctly put, perception requires cognition, the use of a "knowing" facility—feeling or thinking—and it is the coupling of the brain to vital organ of feeling and the mental organ of thinking that makes the brain a quantum brain.

## The Secret

You have now discovered the secret of the universe: you create your own reality. Why not use your creative power to manifest your favorite car, a big house, an unlimited bank account, all the things that you have always wanted? In the 1970s, when the physicist Fred Alan Wolf pronounced this wisdom, "we create our own reality," religious sects opened up shop teaching it, and some practitioners of the human potential movement taught workshops. I actually participated in one of these workshops called *Life Spring* and tried to learn the art of creating parking space for my car in downtown Portland, Oregon, where the workshop was taking place; I never succeeded in creating a parking space by the way. I drove to the downtown for five consecutive days with hope but always ended up paying for a parking garage with frustration.

So again, you in your conscious ego do not create reality, quantum physics is not telling us that. The power is there but is in the transcendent domain in the form of downward causation. And quantum physics does good, it tells us the mechanics of how the power comes into play. The power lies in choice, in our freedom to choose creatively from the quantum possibilities offered to us. Again, notice the nontrivial nature of the material universe. It is the material interactions, their upward causation that creates the material possibilities we process in the unconscious out of which nonlocal consciousness makes the choice for physical events. Both upward and downward causation is important to create the material world.

Thus, the questions of manifestation for the ego are: How do I become creative? How do I achieve access to nonlocal consciousness and its power of downward causation? Can I use this access and causal power to become increasingly happy? How?

## The Tao and the Science of Happiness

Some decades ago, the physicist Fritjof Capra wrote a book with a great title: *The Tao of Physics*. The book made considerable impact on the development of this new science to replace the old materialist science.

What is the Tao of Physics? Fritjof gives a very long answer. Is there only an incredibly long answer to the enunciation of *The Tao of happiness*?

I don't think so. The *Tao* in the original Chinese Taoism means "the absolute ground of being". The Tao comes to us in two modalities—the transcendent yin and the immanent yang—says Lao Tzu, the great master. So, in the language of quantum physics, Tao is consciousness as the ground of being, yin takes us to transcendent waves of possibility, yang is the movement in immanent actuality. In terms of how we process, we process yin with stillness; we use yang to develop various conditioned movements. Therefore, in the creative process, yang represents our movement, do-do-do, yin represents stillness, be. And creativity thrives when we alternate between them—do-be-do-be-do.

The essence of Taoist science of happiness is this: in the nature of things and how they change, there will be imbalances of yin and yang. These imbalances bring us suffering and unhappiness. The recipe for wholeness or happiness is simple: balance and harmonize the yin and yang.

For the record, the quantum science of happiness we've developed here agrees. *Yang* is movement, drive to do, *yin* is stillness, to be. For wellness, we have to use them both in a harmonized way. The Tao of quantum happiness is achieved when we develop the ability of living in this harmony that some psychologists call ''the flow experience'' mentioned before.

One loose end remains. The paradox of the mystical experience of Oneness, the paradox that we started this chapter with. But no worries, keep reading and it will all be revealed with the turn of a page.

# CHAPTER 6

# The Mystics Claim: "Experiencing" the Unconscious Oneness

The term "consciousness" entered the human vocabulary (via the Sanskrit word *Brahman*; the English word is fairly recent) because mystics claimed that they have experienced "Oneness," a state without separation, without subject-object split, something today we call a state of "unconscious." In Sanskrit, these so-called "experiences" are called Nirvikalpa Samadhi (Samadhi without separateness of subject and object). In contrast, the spontaneous experiences involving the quantum self are called Savikalpa Samadhi, Samadhi with separateness, Samadhi with subject-object split.

The paradox here is quite tangible. One mystic I met, the philosopher Franklin Merrell-Wolff used the word "imperience," a word he coined, as a way to distinguish and clarify between the two Samadhis, Savikalpa experience and Nirvikalpa imperience.

The paradox of the Nirvikalpa baffled me for years. The reason I kept at trying to understand it is that if the mystics' claim is right, then their imperience is verifying the metaphysical assertion of the quantum worldview—consciousness is the ground of all being. It's been said that that you can never fully verify metaphysical truth, but there it is. Quantum worldview is an exception: it is "experimental metaphysics" (a phrase coined by philosopher Abner Shimony).

Then one day, the answer came to me. The Nirvikalpa, beyond the brain experience to most scientists is something incredible, as it may be to you as well. But look at the phenomenon through the wisdom of quantum physics, the concept of delayed choice; you will be amazed at what you discover.

## The Delayed Choice Experiment

The physicist John Wheeler suggested an experiment to demonstrate that conscious choice is crucial in the shaping of manifest reality even on a delayed basis. This is called ''the delayed-choice experiment" and has been duly verified in the laboratory.

To get a better understanding of the concept of delayed choice, consider the macro world delayed choice experiment carried out successfully by the physicist/parapsychologist Helmut Schmidt and collaborators in 1993.

Originally, Schmidt had been researching psychokinesis, moving matter through conscious intentions, over many years with some measure of success. Some of these experiments involved random number generators that generate random sequences of zeroes and ones using random radioactive decay processes.

His 1993 experiment was revolutionary because, with tremendous ingenuity, Schmidt was able to combine his psychokinetic experiments with random number generators and the idea of the delayed-choice experiment. In this experiment, the radioactive decay was detected by electronic counters, resulting in the computer generation of random number sequences that were then recorded on floppy disks. With utmost care-making sure that no observer saw them- the computer even made a printout of the scores; then the printout was mechanically sealed and only then a human being sent the sealed envelope to an independent researcher, who left the seal intact.

A few months later, the independent researcher instructed the psychics to try to influence the random numbers generated in a specific direction, to produce either more zeros or more ones. The psychics tried to influence the random number sequence in the direction proposed by the independent researcher. Only after they had completed this stage, did the independent researcher open the sealed envelope to check the printout to see if there was a deviation in the direction instructed.

Schmidt found a statistically significant effect. Somehow his psychics were able to influence even a macroscopic printout of data that, according to conventional wisdom, had been taken months ago. The conclusion is inescapable and irrefutable. All objects in a causal string remain in possibility, even macroscopic objects, until consciousness chooses from the possibilities and an event of actualization occurs. Then it all manifests, retroactively, going backward in time.

So, the explanation of the mystics' experience of Nirvikalpa Samadhi is to be found in delayed choice.

The Nirvikalpa-mystics draw their "imperiences" from the most rarefied aspect of the unconscious—the previously unmanifest quantum unconscious. According to legends, there are two types of Nirvikalpa. In the first type, the mystics talk about images of the archetypes of the Platonic vintage—gods and goddesses in Hinduism, angels and archangels in Christianity, the Jungian archetypes in modern psychology. An excellent example is the Indian mystic Ramakrishna's repeated encounter with Goddess Kali.

But the same Ramakrishna, after being told by a woman yogini that there is a "Samadhi even higher" than this, persevered and had and reported an imperience of no qualification at all, no description of it he said is possible. Obviously, this is the ultimate, consciousness as it were. It is beyond even the archetypes, beyond physical laws, beyond quantum physics. This is Nirvikalpa of the second type, about which no words can accurately describe.

The Nirvikalpa of the first kind is the state of highest happiness on our scale, Level 6. This is what is called by the Sanskrit word *Turiya*, or the fourth state of consciousness beside the three familiar ones—wakefulness, dream, and deep sleep. This is the foundational "ground of being" of quantum physics.

Our legends tell us, that when the mystics come back from Nirvikalpa to ordinary consciousness, there is so much joy there, that people in the proximity can feel it, that they too are affected by the energy.

For those of us who are aficionados of quantum science, the best part of documenting Nirvikalpa Samadhi, is that this demonstrates that a direct experiential verification of the metaphysics of quantum science is feasible; everyone in principle can "see" for themselves, overcoming the ego perspective of denial.

Are there other cases of such delayed choice phenomena in our experience? One example is how we get a preconscious—the zone between unconscious and normal conscious awareness (for details, read *The Quantum Brain*). Another great example is the well-documented near-death experience or NDE. I have written about NDE and its delayed-choice explanation in many of my earlier books. Read *See the World as a Five-Layered Cake: The Quantum Science of Consciousness and Its Experiences* for a discussion about NDE.

# CHAPTER 7

# The Multiplicity of Our Experiences

*Millennia ago, in India, a curious boy asked his father—a wise teacher—"Father, what is the nature of reality?" The father, though pleased with the question does not answer directly, "Why don't you meditate and find out for yourself?" The son meditates for a while, gets an idea, and goes to his father for verification. "Reality is matter—the stuff of which my body is made, the stuff of the food that I eat." The father approves. "Yes," he says, "But meditate some more." The boy goes away, meditates, and after a while, based on his experience no doubt, has another idea. "Reality is the vital body, the container of energy that I feel-vitality," he declares to his father this time. The father approves but encourages him to meditate some more. Once again, the boy does what he is told; soon he has another idea. "Reality is mind, the vehicle with which we think and explore meaning, father." Father says, "Yes, but go deeper."*

*The son is determined. This time he meditates and meditates and finally a shiver runs down his spine as he discovers intuition and quickly runs to his father. "Father, father. I found it, I found it! Reality is stuff from which our sciences come from, the context of what matter does, what vital energy movements are all about, the contexts of our thinking, even the values to live by." He is talking about the archetypes of course. A smile breaks on his father's face. But he says. "Good. But go deeper my son." By now, the son is really motivated, and meditates again and soon discovers the oneness of everything, that reality is one and only, without limits or boundaries. His being fills with joy and a certainty comes to him. This is it. He does not go back to his father anymore, there is no need to confirm what he now knows as...truth.*

This story is from the Upanishads. This is probably the earliest reference to the four types of our experiences: sensing, feeling, thinking, and intuiting and four types of bodies that we have where we experience these four things. The last discovery is one of oneness—consciousness—itself, the ground of all being, consisting of all these four worlds of potentialities as we call it today in quantum lingo.

Of the four experiences, the physical—sensing—is very obvious, but the others are not. It is not easy to feel our vital energies in the body, pure feelings. We

usually experience feelings mixed with thoughts—
objects that we call emotions. Only if we develop
a sensitivity to our body, can we feel pure feelings.
Today, we are not in touch with our body as we could
be, we are very much brain-centered creatures. James
Joyce wrote about one of his characters, "Mr. Duffy
lives a little distance from his body." These days, we
are all "Mr. Duffy" to a greater degree (men) and Ms.
Duffy to a lesser degree (women). You may think the
existence of the mind should be easy to tell since we
are always thinking. Don't we need a mind for doing
our thinking? Thinking is associated with the brain;
how do we know that thinking does not come from
the brain itself?

As for intuition, it is kind of a fleeting experience;
after all we discover it only if we follow up an intuitive thought—those special thoughts that come with
a gut feeling that, although often non-rational, has a
grain of truth! Should we take our intuitions seriously?
Does it really exist? It takes, patience, meditation, and
creativity to find out.

In modern psychology, Carl Jung went about discovering the four-fold nature of experiences in a different way altogether. Jung was studying types of personalities with which people process their experiences.
He found four types of personalities: sensing, feeling,
thinking, and intuiting. The sensing personalities look
at the world through their senses, primarily valuing
the physical. The feeling types value their feelings over
their other experiences. The thinking type is rational-

ity dominated. Finally, the intuiting types live their lives on the basis of their intuitions, an understanding that goes beyond conscious reasoning.

The good news is that today quantum science is validating for us what the authors of the Upanishads had discovered through meditation and creativity, and what Jung had discovered through empirical data. In this way, quantum science that assumes the four-fold nature of experience has a solid scientific basis. How do we know vital energies are not material energies? How do we know mind is not brain? How do we know our supramental intuitions are not just some sort of aberration or oddity? In Chapter 5, I have shown how quantum physics leads us to the inescapable conclusion that consciousness, not matter, is the ground of all being. Today, there are satisfying scientific answers to all these other questions as well: our vital energy feelings are the movement of vital software associated with the physical hardware that we call the organs; the neocortex makes representation-software-of mental meaning. The relationship of the vital and the mental to the physical is not one of cause-effect as materialists assume, but rather the result of what in quantum physics we call "correlation" or "entanglement."

Materialists think MRI—Magnetic Resonance Imaging—pictures of the brain states undergoing change as we think different thoughts, show that our mind is brain. But look at the same data from the "brain is correlated with the mind" perspective. What then? The MRI pictures are providing us a measure of the mental state by showing its effect on the brain state.

No, we cannot measure the nonphysical mind with our physical apparatuses, but we can measure the effect of the mind on the brain!

Can we measure the vital energies, the movements of the vital blueprints of our organs? The body organs, the nonlocal correlates of the vital blueprints, are not electrical; it is hard to measure simultaneous changes occurring in them as our mood swings. But guess what? An unexpected breakthrough has occurred!

We have a bioelectric body in addition to our biochemical body. People have been claiming seeing auras around people for millennia, but few scientists have taken them seriously. Well, now it is fact. The aura is due to a bioelectric body that surrounds our biochemical body.

Kirlian photography was discovered by the Russian scientists Semyon and Valentina Kirlian. It involves the use of an electric transformer called a Tesla coil (designed by inventor Nikola Tesla in 1891) which is connected to two metal plates. A person's finger is placed between the plates where a piece of film touches it. When electricity is turned on what the film records is called a Kirlian photograph of the finger.

Typically, Kirlian photographs show an "aura" around the living object. Proponents of Kirlian photography claim that the color and intensity of the aura are descriptors of the emotional state of the person (whose finger is being used in taking the photograph).

For example, red and blotchy aura corresponds to the emotion of anxiety. A glow in the aura indicates relaxation, and so forth.

Changes in vital energy as in mood swings, in turn change the programs that run the organs whose functions also change, reflecting the mood fluctuations. The photograph is measuring the change in the physical bioelectric level, but because the physical level changes are correlated with the vital level changes, indirectly we are measuring the latter as well.

Over the years these techniques of measuring changes in the bioelectric body in response to changes in the vital body have grown much in sophistication. My hypothesis is that the entire purpose of the bioelectric body is to provide us with a measurement device for our vital body.

## Quantum Psycho-Physical Parallelism

A short summary: Consciousness is the ground of all being and in it and inseparable from it there are four parallel worlds of potentiality: the physical, the vital, the mental, and the archetypal or supramental. The conversion of potentiality to actuality in each of these worlds gives us the four types of experience: sensing, feeling, thinking, and intuiting respectively (*Figure10*).

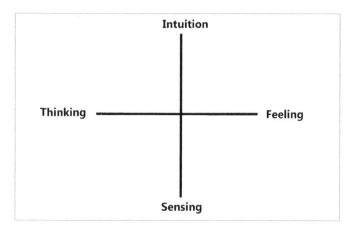

*Figure 10: The Quantum Psycho-physical parallelism: each of our four types of experiences comes from each of four parallel worlds of potentiality. Consciousness meditates and maintains the parallelism.*

Consciousness nonlocally mediates communication between the four worlds; consciousness maintains their goings on in parallel; in this way dualism is avoided.

Imagine you are looking at a rose that someone sent you:

- There is a physical perception (sensing) of a rose.

- There is a mental thought of meaning behind the sensing of the rose.

- There is a feeling of romance.

- There is an intuition of the archetype of beauty.

Where do the meaning, feeling and the archetypal content come from? Consciousness actualizes them, too, along with your physical perception of the rose from the parallel domain of potentialities.

## The External-Internal Dichotomy

Quantum psychology forces us to think about the physical and mental worlds differently from how we are used to thinking of them. Normally, we think of both these worlds as made of substances. Sure, the mental substance is subtle, we cannot quantify it in the same way as we can the physical, but it is still a substance, or so we think. We need to change this view. Even the physical is not substance in the ordinary sense, let alone the mental. Both physical and mental worlds remain as possibilities until consciousness gives them substantiality by actualizing an experience.

But even so there are differences between physical and mental substances when we experience them. One big difference is the grossness, externality of the macro world of our shared perception of the physical domain. In comparison, the mental world is experienced as subtle, internal.

As the great philosopher and mathematician Descartes correctly intuited, mental substance is indivisible. For this substance, then, there is no reduction to smaller and smaller, there is no micro out of which the macro is made. So, the mental world is considered whole, one that physicists sometimes call an infinite medium. There can be waves in such infinite media, modes of movement that can be identified as quantum possibility waves. In between collapses and experiences, all mental modes, big or small, are subject to rapid quantum movement; they quickly expand and become large pools of possible meanings. What this means is that between my actualization and yours, between my thinking and your thinking, the quantum mental modes would have expanded in possibility so much that it becomes unlikely that you will actualize the same thought as me. Therefore, two different people cannot ordinarily share thoughts; thoughts are private, they are experienced internally.

This internality is proof positive that mind is quantum, and its arena is infinite with no micro-macro division. And by the same token of internality, we can safely assume that the vital world of feeling and the supramental world of intuition are also quantum worlds.

So, what's the bottom line? When all is said and done, realize that only the material world can give us a tangled hierarchy which is why the material world is essential for manifestation of any and all our experiences. A disembodied entity cannot have experiences.

## Balancing Outer and Inner

What is psychologically normal? A long time ago, a psych professor defined it for me in a practical way: normal are those people who can cope with their neurosis in most situations and with the help of some occasional therapy if the going gets tough. Then she playfully added.. "Of course, most therapies are also just advanced coping mechanisms."

In quantum science, normal is primarily maintaining a healthy internal life, the ability to have a satisfactory internal place to live. And that may need occasional psychotherapy, but as you will see, psychotherapy in quantum style is more than providing a coping mechanism, it also helps to maintain balance between the various dichotomous aspects of the human condition. One of the major dichotomies is the external/internal dichotomy.

We are supposed to have grown into a normal adult when we have sufficient ego-repertoire to handle most situations and stimuli of our world. Now realize this! For followers of materialist science, the world is very narrow, just the material matters. Unfortunately for your psychological well-being, the challenging part is what the situations and stimuli arouse in your internal worlds of mental and vital. So cognitive/behavioral approach to psychology will not be very helpful to define a psychologically normal happy human adult. Information processing would not help either. The worst part of information overload of today's youth is that it tilts them off balance way in favor of the physical (information is meaning coded into symbols), sacrificing the mental.

In quantum psychology, we ask questions like, what is going on in my meaning life? What is going on in my feeling life, emotional life, archetypal life? We recognize from the get-go, that in the waking awareness, the physical clamors take up too much of our attention. How do you loosen up the dominance of the physical/external to sort out how your meaning and emotional and intuitional lives are going?

Are people not normal and happy if they don't pay attention to meaning, feeling, and intuition? Realize that much of what we call neurosis results from our lack of attention to the internal—the worlds of meaning, emotions, and intuitions. There are two phenomena that help us bring our meaning life to the forefront of the psyche: dreams and synchronicity. There is one phenomenon, the chakras in our body, paying attention to which brings us to the appreciation of pure feelings and positive emotions. There is the phenomenon of creativity where all three meaning, feeling, and archetypes get attention. To balance and integrate the internal and external, it's vitally important that we pay attention to these phenomena.

## Back to the Polarization of the Psychology Profession: Hierarchy of Needs

We have discussed in Chapter 1 the polarization of the psychologies into two groups: 1) cognitive-behavioral, and 2) depth and transpersonal. The two groups subscribe to different worldviews. For group 1, the worldview is matter-based; for group 2, the worldview is consciousness-based. We also pointed out that quantum psychology, by integrating the materialist metaphysics within the idealist metaphysics integrates the two groups of psychology.

And now you can see the beauty of the quantum approach. With materialist psychology, we can only deal with people's survival needs. Indeed, at the stage of evolution we are in, most people live in the survival mode. In this mode, the answers to your mental-emotional problems that require therapy by and large can be given from the mechanistic approach of the first group.

The problem arises when your survival needs are satisfied, and you have become aware of your higher needs. Then you need the consciousness-based approach. This hierarchy of needs was discovered and emphasized by Abraham Maslow.

Does this mean that people of survival needs can ignore quantum psychology? One wishes it was so simple. Human beings live in societies. Human beings need relationship and here is where the materialist approach of treating you as independent separate objects is not going to work. You need causally potent consciousness to engage in relationships, you need meaning and purpose.

People who engage higher needs have discovered spiritual values—the archetypes. When they embody and live these values, the quality of their living improves enormously. Naturally, they want to bring the same quality of living to their community which is largely ignorant of the human potentiality. Thus, is created higher education, education to enlighten the ignorant by removing the ignorance.

In this way we created spiritual traditions and civilizations. Here again today, people mistakenly identify material affluence and technological progress as marks of civilization. The word actually indicates the society's ability of civil behavior to all, irrespective of color, creed, sex, sexual preference, wealth, social status, etc.

Unfortunately, the limitations of our brain and body manages to dogmatize all systems of living to serve the power of a few elites. In this way, spiritual wisdom traditions degenerated into organized religions and eventually, civilizations were undermined.

Science is also a knowledge system. The spiritual wisdom traditions used intuition and creativity-based insights for theory building and experience to verify them. Science did one step better: creative theory based on experience, experimental data to verify the theory. For a while science and religion cooperated: science for the world of nonliving, religion for the world of the humans.

Of course, the success of the old science in the material world and to some extent even for the living world did not extend to psychology. It is the polarization of psychologies that must have been one of the important contributing factors toward the formulation and eventual widespread acceptance of the materialist dogma—material monism.

Of course, religions saw materialist science as a power play to demolish religions. If the world of matter is everything, there is no room for God, downward causation, and spiritual values. Materialist science did not have any credibility with religious people and more. Most nonscientists, especially people of the creative arts did not experientially subscribe to material monism; but they acquiesced.

Can one live without spiritual values? One can but at what price! We have to give up the idea of higher needs, human potentiality, and civilization. This is what is happening to America and most of the world today.

The materialist science has forced social thinkers to formulate an ad hoc philosophy called humanism that coopts spiritual values as human values. How do people follow them? Not being a part of the regular experience of human beings locked into survival needs, these values are imposed upon them as "politically correct." It is this revolt against political correctness that created the phenomenon of Donald Trump.

Well, Trump maybe in the past but the problem remains, how to deal with mental health of both groups of people: those acquiescing to valueless materialist science and imposing values on others using politics and those who have been traditionally confused about the values due to their religious dogmas. The answer is of course: education, higher education in the true meaning of the phrase.

In this way, quantum psychologists will have a dual role to play: as healers as well as educators. If you follow quantum psychology and begin to climb the ladder of happiness to Level 3 and beyond, you will find yourself transformed; your character will have changed. Maslow hinted at this; he called it self-actualization. That is the entrance requirement for a teacher of higher education—quantum style.

# CHAPTER 8

# Discovering Happiness Within the Mind-Brain Relationship

Consider this—just because thoughts always occur in association with the brain—the mind is not of the brain. In other words, the brain does not cause or create mental thought. The mind's essence is meaning processing and the mind is not brain as materialists say because brain looked upon as a step-by-step operating computer as materialists correctly theorize, cannot process meaning.

It can be confusing because the mind has content that can be coded as information or symbols. When we experience the coded content, we then experience meaning, and the meaning comes so automatically we take it for granted as part of the content. But truly, meaning is another category of logic; it is subtle, not computable. And if you are honest, it does not take you long to realize that thinking about meaning to discover new meanings for yourself is more satisfying to you than processing meaning in an automatic way, solely as information.

Imagine that your brain is looking at a TV set. There are movements of physical objects that show up as electrons on the TV screen. Light photons from the screen move to your eye and interact with matter in the eye and subsequently some of the rest of the brain. Now, the brain scientist can summarize the resulting information as a brain state of some detail. However, what you experience when your brain looks at the screen and there is a love scene, or a situation comedy is not as easily summarized, because somehow meaning appears. That experience, that meaning, is not part of what the brain scientist can tell you about, the brain state. As it turns out, your mind is providing the meaning.

Artificial intelligence researchers attempt to construct programmed computers that can think. Indeed, today computer programs can generate contents of thought versatile enough to fool a human being, once thought to be a sufficient condition for a computer to be called intelligent. But as mentioned earlier, the philosopher John Searle first pointed out that apart from content, thoughts also involve meaning, and this latter a computer, being a symbol processing machine, can never process. Our human meanings have been fed to the computer as programs of symbols processing symbols building a large repertoire. When you talk to the program, your meanings are again fed to the computer as information and become symbols. The computer programs look for programmed cues that trigger the programmed response still in symbols. And another program converts these symbols back to human meanings. All is mechanical, the computer never has to deal with meanings, it never has to understand, it cannot; this is Searle's point. In 1991, the mathematical physicist Sir Roger Penrose perfected Searle's proof with application of mathematics.

We need a nonphysical mind to process meaning, and consciousness to understand. This is what quantum psychology provides.

## The Quantum Nature of the Mind and Other Objects of the Psyche

Internality is proof positive that the mind is quantum. There are other ways that show evidence of the quantum nature of thoughts-such as- thoughts can be nonlocal and discontinuous, very quantum-like, in some of their operation. Nonlocality of the mind is revealed in such phenomena as mental telepathy and distant viewing; Nonlocality is signal less communication possible only for quantum objects. Discontinuity is revealed in the phenomenon of creativity in which we discover new meaning of value. As mentioned before, when electrons jump from one atomic orbit to another, they never go through the intermediate space. Similarly, when we experience a creative insight, the experience is sudden without intermediate steps of reasoned algorithms. The signature of the discontinuity of a creative thought is the surprise, the reason creative experiences are called "AHA!" experiences.

The same quantum attributes—internality, nonlocality, and discontinuity are found for feelings and intuitions as well. So, we can conclude that all our internal objects are quantum.

## The Nature of Memory

In the process of perception/cognition, consciousness uses the brain to make a memory-trigger involving neuronal circuits with correlated mental memory consisting of a meaningful image. Subsequently, the brain memory is triggered in response to a stimulus, the correlated mental memory also plays out.

Memory retrieval is a difficult problem of brain science. We recall computer memory by button pushing. But where is the button to push for a brain? Sure, a neurosurgeon can cut open the human skull and poke suitable areas of the brain with an electrode, and there comes memory! But we do not do it that way; we seem to do it by intention. In quantum psychology, brain memory and its associated mental meaning both are quantum (determined) possibilities in the unconscious. When we intend, unconscious cooperates (this is the law!) and collapses the appropriate memory.

The quantum way of looking at memory recall also agrees very well with the experimental findings of neurosurgeon Wilder Penfield. Penfield researched extensively with epileptic patients probing their brain with electrodes in search of the so-called memory "engram" (a unit of cognitive information stored in the brain). He did find groups of neurons which, when activated played out even elaborate memories of entire symphonies! How can a little piece of the brain contain so much memory? In quantum science, there is a correlated nonphysical mental memory to a little neuronal circuit to explain such elaborate memory recall!

There are other aspects of memory that are puzzling. We all experience, and neurophysiologists have found much data corroborating our experience, that there are three kinds of memory: working memory, short term memory, and long-term memory. Why three kinds? It is somewhat puzzling!

On closer inspection, we find that working memory is for insignificant stuff—stuff without meaning. Mechanical at best. Consciousness and its meaning-giving mind is not really engaged. Cognitive scientists do not even consider it as a separate category.

Why short-term memory and long-term memory for meaningful stuff? Why not just one kind? We reinforce memory retrieval by repeated recall. And we use these recalls not only to reinforce the memory, but also to reconstruct them with the help and influence of other memories of same and similar stimulus-response situations. That is how we build memory compatible to the self-image we project—the personality masks.

When we finally settle on a particular piece of memory (when it is in equilibrium with our self-image) that is when it becomes stored as a "permanent" memory. This is the memory that even Alzheimer patients can recall in the early stages!

It is estimated that it takes roughly about ten years of processing at the short-term level before we make them long term. The lesson to remember here is that memories that we recall are not "facts," they are reconstructive and are constantly in flux during a period. You should always remember this when recalling memory in connection to your relationships: each of us will have somewhat different memories, connected to the same event. The Japanese movie *Rashomon* illustrated this idea beautifully and is the basis for "The Rashomon Effect" that describes a situation in which an event is given contradictory interpretations or descriptions by the individuals involved.

## From Information to Meaning and Happiness

There is a great question before us. How do we live in this information-based culture and still find meaning in our lives? Mind you, on so many levels, the world of so-called "higher" education has become a wasteland as far as meaning is concerned. Physicists routinely say there is no point in the universe. Bio-philosophers assert that just like genes help build the physical body, there are cultural "memes"—bits of information—of evolutionary origin that make up what we experience as mind. The truth is, meaning does not fit the metaphysics of scientific materialism's the "all-is-matter philosophy!"

A matter-based culture invariably gravitates toward making it appear that all that is needed is information, you don't need to bother about meaning. At worst, let other people—the elite—provide the meaning. So how do you go from this to a meaning-based mindset so that you can participate in the grand scheme of the universe?

First, notice that all you have learned from your education is other people's meanings of a particular subject or area of study. To reverse this, start giving meaning to stuff that you experience yourself: of art, of poetry; however unsophisticated as they may sound, take your own meanings more seriously than other people's meanings. It takes a while, but you get the hang of it sooner or later and it becomes fun. Then one day, you discover a new meaning of an experience that nobody else has thought of and there you are. You have become a person who is truly an individual who can be enthused about how to become an original human being, which is a great achievement. This will bring you satisfaction, happiness.

Back in the 70s, when I was trying to be more of an individual, I did a lot of work with *Zen Koans*, those very puzzling statements, parables, and questions that the Zen Buddhist tradition has developed. Questions like "What was your name before you were born?"

One very effective way of getting into personal meanings is to engage with your own dreams. In quantum psychology, dreams are seen as made up of mental meaning represented by pictures made up from the Rorschach (as in ink blot) of brain noise. If it is a little hard to analyze your own dreams for hidden meaning, do the analysis with the help of a friend. You can analyze each other's dreams. Dream analysis can be a journey of self-discovery of profound satisfaction.

Of course, the way to do all this systematically is to creatively engage with phenomena looking for new meaning. Quantum science teaches us the subtleties of the creative process to do exactly that.

By the way, are you still puzzling over that *Zen Koan*, "What was your name before you were born?" The quantum answer to that question is: Possibility.

## Synchronicity

In quantum psychology, synchronicities are events of meaningful coincidence consisting of one external and one internal event of quantum collapse precipitated by a common cause—consciousness. Synchronicities are examples of consciousness reaching out to you to show the way. They expand your consciousness when you see the meaning you feel happy.

An example from Carl Jung will make the specialness of synchronicity experiences for mental health quite clear. Jung was dealing with a client, a young woman, who was psychologically inaccessible, and did not respond to Jung's repeated attempts to sweeten her rationalism. Jung was desperately hoping that something unexpected and irrational would turn up, helping Jung to break through the woman's intellectual shell.

And then the following synchronistic event took place:

*"I was sitting opposite her one day, with my back to the window…. She had an impressive dream*

*the night before, in which someone had given her a golden scarab—a costly piece of jewelry. While she was still telling me the dream, I heard something behind me gently tapping on the window. I turned around and saw that it was a fairly large flying insect that was knocking against the window pane. I opened the window immediately and caught the insect in the air as it flew in. It was a scarabaeidae beetle, or common rose-chafer (Cetoniaaurata), whose gold-green color most nearly resembles that of a golden scarab. I handed the beetle to my patient with the words, "Here is your scarab."*

(*The Portable Jung*, Joseph Campbell (Ed.))

This synchronistic appearance of the "dream scarab" in this patient's inside awareness and the beetle/scarab in her outer awareness broke through the young woman's intellectual shell and she became psychologically accessible to her therapist, Jung.

Synchronistic events like this happen to everyone in need of a breakthrough in connection with romance, therapy, creativity, meaning-of-life questions in general, just to name a few contexts.

More explicitly, in Jung's thinking synchronistic occurrences are traceable to objects of the collective unconscious—the Jungian archetypes. The Jungian archetypes are representations of the Platonic archetypes.

If you want to incorporate meaning in your life, synchronicity offers you a viable means. Allow me to share a few examples of how creative people, the explorers of new meaning, used synchronistic experiences.

Dajian Huineng, the sixth patriarch of Chinese Chan Buddhism, was living with his mother in poverty and selling wood in a marketplace. One day, he delivered firewood to a customer, wherein he met a man reciting the Diamond Sutra. "On hearing the words of the scripture, my mind opened up and I understood" he was suddenly enlightened, which eventually led Huineng to become regarded as the founder of *the Sudden Enlightenment Southern Chan School of Buddhism,* which focuses on an immediate and direct attainment of Buddhist enlightenment.

Alexander Calder was visiting an art gallery that displayed the abstract art of Piet Mondrian, and in a flash of inspiration, he had thought of using abstract pieces in his moving sculptures, which would lead him to become the world-renowned pioneer of mobile sculpture.

Five-year old Albert Einstein was sick in bed when his father brought him a magnetic compass. Seeing the needle of the compass pointing to the north no matter how he turned the case containing the magnet gave, brought forth a sense of wonder in Einstein, which pervaded and guided his lifetime of scientific work.

The Nobel laureate poet Rabindranath Tagore saw raindrops falling on a leaf, and in that moment, two sentences of a little verse rhymed in the original Bengali came to his mind. The verse can be translated thus: It rains, the leaves tremble. Later, Tagore wrote about this experience as follows:

> *"The rhythmic picture of tremulous leaves beaten by the rain opened before my mind the world which does not merely carry information, but a harmony with my being. The unmeaning fragments lost their individual isolation and my mind reveled in the unity of a vision."*
>
> (Tagore, *The Religion of Man*, p. 93)

Huineng, Calder, Einstein, and Tagore woke up to the purposiveness of the universe as a direct result of their synchronistic experiences. And they dedicated their lives to the service of the archetypes, to make a better representation of truth for Einstein, of beauty and love for Tagore, self, and enlightenment for Huineng and a deep sense of purpose in the beauty of movement, for Calder.

## Mythology as a Guideline for Programming of the Mind and Vital

In the quantum worldview, the world cannot run entirely on laws, knowledge, and logic. In quantum-based science within the primacy of consciousness, matter is hardware in computer lingo. We not only use matter to represent consciousness in the form of the self, but also to make software of our subtle experiences in the form of brain memory, epigenetic programming for the body organs, and their modifications. The material hardware indeed follows physical laws. But just as in the working of our silicon computers, the hardware laws can tell us nothing about the behavior of the software.

In the silicon computer, we make software to map our mental storylines via algorithms and process them consciously. We do exactly the same thing with our bio-computer except that there is no algorithm, at least not always. Do these story lines have any order at all? Of course, they do; if they did not there would be no arts, no humanities to learn about. No civilization to build. The order comes from guidelines from the supramental Platonic archetypes; our mythology is the history of the play of these guidelines. As philosopher William Irwin Thomson wrote, "Mythology is the history of the soul." The soul, in quantum psychology, is defined as our "supramental body"—which would be a birthing of a newly formed person that was created out of a connection to the same primal source that created the physical universe—albeit a facsimile built from mental and vital representations of the archetypes.

One of these mythical story lines that play a very important role in personal growth toward increasing happiness is called the *Hero's Journey*. In the first stage, the hero departs on a journey in search of finding truth or wisdom (often after ignoring "the call" many times over) to the greater meanings of life. In the second stage, the hero, through many trials and tribulation, triumphs, and failures, finally discovers wisdom. Then in the third and final stage, the hero returns triumphant, a resurrected soul, very different than the person who they once were.

In another mythological story of enormous importance to the psychology of the explorer is the myth of the *Holy Grail*: there is something wrong in the Kingdom, but at first our hero sees it, but does not say anything because of socio-cultural conditioning. Only after much work (hero's journey?), the hero gets enough courage to ask, "What's wrong here?" and then sets about making things right again, and the Kingdom is healed.

These are general myths to follow, they are for everybody. How do you know your personal myth, your particular meaning, your particular archetypal context of meaning that you want to explore? That's where dreams can help, as can intuition and memories of reincarnation recall that we'll discuss in another chapter.

The mythologist Joseph Campbell used to advise people, "Follow your bliss". Quantum psychology agrees with a little addition: find your archetype and follow it. In time, you will find your bliss, for what you are seeking the most, is also waiting for you to discover it.

# CHAPTER 9

# Happiness at the Chakras: Vital Energies and Their Relationship to the Body

As I stated earlier, the feelings of vital energies are associated with body organs, just as thoughts are associated with the neo-cortex of the brain. Another way of saying it would be that mind, mental potentialities, are embodied in the brain as mental software; and similarly, the vital body potentialities are embodied in the physical body organs as vital software (that includes the brain).

Let's go to the basics of the biology of consciousness. The conventional dogma of molecular biology is that biology is chemistry and that there is no difference between the living and the nonliving. The biology of consciousness begins with the bold (but obvious) assertion that life is fundamentally different from nonlife. A single living cell represents consciousness, albeit in a rudimentary way, as a cellular self by virtue of having a tangled hierarchy. For details, read the book *The Quantum Brain*.

One important part of the story of biology, is evolution from the simple single cell to the complex human beings that we are. Along the way, cellular complexes called organs came along that perform specific biological functions. Like physical laws, these biological functions are also part of the archetype of truth and belong to the archetypal world. And just as consciousness uses the quantum mind as an intermediary to map archetypal contexts in our brain, similarly, consciousness uses a quantum intermediary to represent the biological functions in the physical body organs.

Biological morphogenesis is the formal name of biological organ making. It has the problem of what is called cell differentiation. All organisms begin from a single cell embryo that then divides making exact replica of itself containing identical DNA. But cells must be differentiated on their way to making organs because cells in different organs perform very different functions. The genes in the cells of different organs are activated differently to make different sets of proteins, thus different functions. The biologist Rupert Sheldrake first proposed that these activation programs are epigenetic; they come from morphogenetic fields that must be nonphysical organizing principles. Morpho means form, genesis means creation. But these fields have more do with function than form; so, I call them *liturgical fields* (liturgical means functional) or to avoid confusion liturgical/morphogenetic fields. Now we must recognize the mediating role of nonlocal consciousness between the liturgical/morphogenetic fields and biological forms. Cell differentiation works as if the cell knows where in the body it is. In other words, cell differentiation smacks of nonlocality, the action of nonlocal consciousness.

You can also think of the liturgical/morphogenetic fields as blueprints of vital software. An architect uses a blueprint to make a house. Similarly, consciousness uses a liturgical/morphogenetic field as blueprints to program biological functions into the organ—the vital software of the organ hardware. And similarly, that is how consciousness uses the neo-cortex to make representations of mental meaning.

In summary, the liturgical/morphogenetic fields are blueprints of *epigenetic* software that guides the turn on or off the genes that make protein for organ functioning. Finally, what we normally feel as movements of vital energy are the movements of actualization of liturgical/morphogenetic fields in the form of the vital software. For vital creativity, when a new organ function is awakened, we experience the movement of new liturgical/morphogenetic fields.

## Developing the Visceral Awareness of Vital Energy Movements

When I started consciousness research, back in the late 1970s and early 1980s, psych departments were quite open to new ideas, and I hobnobbed quite a bit with University of Oregon Psych department colleagues. Then, one morning when I got an urgent call from a psych professor to come over and see a demonstration of something weird, I was not surprised. "We need a hard scientist to check out the authenticity of this guy. You are a hard scientist. Please come," my colleague pleaded. He did not have to plead too much; my curiosity was aroused, so I went.

The demonstration was simple. The fellow claimed that his palms were energized. He insisted that if one of us put our outstretched palm (right or left) in the gap between his outstretched palms, we would be able to feel vital energy.

So, one by one the psych professors took turns, but none of them felt anything discerning. I was the last person to test the guy. As I put my palm between his, Wham-O! I felt a surge of tingles!

I lost my credibility that day with my psych colleagues—they claimed I was too gullible. But my own curiosity was aroused. I grew up in India, where vital energy is not exactly a stranger. It is called *prana*.

It took me many years to achieve a theoretical understanding of how the guy had energized his palm so others could feel the energy. But of course, if we rub the skin of palms together, the liturgical/morphogenetic blueprints correlated with the skin get aroused and it is this movement that we feel as tingles, as vital energy.

So, this is a simple way to begin your exploration of feeling vital energy in your body. Matter of fact, you've had such experiences before. If you recall, when you fell in love, your first time back when you were a teenager, you felt similar tingles in your heart chakra, maybe even throbs. Explore energizing your heart chakra with your energized palms; you may be able to do it even without touching your chest, leaving no doubt that something nonlocal may be taking place, something that at first might seem unusual.

As you become familiar with the "feel" of vital energy, one of these days when you are in the throes of strong emotions suddenly visceral awareness of feeling will come to you, no doubt. This is a crucial aspect of the exploration of emotional intelligence—quantum style—a critical component in the pursuit of happiness.

## Chakras

In the chakra psychology of the East, feelings are recognized to be associated with seven major centers of our body—the chakras—where we feel our feelings. But through the centuries, although the idea of the chakras has found much empirical validations from spiritual disciplines, not much theoretical understanding has come. Now, finally, with the idea of non-physical liturgical/morphogenetic blueprints of organ software, an explanation of the chakras, where feelings originate and why, can be given. First, look at the major chakras (*Figure11*) and the feelings most people experience therein.

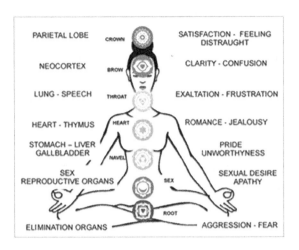

*Figure 11: The seven major chakras*

Notice that each of them is located near major organs for our body's biological functioning. Second, when you experience emotions, develop sensitivity to your body so you can trace the emotions to a feeling in the body at one of the chakra points. Make a note of the specific feeling you experience at each of these chakras. Third, realize that feelings of vital energy are the movements of the liturgical/morphogenetic blueprints of organ software that are correlated with the physical organs. In this way, every physical organ has a vital counterpart, a V-organ (*Figure12*).

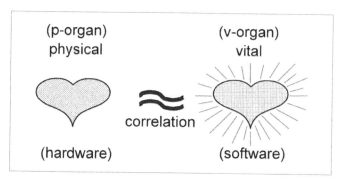

*Figure 12: A physical organ (P-organ) has
a correlated vital organ (V-organ)*

Let's call the conglomerates of all the liturgical/mor-
phogenetic software—V-Organs—correlated with
each of the physical organs-our vital body.

I will give further details of chakra psychology later
in this chapter. But here I will share with you how hard
it was for me, (at the time a materialist intellectual) to
get into the experience of the chakras, even though I
was open and curious about the concept.

In 1983, I was attending a workshop by the physi-
cian/spiritual teacher Richard Moss. Richard (along
with his colleagues) gave each one of us a "chakra
healing." Afterwards, there was a discussion, and many
were telling of their experiences in glorious terms. The
twenty-five people I shared the session with seemed to
have some sort of energy exchange, while I had hardly
any experience, and felt totally left out. Like "What am
I doing here?" Finally, I could not hold it any longer
and raised my arm.

"Yes, Amit."

"Richard, looks like you gave all these experiences to all these people, why not me? "

Richard said, "Amit, I can only open the door for you. It is you who has to pass through it."

"Sounds well and dandy. So, you are saying all these people passed through the door and I chose not to?"

"That's for you to decide. All these people left their selves at the door. That's the trick. Then you enter."

"But I am a scientist. I want to be there when it happens." I blurted out. Everybody was laughing. And I realized my mistake. In the next few days, I received ample doses of Richard's prescription medicine—juicy physicality consisting of intimate hugs, especially from women. After that and a few more sessions of chakra healing, I got it. I could experience energy in my chakras, the nonlocal connecting points for the V-Organs.

Truly, the experience of energy at the chakras can change your worldview. Many scientific materialists get stuck with the question; can macro physical bodies be quantum? Their answer is always as resounding "No." I explained in an earlier chapter, that macro material objects are approximately Newtonian. However, experiencing energy at any chakra will convince you of a vital counterpart of the physical organ whose energy movement you are experiencing. From that it is simple logic that this V-Organ must be correlated to the physical organ at the chakra. Since the V-organ is quantum, a macro-physical organ in our body gets to be quantum also when we experience its movement. Realize that it is the correlation with the vital counterpart that makes a macrophysical organ quantum.

## Chakra Psychology in the Light of the Quantum

Chakra psychology is a developed branch of Eastern yoga psychology. The idea is that consciousness identifies with each chakra in a unique way depending on the chakra's function. The term "chakra" is from a Sanskrit word meaning "wheel" or "disk." This should remind you of the circularity of tangled hierarchy. Were the ancient yogis intuiting tangled hierarchy and self-identity at the chakras?

Below is a chakra-by-chakra description of what the chakra psychology tells us about our chakras examined under the light of quantum psychology.

As you read the descriptions, take note that the chakras are more or less along the spine. Why do the chiropractors and osteopaths pay so much attention to align the spine? The underlying assumption is that the misalignment of the spine suggests unbalanced chakras. So, these specialists try to re-balance the chakras, which in turn gives relief to the affected areas.

## The Sacral or the Root Chakra

The root chakra is situated at the base of your spine. The organs it represents are the excretory organs. The biological function of catabolism is the breakdown of complex molecules in living organisms to form simpler ones and excretion of wastes of the body. In response to a stimulus, if you pay excess attention to this chakra, the feeling would be aggression; if your attention moves away in a hurry, the feeling is fear. For example, if a Bengal tiger suddenly appeared out of nowhere, it promptly takes your attention away, and you would feel fear. This, of course, would be good for you needing to take appropriate action-which in this case would be flight-not fight.

With evolution, however, the brain has largely taken over the control of the function of this chakra; there is indeed a corresponding instinctual brain circuit of emotion. And then the feelings associated with this chakra, aggression, or fear, are relegated to the more or less unconscious activity in the midbrain.

With further "opening" of this chakra via engaging creativity, the feeling at this chakra would be a feeling of "rootedness" and security.

Perhaps the worst aspect of energy blocks at the root chakra (for which chronic constipation is a symptom) is not feeling grounded: you lack the ability to be at the present moment let alone enjoy the moment. You are always anxiously revisiting the past for what went wrong and why it is making you anxious or weaving a future that will make ever more demand on you; this will create more fear and more anxiety. You become a pessimist. You may end up a loner because nobody can handle your fear and anxiety.

In this way, not keeping attention to root chakra energy and not engaging creativity, can lead to paranoia, anxiety neurosis, and panic attacks. And keep you from happiness. Alternatively, paying attention and being creative helps to keep this chakra fully engaged and open, and enables you to courageously explore your archetypes even though the society around you might not be in alignment.

## Sex Chakra

The primary biological function associated with the sex chakra is reproduction. For this you need a partner. Here again, the brain takes over; so, the brain circuit of sexual instinct drives you toward finding sexual partners—the sex drive. When mind puts meaning on the feelings associated with the sex chakra, sexual act is recognized as pleasure full. In this way, pleasure enters the equation for sex. The sex chakra is located in the lower abdomen.

During the 2012 election cycle, there was great political debate in America, as to whether we should have sex primarily for reproduction and only secondarily for pleasure or vice versa. People who are religious value reproduction over pleasure and people who are more science minded value pleasure over reproduction. In the debate, what got lost in all the rhetoric was the third aspect of sexuality which is—relationship.

In materialist science, we are looked upon as machines, reproductive machines to be sure, but machines, nonetheless. So, neither the self nor the "other" exists. In quantum psychology, we are humans with a self; and so is a partner, a human with a self-identity. For humans, the challenge of sexuality is to use it for an intimate relationship with another human that is unique about sex.

We can use sex for self-gratification, as a conquest in the service of narcissism, or we can use sex as in romance and use romance as an entry point for the archetypal exploration of love.

## The Navel Chakra

The biological function here is anabolism—the positive side of metabolism. When the chakra is only part open as is normal, the feeling is an assured body identity. The Japanese have known this for centuries and they call this chakra as body identity—the site of the body-ego—*hara*. When activated in excess, the feelings experienced are pride and narcissism. If it is a deficit of attention; the associated feeling is unworthiness.

When the brain enters the picture, the corresponding instinctual brain circuit dominates behavior. The feelings at the navel chakra likewise become part of our unconscious suppression-repression dynamic.

When an unconscious feeling of unworthiness surfaces what happens? There are two poles of possible behavior: one is to continue to hide it and behave like a narcissistic diva, as self-centered as can be. The other pole of behavior is to try to please the other to prove your worthiness to him/her.

Here is a culturally encouraged male-female difference: males are encouraged in most cultures to act as narcissistic, the females as pleasers. Most males learn to use sex to boost their body ego and some men become sexual predators and conquesters.

Most cultures do not allow the females to be promiscuous; so, most females never recover from their habits of pleasing others. In fact, they become more and more dependent on others for the vicarious feeling of worthiness. They become needy.

Some of the female divas do use sexuality to boost the body-ego. They are typically the independent women in traditional societies.

A dynamic change takes place when you cultivate body-awareness and appreciate visceral feelings and your navel chakra opens further. You begin to pay attention to the energies in the navel and cultivate self-worth. No longer do you need to please compulsively; nor do you need to hide your unworthiness behind the veil of a diva. Most of all, opening and cultivating this chakra is a necessary ingredient for becoming independent and eventually an original individual.

## The Heart Chakra

The heart chakra is the center of the feeling of romantic love. When you fall in love romantically with a partner and vice versa, there is no "me-not me" distinction between you and your partner; that immune system thymus gland function of distinction between "me" and "not me" is suspended for both of you. This temporary suspension of the immune system function in the form of the thymus gland is the prerequisite for the heart to open to a new function besides pumping blood—romantic love.

The feelings we get at the heart chakra during a romantic episode are so strong that even the most insensitive among us are not oblivious of these feelings; so, nobody can totally deny them. Even in this materialist age, the connection of heart and romance is acknowledged, and proven to a great extent.

Of course, people's minds respond to the feelings that arise, and often experience the resulting emotion tainted by the socio-cultural conditioning. Usually for men, these conditionings are not particularly liable to produce "love the other" oriented response; most cultures in the West encourage their men to be independent rugged individuals, not emotional and other oriented.

In this way, suppression of feelings of vulnerability (that arises when immune defense is suspended albeit temporarily) leads to adult men in the Western culture to become "iron men" who literally are unable to open up to love to anyone including a romantic partner even during a romantic episode.

On top of this, here also, the brain interferes through what is called psycho-neuro-immunological connection giving the experience of romantic love a molecular pleasure-boost no doubt; unfortunately, the boost does not last long because the associated brain neurochemicals of pleasure dry up.

Exceptions to the iron men syndrome are relatively rare; so, our popular stories constantly mythologize and talk about childhood buddies and college buddies with nostalgia, but in truth how common are they? It is much more common to see kids and young adults mingle because of their common interests, games etc. It is also not uncommon for such men to develop homophobia.

Freud theorized that most love is driven by libido and sexuality. A sudden feeling of love towards your own mother maybe a sign of Oedipus complex, Freudians tend to say. But it could be the other way around. Because men feel uneasy when their unconscious erupts with these feelings, they develop the Oedipus complex as part of the repression dynamic.

For women in the West, it is quite different. Women have an exclusive brain circuit, the maternity instinct, which activates at puberty. And even before puberty, most cultures encourage their little girls to be other love oriented in preparation for their future motherhood. So, adult women have grown up being quite sensitive to all their heart chakra feelings. Of course, their situation is not so great either because of suppression of self-worth at the third chakra (navel).

There are women who suppress the heart more like men and for some of them there is a danger for homophobia and Electra complex in the way explained above. But I think on the whole it is fair to say that these are relatively less prevalent problems among the female of our population.

The heart chakra is a chakra where one of the most important spiritual higher values, namely love, is represented as a feeling. All the subsequent higher chakras also are places where important higher values are represented as feelings.

## Negative Emotions at the Heart Chakra

There are also negative emotions associated with the heart. It is all good when your heart is occasionally open towards someone, but if your navel is not simultaneously open, what then? Then the relationship often cannot keep pace with the expectations and vulnerability of an open heart. So often what happens is jealousy and hurt—vital energy goes out from the heart to the navel. And ongoing hurt leads to bitterness.

There may also be grieving associated with the termination of a love episode. And when grieving comes together with bitterness, the result can be devastating, leading to hostility.

In therapy, the therapist has to work on the subject's letting go and acceptance: letting go of neediness and expectations, letting go of the past. And then, working on forgiveness, first of the subjects themselves and then the objects of their anger.

Generally speaking, these negative emotions associated with love can be mostly avoided by having a balance between the navel and the heart chakras.

## Higher Chakras

The throat chakra is the chakra of expressive organs, and the associated feelings are positive when we are free to express and negative when our freedom to express is suppressed.

Our creativity depends on how open this chakra is. In this way, it is very important to encourage children to express and engage in practices to keep this chakra open, creative. Singing in the shower is an excellent exercise for that.

The brow chakra organ is the prefrontal cortex located right behind your forehead. This organ is the seat of our ego-self, mental thought, and decision-making. When this chakra is partially open, and this is the case with most of us, it caters to rational thought. You will notice energy in your brow chakra when you concentrate on intellectual thinking. The feeling of clarity that has an intellectual origin is not so great. But when this chakra fully opens, our intuitive facility also opens up. Then the energy of clarity is truly spectacular.

On the negative side, if you don't pay attention to the brow chakra, which is you have a problem with focusing, you will suffer chronic confusion about intellectual matters.

The crown chakra organ is the parietal lobe at the top of the head that is associated with our body image. When partially open, the feelings are mostly concerned about the body image, "How do I look?"

When the function of the parietal lobe is suspended, the physical body identity shift to subtle body identity as in out of the body experiences that many people report. There is some neuroscience evidence for this thanks to neuroscientist Mario Beauregard, but more research is needed in this area.

## Brain Circuits

Materialists think that emotions originate in the brain, that is, emotions are brain epiphenomena (a secondary mental phenomenon); more exactly, they posit that emotions are brain's response to certain stimuli. They come to play a role in the body through the nervous system and via the so-called molecules of emotion, neuropeptides, and such.

Quantum psychology says that we feel feelings at the chakras directly in response to a stimulus as well if the stimulus is a living body. Via nonlocality.

What confuses the brain scientist (and also many of us) is that there are limbic brain circuits that also respond to stimuli that stimulate the low chakras. Why were these brain circuits made at the mid-brain during evolution? Efficiency.

Without some central control we would be rather inefficient in responding to a dangerous stimulus. For example, neurophysiologists generally agree that a stimulus of fear bypasses the neocortex going directly to the brain area of the Thalamus which relays it to the brain area of amygdala where the response is, on to the execution of the flight or fight response at the motor areas of action (*Figure13*).

This is a programmed response learned perhaps millions of years ago, when life was a lot more challenging for our evolutionary ancestors, the mammals. The conscious self would take too long to process the danger; hence the unconscious would very promptly kick into action bypassing the neocortex in order to keep us alive.

What we experience consciously in such an event— like a Bengal tiger crossing our path—an instinctual universal emotion of fear—feeling plus the meaning given to it—comes from the memory of humanity's collective unconscious. We will refer to the totality of the unconscious response as caused by the instinctual negative emotional brain circuits. In other words, the instinctual negative emotion is the movement of universal vital software guiding these brain circuits.

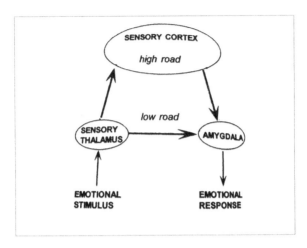

*Figure 13: Stimuli producing negative emotions go directly via the thalamus to the amygdala by-passing the neocortex (Ledoux, J., 1996, The Emotional Brain, N.Y.: Simon & Schuster)*

When the human mind of the current culture enters the picture, the mind melodramatizes and creates tigers out of other human beings like a boss or even a spouse. When we simulate an instinctual emotion through such imagination, a process I call mentalization of emotions, we make additional emotional software. But this is personal software, not universal.

Why is this distinction of universal and personal software of emotions important? The personal software of emotions is readily reprogrammable; but this is not the case of the universal software of emotions.

We mainly discussed the brain take-over of the low chakras, but there is the psycho-neuro-immuno-gastro-intestinology: brain has ongoing two-way communication with the immune system (of the heart chakra) and the gastro-intestinal system (of the navel chakra). So, brain's control is wider. For example, the brain circuits of jealousy, competitiveness, and domination, all are connected to the suppression of love energy at the heart and the navel that happened out of survival necessity during our evolution.

## Self-Identity at the Chakras

Remember that your "experiencing self" is tied up with the engagement of a tangled hierarchy. And that requires a cognition and memory apparatus such as in the neo-cortex. So initially I thought our visceral experience of the feeling has to wait until the mind gives meaning to the feeling and tangled hierarchical quantum measurement takes place in the brow chakra, neocortex; only then would you experience feeling, always mixed with thought, as an emotion. This is how most people experience feeling.

But wait! While men generally accept that their self is centered in the head, quite a few women claim that their heart "talks" to them because they know how to listen to their heart. Is this mere metaphor for women's emotionality or is there a scientific basis for it? The plot thickens further when many mystical traditions refer to the spiritual journey as a journey inward—towards the heart.

There is more than a metaphor here. First, the immune system is the second most important body organ. Scientists are discovering that the immune system has quite a bit of autonomy.

Second, everyone knows the neocortex needs sleep every night; sleep-depravation is bad for both physical and mental health. It is easy to connect the thymus gland (of the immune system) with romantic love; romance is when the immune system function of distinguishing between me and not me is suspended. That is when the heart shines forth with romance. So why do we need love? The answer must be to give the immune system some rest. If the immune system is denied rest, immune system malfunction will occur, and this leads to many disorders such as autoimmune disease, heart disease, and cancer.

Notice that out of all the organs of the body, only the neocortex, the immune system, and the gastrointestinal system (in the form of fasting) need regular rest. What do they have in common? The neo-cortex has autonomy; it also has a tangled hierarchy, and it thereby acquires a self. The immune system has autonomy; does it also have a self?

A major surprise of neuroscience is the recent discovery of a large group of neurons in the heart chakra, as much touted by the Heart Math Institute, which has been attracting our attention for some time. There is a cognition system at the heart chakra—where the organs of the thymus gland and the heart are located; the feeling of love is an excellent way to cognize. With the bundle of nerve available, there is also the capacity to make memory. Cognition and memory—the two systems that make a tangled hierarchy in the brain— and the heart has them too. So, the heart chakra has a self: the experience of pure feeling by itself can actual ize at the heart without the brain's help.

More recently, neuroscientists have also discovered another little brain, a big bundle of nerves at the navel chakra. The navel chakra has a cognition apparatus, it cognizes with the feeling of self-worth, self-love. Its little brain gives it a memory apparatus. The combination makes a tangled hierarchy and manifests a self-identity centered at the navel.

The Japanese culture calls the navel center "hara" or self of the body; at least one spiritual culture has recognized even this center of the self for hundreds of years. To be fair, even in our modern culture, creative men do talk about gut feelings that tell them about the veracity of a creative experience.

The important questions are: why do males among us not hear the small voice of the heart and why do women miss the small voice of the navel chakra, those pure feelings associated with the actualization of experience at these chakras? This has to do with evolution and culture and is perhaps the main contributing factor for the male-female dichotomy.

## Energy Psychology

The awareness of vital energy, as my own experience shows, has been slow among professional psychologists. However, evidence of it has been abundant since the 1960s when such things as massage and Rolfing (a very tough form of massage) became popular. In retrospect, what is massage but releasing the memory of emotional episodes that leave one with unrelaxed muscles? Only when you relax the muscles with acupressure like massaging or, better yet, Rolfing, will the correlated negative emotions come up and release.

I met the psychologist Roger Callahan in 1997 at a conference when he talked to me about a new therapy called Thought Field Therapy that he had developed and that is very useful for healing most phobias. This method advocates the releasing of stored negative emotions, through specialized tapping with the fingers at various meridian points on the upper body and other selected areas and voila! Even stubborn cases of phobia have been reported to have been treated successfully in this way.

More recent variations of the same general idea go by the name of energy psychology and also uses tapping different areas of the body (one brand of this that Sunita uses in her practice is EFT—Emotional Freedom Techniques).

I will end this section with still another myth for you to remember, this one from Indian mythology. The gods and the demons get together in their quest for the potion of immortality—*amrita*. To that purpose, they churn the ocean with the help of a great snake named Basuki. And indeed, after some churning, the beautiful charmer goddess Mohini comes up with the vessel of amrita. She gets busy charming the demons while the gods drink up all the amrita. When the demons became aware of how they were cheated, they became angry and demanded another churning of the ocean! Basuki reluctantly agrees, but he was tired and what came up this time was poison vomited by Basuki himself! And now everybody's health on Earth was threatened. How to save humanity, who can do it but the great god of goodness, Shiva? Indeed, Shiva drank up the poison that was so potent that even Shiva's throat became blue. But humanity was saved!

The message is clear. The gods—representing positivity—are immortal, but demons—representing negativity—are not. In your search for emotional intelligence, always be heartened by this myth and the lessons it presents.

## The Challenge of Mental/Emotional Health

In quantum psychology, the challenge of mental health is one of conscious control: if we have conscious control over how we behave in various situations under different stimuli, we are deemed normal, more or less. If our behavior has lapses of lack of control, we label it as neurotic behavior. On the other hand, if the behavior reflects that the people so behaving are more or less out of conscious control, that is, unconscious has more or less taken over the control, we say these people are psychotic.

It has been said that, "everyone is at least a little bit neurotic." Nevertheless, more recently beginning with the 1960's, we have the concept of positive mental health. Exactly who has positive mental health? In quantum psychology, we say, people have positive mental health when instead of the personal unconscious, the quantum unconscious—the domain of potentiality beyond our personal and collective unconscious—takes over some of the causal authority over our conscious behavior. There can still be neurosis, but the neurotic episodes keep getting shorter and shorter.

Ordinary people have much at stake in avoiding ongoing neurosis and in learning how to move to normal stability and even on to positive mental health. And then it helps to know that you have the freedom to change and take charge of your mental and emotional health.

The same holds true for society as well, for this is a crucial breakthrough. Right from the get-go, one of the defects of the behavioral approach stands out: the question of responsibility. If we are conditioned machines, why should we be held responsible for our behavior? We have to recognize the causal efficacy of individual choice before we ascribe people responsibility.

The religious labeling of yourself as "sinner" does not do you any good if the only recipe for healing is to "confess."

So, it should be clear that a sensible science that offers you relief from neurosis and aspire for "normal" or positive mental health and happiness has to have the following basic ingredients:

1. You can make your experiences count; they don't just have to be trivial information processing. If they have meaning and value, especially spiritual value, then suitably contextualized, they can bring happiness.

2. You have a free willing self; you can choose the context in which to validate your experience and you also have the responsibility for your choice

3. Not only is it important how comfortably you live in the external world (which even the materialist science acknowledges as relevant) but also how you live in your internal world— your psyche. Here the materialist worldview has very limited offerings.

Quantum psychology is designed to have all three basic ingredients to build an effective psychotherapeutic program around it for the prevention and treatment of neurosis and this should be comforting. Additionally, quantum psychology gives us fundamentally a positive psychology designed for taking you to the ultimate peaks of mental health and happiness.

Much of the advancement of physical health and longevity that we see today is due to our use of better external hygiene. Similarly, the quantum psychology is attracting our attention to giving equal importance to better internal hygiene. Indeed, the quest for happiness result in a huge reduction of emotional stress and recent research is connecting this to be a crucial factor for longevity.

## Influencing Factors for Internal Hygiene

For physical disease a breakthrough discovery was that of our vulnerability to bacteria and viruses. For the psyche, negative emotions are the equivalent of bacteria and viruses, and to top it off, they are, through evolution, built into our brain as negative emotional brain circuits.

And the analogy does not end there. Like bacteria and viruses of the physical, we are susceptible to pick up other people's negative emotions via even locally operating our own mirror neurons, a phenomenon called sympathy.

Additionally, there is a new problem for the psyche. Any negative emotions we suppress become a part of the personal unconscious, ready to surface any time and create difficulties. The tendency to suppress is well-intended; if we express, it affects other people, possibly producing inefficiency in our relationships, especially for professional work. So, Westerners generally, and males even more than female, suppress their emotions.

Now realize that the balance-restoring mechanism—positive emotions—(with a few exceptions) are not built into us organically. To top it off, positive feelings come to us along with intuitive thoughts; we need to develop sensitivity even to be aware of them, let alone explore them enough to make new circuits.

Some of the suppression/repression dynamic begins to form when we are children, when our freedom to choose is still developing, and we are vulnerable to abuse. In the past, societies generally have not taken much responsibility toward parental education and equip parents with sensitivity in their treatment of children.

Some of the suppression/repression dynamic takes place because of our cultural suppression of the contribution of the vital-sensory software as well as the vital-mental software in the affairs of the psyche. Most people of the West are simply ignorant of these contributions.

In quantum psychology, we recognize all this and concentrate on preventive medicine:

1. We firmly advocate for cleaning up the unconscious;

2. We solidly encourage balancing negative emotions through building positive emotional brain circuits;

3. We teach body sensitivity via chakra psychology—chakra balancing;

4. We teach people vulnerability, to give up the immune defense (those vital-sensory and especially those vital-mental software connected with the immune system) when the relationship demands it;

And finally, we strongly emphasize:

5. Creativity—even for "normal" people so that not only is the personal unconscious (where neurotic stuff is suppressed) engaged, but also the quantum unconscious with creative stuff of healing is occasionally accessed.

# CHAPTER 10
# Intuitions and Archetypes

Objects of our intuitions are what Plato called archetypes Sri Aurobindo called the domain of the archetypes *the supramental.* I previously commented that the body organs make representations of the morphogenetic field-source of our vital energy feelings (personal vital software) and the neocortex makes representations of mental meaning (personal mental software). But it is a fact that as of now we do not possess the capacity of making direct physical representations of the supramental archetypes.

How then do we experience intuitions? For the actualization, we have to go to the mental and the vital route.

For example, a mental representation can be made of the archetypal possibility; only then can the existing tangled hierarchy of the brain can engage, and consciousness gets to collapse an intuitive experience along with its representation in thought.

In this way, an intuition cannot be directly experienced, but it sets off the making of mental potentialities that ends in eventual tangled hierarchical collapse. In this quantum-self experience, mind has given a new meaning of the archetype.

But of course, if we are not sensitive, we will miss the quantum self-experience and further processing of the reflection in the mirror of memory will take place. The more spontaneous the whole sequence—primary and secondary collapses—is, the greater our chances to catch the spiritual joy of an archetypal experience. No wonder not all people report such joy; instead, many people report being troubled by an intuition. This is because intuitions have truth value that we cognize, and that makes us uneasy.

On the other hand, there is nothing rarefied about intuition; it is potentially everybody's everyday phenomenon to be experienced.

There is also an affective quality of archetypal experiences. Some of our intuitions give us a "gut feeling" or a sensation that can be called "sweet to the heart." The reason is that archetypes can not only be represented in the mind as mental meaning but also in our vital body as elevated feelings-vital energy movements connected with our higher chakras. For example, the intuition of the archetype of love can be experienced as a mental thought of love as well as a wonderful feeling in our heart chakra.

How do we know that intuitions are different from rational thought, that they are not creations of thought itself as many materialists' claim? Well, intuitions are a prelude to a full-fledged archetypal creative experience. As Aurobindo points out, the archetypal world is filled with truth—and truth—is one eternal absolute archetype for which not even quantum movement is allowed. What this implies is that archetypes like love have many quantum facets from which we can choose the facet of a particular experience (for example, for love, we can choose romantic love or agape—compassion—which both have many shades); and all the facets have truth-value. So, every time we intuit, the experience has truth-value which is diminished but not eliminated even for a mental or vital representation. So intuitive thoughts always come with a little feeling of "truth" although mental logic maybe telling us otherwise. Sometimes we feel uneasy and wonder if we should follow up this little feeling of truth although it is not strictly rational. Other times, we experience this truth-value as a gut feeling or a tingle in the heart that gives us more incentive to follow up.

If we do follow up the intuitive thought to its source, if we cultivate the requisite sensitivity to intuitions, and learn to creatively explore them, we can verify the archetypal authenticity—truth value—of intuitions directly.

## The Supramental World

The abode of the archetypes that we intuit is called supramental. Why do we need to postulate it thereby authenticating intuitions further?

There is an important theorem in mathematics called *Gödel's theorem,* whose purport is this: whatever mathematical system of algorithms is used to ascertain mathematical truth, if the system is sufficiently elaborate, there is always a proposition within the system that the system cannot prove. Although the mathematician can see the validity of the proposition without a doubt, the algorithmic system of logic is unable to prove it.

In other words, mathematicians, when they discover mathematical laws, jump out of the system—they bring mathematical truth from a transcendent world. This is the world of supramental archetypes that Plato introduced. In the same vein, if mathematical scientific laws guide the behavior of material objects, as in physics and chemistry, they must exist a priori to matter, they must be nonmaterial transcending matter. By the same token, they must also transcend the mind that put together the mathematics.

Science, in general, is the result of our pursuit of the archetype of truth with a two-prong strategy: theory and experiment.

Aside from the physical laws the supramental also acts as the reservoir of the archetypes of biological functions (of which the liturgical/morphogenetic fields are vital representations) and of the archetypes of mental meaning.

Confusion is created because there is no place in the body or the brain where intuitions are memorized for us to recall them to look at them in detail. But there is no need to deny that there is a special type of thought—intuitive thought—that is not necessarily rational by present standards but is not irrational either. They seem to guide us to deeper truth that become part of the reservoir of rational thought in some future time.

It helps to consider that intuitive thoughts are mental representations of archetypes of intuitions.

In psychology, Jung discovered collective memories of humanity that form what he called the "collective unconscious." Jung named the objects of this collective unconscious that often come to us in big dreams also as archetypal symbols. Lest this creates confusion, realize that the Jungian archetypes are mental representations of the Platonic archetypes in this way providing evidence of the point asserted above.

## The Special Case of the Archetype of Truth

Archetypes are quantum multifaceted objects. With one exception, the archetype of truth. Truth is absolute. As previously stated, the archetypal world is a world of truth. Why then is truth not quantum, not multifaceted?

The answer is clear: the universe needs to be created with a fixed set of highly fine-tuned laws. The archetypal universe of potentiality is under absolute truth; so, all the objects of the archetypal domain, all archetypes, have truth value. This is why in creativity, especially in a creative experience directly exploring an archetype, we always know what we know with certainty.

The notion that a fine-tuning of the universe is required to produce manifest life and self-awareness in an otherwise potential universe is called the anthropic principle. It is a sure-fire evidence that there is purpose in the movement of consciousness.

## The Archetype of Wholeness

Both physical and mental health, (and happiness itself) is characterized by wholeness when the parts involved are all synchronized to act as a whole; lack of wholeness on the other hand is experienced as unhappiness, disease, and depression.

The only wholeness that we can totally and absolutely count on, is the wholeness of oneness, of consciousness itself, with no subject-object split. This undivided whole is of course unconscious in us. Short of spiritual enlightenment we cannot experience it, but we can be it, as we are in deep sleep and unconscious processing. So deep sleep and some unconscious processing are essential elements of good physical and mental health.

Unfortunately, while the need of sleep is more or less recognized, unconscious processing is underrated in our materialist do-do-do culture. To live the quantum worldview, we promote unconscious processing in our culture by emphasizing the importance of slowing down. Instead of fast food, try slow food; instead of.. fast hands in physical contact, experience slow hands. Instead of fast sex, affirm and engage in... slow sex.

We also, as mental health practitioners, suggest yoga, Tai Chi, martial arts, meditation etc. All these practices slow you down; that is one of their many objectives.

How do we approach wholeness in conscious processing? We approach it as an archetype to explore. When we get mentally disturbed or emotionally traumatized, the tendency is to look at the discomfort as inconvenient suffering and we suppress it if we can. Perhaps we seek out a behavioral/cognitive therapist and ask for a "quick fix" which will enable us to cope with the mental/emotional stress. But ability of coping with stress does not put us in ease. When you realize it, you will be interested in mental/emotional health as a way of regaining wholeness. You will want health not only at the level of where you don't suffer, but also at the level you want to optimize your wholeness which brings satisfaction and happiness.

According to Traditional Chinese Medicine (TCM), wholeness is about balancing and harmonizing yin and yang, the "be" and "do" aspects of the whole process of creativity. This is also true of the vital-physical, as well as the mental situation.

Einstein said, "Creativity takes courage." Courage is needed to invite the archetypes in your life, once again irrespective of how many times you have explored them before. Courage is required to heed to the quantum self-giving up the ego-control. In this way you transition from material pleasure centered happiness to spiritual joy-centered happiness of expansion of consciousness.

## Ethics: The Archetype of Goodness

Spiritual traditions put one of the ideals of the human being this way: as above, so below. As Jesus taught, when you integrate above and the below, it is a step toward entering the "kingdom of heaven." So, for TCM, this integration is about balancing yin and yang, unmanifest and manifest, conditioning and creativity that fits right on with the quantum worldview.

But there is a narrower interpretation of what it means to integrate above and below, namely heavenly values (the good) and earthly values (the evil). Depth psychologists, beginning with Freud, look at it differently. Freud had three concepts, the Id, the ego, and the superego. The Id is the subconscious, suppressed and repressed emotions and (mostly) childhood traumas. Ego is the conscious I, the subject pole of our everyday waking awareness. Although Freud did not define the ego the way we have done it in quantum psychology, I don't think Freudians will object too much if we continue to say that the ego is the normal ego/character/persona as defined in this book. The superego is also unconscious; it is the result of parental, religious, and socio-cultural dos and don'ts. In the old days, we called it conscience, and everybody except psychopaths and sociopaths could be counted on to have it to a greater or lesser degree. Under materialist science, the concepts of ethics and morality on which the conscience was based, have become blurred and uncertain.

For socio-biologists, our negative emotional brain circuits are the true determinants of our behavior along with other genetic and environmental conditioning. Additionally, they do allow for cultural "memes" to have some effect on your behavior which include social & cultural dos and don'ts and so have some similarity to the concept of conscience.

Religions do not entirely disagree with the socio-biological pessimism about the human being. They identify this aspect as the "evil in us" and suggest that we balance it with "good," (and God) that religions are meant to teach us. Indeed, in past religious cultures, people strove toward morality, trying to build positive emotional brain circuits on the basis of the religious and ethical teachings. Unfortunately, positive emotional brain circuits built in this way are nowhere close to balancing the strangle hold the negative instinctual ones have on us. And Freudians would agree, the Id always beats the superego, Mr. Hyde triumphs over Dr. Jekyll in the final reckoning.

It is plain to see, that under materialism, the situation is getting worse. These days, we debate with materialists if ethics applies to the human condition at all. Is it scientific, or is it just a convenient bunch of politically correct social rules, a necessity, even if pretense, for some sort of maintenance of civilization, civilized behavior?

In quantum psychology, these debates are unnecessary; even irrelevant. We are all potentially inter-connectable through our common consciousness; so, ethics is compulsory once you actualize your oneness with another, once you enter a relationship. However, if you are ignorant of this truth, it is the duty of the society and culture to teach you about the oneness, about your moral covenant to remain open to correlation with any human being irrespective of race, sex, sexual preference, etc., about the archetype of good-ness, about how to directly investigate this archetype through your creativity, and so forth. In other words, ethics must be emphasized as a critical component of psychological education.

# CHAPTER 11

# Regaining the Promise of Paradise

Consciousness comes to us via quantum measurement in the tangled hierarchical brain in the form of the quantum self—a numinous experience of the present moment. The quantum self is cosmic, tangled hierarchical, and the experience reminds you who you really are—the unity that we call paradise—instantly. We often lose this access to paradise and forget unity in two steps.

## The Ego / Character

Of course, the biggest barrier to access the quantum self for most people is that ordinary state of "I" they experience, colloquially called the ego. Ego is the biggest barrier because its nature is to maintain a status quo, a control that it feels it must retain over its affairs. How then does this ego arise if our initial response to every stimulus (that is not a replay of memory) is the quantum self?

Every time the tangled hierarchical apparatus of the brain finishes the processing of a stimulus, it makes a mental memory of the cognition of the stimulus. Next time the same stimulus arrives at the brain, the memory plays back giving a secondary stimulus, a reflected image so to speak. So, the quantum cognition system has to respond not only to the primary stimulus but also the secondary stimulus. You can think this kind of what is called pre-conscious processing, as a reflection in the mirror of memory. Experiments show that after the initial quantum self-response, it takes on the average 500 milliseconds of secondary processing of the stimulus to reach a stage where we become conscious of it. What a repeated reflection in the mirror of memory does is to bias the system to respond in favor of the previous response. In this way many such reflections produce what psychologists call—conditioning.

Therefore, repeatedly learning the response to stimuli with such stimulus-response reinforcement mechanisms produces an entire pattern of conditioned habits and learned repertoire of a human self that we call our ego's character and habit patterns. At this level, the behavior is much like how behaviorists think of the ego—a bunch of conditioned patterns acting out behavior. We are acting out a verb without much of the feeling of being a noun; in other words, our "I" is being objectified to "I/me." Instead of experiencing "I am smiling," we experience "smiling is happening (to me)."

## Ego / Character / Persona

As it turns out, the ego that we normally experience is what some psychologists correctly call ego/persona; it is simple hierarchical, not tangled hierarchical; with the acquiring of ego-persona, we literally become the chooser and doer. We choose from our learned programs and act on it.

What is it that converts a bunch of character patterns and learned repertoire to a simple hierarchical chooser/doer? First of all, the conditioning accompanying any learning of a stimulus is not 100% for any response. In practice, we learn a series of responses to the same stimulus with a varying amount of probability weighting. Second, memory making is a complex process: there is short-term memory and long-term memory. So, when we make reference to a reflection in the mirror of memory, which memory are we talking about? Third, we have the ability to be conscious of being conscious and we can play this ad infinitum and often do. In this way, we can change the probability weighting of our responses to an external stimulus via introspection. The net effect is that we seem to be choosing our behavior for a particular situation from a whole spectrum of behaviors, a bunch of programs that we identify with at that moment. This is our simple hierarchical ego/character/persona or me-me-me.

In this way, our ego/character persona can occasionally be inauthentic. The service of the self-image tends to become more important than the adherence to truth. An authentic ego would be one in which all the personas are congruent with the character.

A striking difference between the ego/character/persona and the quantum self is this: in our ego/character/persona, we can witness ourselves acting this way or that way; the ego/character/ persona can be seen as an object. We can even witness our witnessing, ad infinitum it seems. In contrast, think of the quantum self as the pure witness, with no reference point to "the me."

## Torn Between Two Selves?

In this way, we literally are capable of identifying with two selves: the quantum self and the ego/character/ persona. In between them is the preconscious—during the five hundred millisecond processing time. Neuroscience data validates all this. Read the already cited book, *The Quantum Brain*.

> *This Zen story perfectly illustrates both modalities of the self. Two monks were about to cross a shallow but muddy river. Just then, a maiden appeared on the scene in beautiful clothes that went all the way to her ankles. Naturally, the maiden was hesitating to step into the river lest her attire got ruined. One of the monks asked for permission to help her, and when she agreed, he picked her right up and walked across the river and gently put her down. The maiden thanked the monk and went her way. The other monk soon caught up with the first and they both continued on their journey.*
>
> *After about an hour the second monk spoke. He was upset. "Brother, you did something very wrong back there, you know. We monks are not*

*supposed to touch women, let alone carry them*
*for so long as it took you to go across the river,*
*a full five minutes, and you held her so close."*

   *The first monk thought for a moment and*
*responded, "Brother, I carried the maiden for a*
*mere five minutes, and put her down, but you*
*are still carrying her."*

The first monk performed an act of compassion responding to his intuition that the maiden was needing help,
and thus was acting from the quantum self. The second
monk was thinking from his conditioned ego/character/
persona and judging mind. So, he suffered.

   The quantum self is the unity self, it is our reminder
of our origin in unity. The ego/character/persona
brings separateness; yet it also brings us some individuality including our own unique character and
personality. It also brings us repertoire of knowledge.

   Developmentally as young children, we don't have
much of the burden of memory, especially the ability
of memory recall; we are naturally more in our quantum self. As we grow up, more memory, more conditioning, more learned repertoire, more ego structure
and ability to recall, and don't forget the call of the
instincts, (especially the sexual instinct that becomes
aroused with puberty) all this and more, contributes
to your adult ego. Negative by-products of the adult
ego include a lot of unwanted pain and suffering. What
next? Should you now try to go back to your quantum
self and live in unity, in wholeness, in peace as some

of the ancient spiritual traditions suggest? Can you? Or are you too attached to your seek pleasure-avoid pain dynamics, especially since materialist scientists approves that lifestyle?

At least close fifty percent of America's population believes in God or a higher power. In my opinion, which means that these people are a little torn between the two selves, ego, and the quantum. But if the ego identity has to be given up, then why develop a strong ego in the first place?

People who live under the aegis of materialism never have to ponder such questions. For them, ignorance is bliss. But they too have the problem of finding satisfaction. "Eat, sleep, have sex, process information with your cell phone, and have a job to earn money so survive" as a way of life does not satisfy everyone and satisfies no one all the time.

Many spiritual traditions tend to say that the unity consciousness is preferable to the ego-separateness. I once heard a Christian preacher on a late-night radio put it this way: "Give your gavel to the Holy Spirit." I took it to mean that we should drop our judgments and surrender to that which is greater than our ego (that we so closely identify with) and "the false self of separation" that does not readily recognize a source greater or outside of itself.

The opportunity that exists (at least in theory), is that we never have to completely identify with the ego. First of all, the conditioning for a particular response is never 100%. We can always say "no" to conditioning and open ourselves to the quantum self. Second, as soon as we become open to intuitions, the forgetfulness that comcs with the ego/character/persona develops a chink in its armor. The latter means that we can always hear the call of the oneness and respond by paying attention to our intuitive facility. And every time we push the ego aside and do that, we get to be in touch with our quantum self! The former means that a creative response to any stimulus is always possible. We can always follow up our intuitions to full bloom creativity which involves prolonged encounters with the quantum self.

And don't get the idea that a weak ego conditioning is more efficient for turning toward oneness or for creativity. Experiments with animal training have discovered the phenomenon of experimental neurosis. If an animal is trained to distinguish between a circle and an ellipse and then a picture of an ellipse is shown which is progressively made more and more ambiguous, (let's say progressively less ellipse and more circle), the animal will show signs of anxiety neurosis; the weak ego cannot handle the ambiguity. Creativity requires the handling of uncertainty and ambiguity; so clearly a strong ego is needed with a lot of repertoires. Turning toward oneness in spite of an adult ego requires what I call inner creativity.

## Is Paradise Lost?

In John Milton's epic poem, *Paradise Lost,* Satan is banished to hell and says, "Better to reign in hell than to serve in heaven." This is a very polarized view of the heavenly quantum self and the ego—the earthly self and their relationship.

The truth is paradise is really never lost. Even when you are in the ego (more or less), the quantum self is not as elusive as you think because:

1. Intuitions are quantum-self experiences and they come to you frequently because the archetypes are attracted to you.

2. More recently, Maslow has spoken of the "peak" experience. I myself have often experienced spiritual joy of a creative experience. I bet you have also experienced occasional bursts of creativity especially during childhood. Recall your first experience of getting the meaning of algebra or learning a song. Where does the spiritual joy of these experiences come from? It is due to an encounter with the quantum self.

3. Then there is also the flow experience. Some forms of it, in sports for example, are even more commonplace than the creative experiences.

4. Our neocortex dominates our ideas of who we are because that is where our dominant self-identity is. This you cannot change easily. But you can learn to be sensitive to intuitive thoughts. You can also learn to be sensitive to

emotions in their visceral aspect and develop a kinship with the chakras. This opens you to vital creativity and further increases your access of the quantum self.

5. Finally, even when you are immersed in the ego, you retain the right to free will and ability to return to the quantum self.

## The Question of Free Will

I want to make the point that even in the ego/character/persona we do retain a modicum of free will. In other words, consciousness goes along with our choice between conditioned alternatives at the ego level. So, in that sense we have free will.

I offer this simplified example of that point. Suppose you are choosing what flavor of ice cream to buy. You have a whole bunch of conditioned habits from a lifetime of experience with different ice cream flavors with varying probability weighting. In a large number of such instances, your behavior will confirm to the probabilities. But in a particular instance, do you get to choose? The answer is a resounding yes! "This time I choose the mint chocolate chip, instead of my usual, cookies and cream." If so inclined, you can really push the limits of choice by getting a waffle cone instead of a regular cone!

The other most important instance of this ego's choice is the freedom to no longer accept our conditioned choices altogether. In general, our picture is that free choice comes to us from the unconscious oneness via the quantum self, and experiments bear this out. There are a whole series of experiments that supports this view and show that a human can flex a finger within 200 milliseconds in response to an external signal, when we are asked to do so voluntarily. It takes a second or more to do that from the time of onset of electrical activity connected with internal stimuli (as when you intend to flex your finger) and unconscious action in the brain, called the readiness potential. The explanation fits the notion that the primary quantum self (and the unconscious beyond) is the leverage point of free choice; even the thought of free-willing at the ego-level does not surface without its processing time of reflection in the mirror of memory. And execution of the "free" will takes even longer.

The neurophysiologist Benjamin Libet asked subjects to flex one hand at the wrist while also noting the position of a spot on a revolving disk (like the second hand of a clock) as to when they formed their intention. A few seconds afterwards, the subjects told the experimenter where the spot was when a conscious will was made, which enabled Libet to calculate the time of that event. Libet found that indeed there is 400 milliseconds or so time lag between the onset of the readiness potential and the awareness of the will to flex the wrist. This further supports the above idea that conscious choice is a function of the quantum self and the internal event of an eventual intention percolates via secondary processing to the ego level and only then we have the thought that we will to flex our wrist. An external observer already can know of our free will by simply looking at the EEG connected to our brain. The ego simply is not free if its choice can be predicted a priori, is it?

However, Libet did discover a twist. Although the will to flex the wrist is formed before we become aware of that will in thought, we are able subsequently to stop our willed action during the 200 or so milliseconds that remains between the actual action and the thought. What is the explanation? Even in our ego/identity, we can say "no" to our conditioning. And this is the key to opening up to creativity. Therefore, intuition and creativity are the pathway back to paradise of eternal happiness.

# CHAPTER 12

# The Science of Mental and Vital Creativity and Manifestation

We all want our deepest intentions to come true; our happiness in part depends on that. The process to engage is the creative process, no doubt about that. There is, however, a recent development. Until now, creativity has largely been looked upon as mental creativity. With quantum psychology to guide us, the road to creativity of the vital is being charted. This enables us a double-barreled attempt for the exploration of archetypes.

Let's discuss the creative process for mental creativity in some detail. The abrupt and spontaneous nature of creative insight is by far the most spectacular aspect of an act of creativity. But all is not discontinuity and insight; what appears as sudden and discontinuous creative insight is actually only one part of a much more extensive process.

The creativity researcher Graham Walla was one of the first to suggest that creative acts involve four stages that are now fairly commonly accepted. These four stages are: preparation, incubation, insight, and manifestation. However, many subsequent researchers have noted (and I agree) that even before preparation begins there is an intuition, an inner nudge of sorts, a vague feeling about a possible problem which needs to be explored. I myself, (based on my own research and my own experiences) added an intermediate stage summarized by the slogan do-be-do-be-do.

The stages are as follows:

## Stage 1: Preparation

Gather facts and existing ideas about your problem and think, think, think. Churn the ideas around in your mind-field, looking at them in every way possible, from every angle and vantage point. The most effective tool in this stage is your imagination. If you aspire for mental health and happiness, seek inspiration from good books, attend healing workshops, and meditate to increase your concentration and mindfulness, and most of all, create new contents for imagination—divergent thinking.

If you are suffering from occasional bouts of neurosis, work with your therapist to explore your emotional trauma suppression dynamics, explore techniques of energy psychology for temporary relief, explore how you handle emotional stress, and all that. Explore many possibilities for healing-divergent thinking. Again, be imaginative. Pay attention to dreams and the meanings they bring you. Practice healing visualizations or visualizations of good mental/emotional health. Be fully aware and open to the synchronicities to guide you.

## Stage 2: Incubation

Relax, relax, relax. The problem is not going anywhere, and meanwhile, you can play, sleep, meditate, and do all the things that relax you.

What does relaxing do? When you relax, your unconscious takes over and combined with preparation—divergent thinking—it creates a myriad of possibilities for the unconscious to process.

How does this happen? You will recall that every thought also arouses a whole bunch of associated memories; whenever you are not thinking all these mental memories return to their original being of a possibility wave of meaning. They all start small as it is when you toss a pebble in a pond to create a ripple effect. And then, just as the water wave grows and grows and the concentric rings become ever larger and spread further and further, so then does your possibility waves of meaning, created by divergent thinking. They act as seeds of huge pools of possibilities of meaning that can mix and mingle creating even more possibility some of which would likely be new.

Sleeping is good for creativity; the adage, "let's sleep on it" produces result because of the unconscious processing involved. Sleep works even better if you don't clutter up your personal unconscious with a lot of day residue and suppressed emotions.

Also, dreams are highly conducive for creativity. It is said when Niels Bohr was working on his model of the atom, he saw the solar-system model of the atom in a dream, suggesting unconscious incubation going on in his psyche that was converging to an insight in his dream.

## Stage 2a: Do-be-do-be-do

It's important to alternate between the doing and being, preparation and incubation. Why the rotation of doing and being? Too much relaxing takes the focus of your unconscious processing away from your problem. Like an evening fire in the fireplace on a winter day, the fire needs occasional stoking to keep it going. So "being" has to be occasionally interrupted by "doing" to regain focus and keep balance and flow intact.

## Stage 3: Illumination

This is the big "AHA!" Insights, answers, visions, and discernments usually show up when you least expect it. Much like a frog jumping off a lily pad, insight is a sudden, quantum leap, the "AHA!" surprise is the signature of discontinuity. I have heard that watching frogs leap was one of Niels Bohr's favorite pastimes. Maybe we all should do that to get inspired.

If it is a quantum leap to the archetypal land— an act of archetypal creativity—the "AHA!" will be accompanied by certainty, a deeply authentic sense of knowing, that is often accompanied by a visceral feeling of energy along the spine, shaking of the knees, gut feeling, or some such thing.

## Stage 4: Manifestation

Don't worry, the fun is not over; it is just beginning! Manifest, evaluate, and verify what you have. It is a lot of fun because this often involves long episodes of flow— interaction between ego-character and the quantum self.

For example, when I am writing a book, I experience many creative insights, which are encounters with my quantum self. I personally experience this as an episode of ideas where I receive lots of creative information and ideas. However, the difficult part for me is translating this information into written word, for which my ego-character is necessary. Making the writing flow with correct grammar etc. is the work of my ego-character in conjunction with my brain. The creative insight is the primary collapse and the meaning my ego-character gives it is the result of secondary collapse(s) of mini-insights. My brain enables me to translate the meaning as information/symbols onto my computer; and in this way the ego-character and the quantum-self works in tandem in a flow for the manifestation to happen in the brain and the computer. It is a balanced and harmonious flow between idea and form, a true partnership at work.

As you climb the ladder of happiness (to reach rungs of more happiness than unhappiness), as you engage in creativity toward inner transformation, the new mentally/emotionally strong you, will manifest. Before the "AHA!" you might have been a mental weakling, tossed around by your unconscious with hardly any conscious control on your emotions, (or even behavior) and now, here you are after the insight with regained faith in your conscious control. But beware; the control is still tentative. To stabilize it, you require repeated encounters with your quantum self, mini quantum leaps, so small that the discontinuity is obscured. Again, this part of the process is experienced as a flow in outer creativity and people having it, often report intense happiness in the form of spiritual joy. The happiness comes from the encounter with the quantum self while the ego's role is to provide expertise to represent the ideas coming from the quantum self.

There are also other considerations. Psychologist Carl Rogers emphasizes that preparation also means developing an open mind, a de-structuring of the existing belief-system(s) that sets the stage for the acceptance of the new. You have to believe (and develop a deep knowing) that you will be healed; you have to have confidence in your therapist and that you are working together toward healing.

In the healing of mental/emotional disease, manifestation often involves lifestyle changes. This may include some cleaning up of the unconscious which Jungian psychology terms "shadow cleansing" and Joan Borysenko calls it "removing the clouds that hides the sun of the quantum self." Within the manifestation stage, there is also a restructuring of the belief system, a definite shift from disease prone to healing-prone personality, from separateness toward wholeness. For people seeking happiness in life, one of the ultimate goals is to live in the flow experience as much as possible.

## The Science of Manifestation

Who doesn't want to manifest his or her desires and ideas? There are books, many of them bestsellers, that proclaim to teach you the secret of manifestation but when you try to apply these simplistic concepts, the methodology falls short. Are these authors wrong? Not entirely, they are just not telling you the whole story.

When you first encounter the quantum worldview with its definitive dictum, consciousness chooses actuality out of the infinite potentially available to it, it is natural to think that we can choose whatever we want to manifest. What's the catch? After reading through the book to this point, you have come to know what the catch is: that which chooses a transformative experience is unity consciousness, not your separate ego. A second important "catch" is that the infinite potentialities are quantum potentialities allowed by the purposive laws of quantum psychology and the movement of consciousness. You have to be in synchrony with them. In spiritual language of the old, you have to get God on your side.

There are three ''I's'' of empowerment for manifestation even before we engage the creative process starting with preparation: Inspiration, Intention, and Intuition. Let's take a deeper look into each of them.

**Inspiration** — an influence or action on a person believed to qualify him or her to receive and communicate sacred revelation. Inspiration comes from our quantum self. Inspiration is a sure-fire way to ascertain that we are in synch with the meaningful purposive movement of consciousness, but why is inspiration necessary? Inspiration is the basis for motivation. The truth is manifestation requires a lot of relaxed focus and you have to be motivated.

Books on the attractor principle make a good point that is worthwhile to remember. The archetypes are attracted to you. So, it behooves you to be attracted to them. As has been stated "Whatever you are seeking, is seeking you." Find and follow your own archetype. That will help to keep you inspired on your journey.

**Intention** — a focused effort and energy on a directed object or outcome. The importance of intention has been very clear ever since Mexican neurophysiologist and psychologist Jacobo Grinberg and his collaborators did their transferred potential experiment (see Chapter 5). How do you hold your intentions?

I suggest you use four steps of intention:

1. Declare your intention from your ego and make it strong. Take ownership of it. If you are not for yourself, who will be?

2. Accept and confirm that you also have a unity nature as a potentiality; and moreover, this

is where your power to choose lies. So, at the second step, you must intend for the greater good as well.

3. Now comes the crucial third step; synchronizing your intended movement with the purposive movement of consciousness. I intend so my intention is in synch with the movement of consciousness. At this level, your intention is like a prayer that religious traditions use for the same purpose.

4. Final step, end with silence…and thanks. You have spoken your intention, now it is time to listen and meditate.

**Intuition** — a process that gives us the ability to know something directly without analytic reasoning, it is a bridge between the conscious and unconscious. Itis a summons from an archetype. Many people call this occurrence of a summon a part of the attractor principle. Archetypes keep calling you because they are attracted to you.

## The Kundalini Phenomenon and Creativity of the Vital

In 1981, I was at the Esalen Institute in Big Sur, California, as a guest lecturer for a week. The late spiritual teacher Osho, (Bhagwan Shree Rajneesh at the time) had a big following in America then. I was invited for a morning meditation with a Rajneesh group and so I went. It was explained that the meditation would consist of four parts. The first was just shaking your body standing in place; (as I discovered it really wakes you up). To begin the second stage, when somebody shouted STOP; the instruction was that we stopped right where we stood and meditate in that standing position for a while.

At the third stage, we began slow dancing to music with eyes closed. I was doing great, but suddenly I bumped into somebody and opened my eyes. There I beheld a pair of bouncing breasts before me! Did I forget to mention that the *Esalen* Institute was quite famous back then for allowing a lot of nudity? Also, did I mention that in spite of being in the USA for some time, I was still not real comfortable with nudity? So, my body reacted in that peculiar protrusion that a man's body is capable of and I was thoroughly embarrassed. Fortunately, the bell rang and that was the signal for the fourth stage: we were supposed to sit down and meditate, which I did. But the feeling of embarrassment persisted, and right then a strong feeling of energy rose from my anus to about my throat, maybe beyond. It was quite a delightful experience.

Now, mind you, I grew up in India and in that culture, everybody knows about kundalini awakening in which you supposedly experience movement of prana (vital energy) from the lowest chakra to the highest one. The Sanskrit word kundalini means coiled up energy. The idea, expressed in quantum terminology, is that the feelings at the two lowest chakras mostly remain in potentiality until a sudden quantum leap of awakening takes place and they are opened, then some of their previously unmanifest potentialities become available for manifestation at the higher chakras. So, at once I romanticized that I had a kundalini awakening experience; but I in the same moment, I was also disappointed that the energy did not rise all the way to the crown chakra as the literature indicates.

Was it an awakening of kundalini energy? I am now sure that it was, but at the time I didn't know. There was surprise; but I am not sure if there was any feeling of certainty about what it was; basically, I was just too ignorant to understand what was taking place in that moment!

In retrospect, I can confirm, that not only does creative vital energy movements authenticate our "AHA!" experiences, but these movements also used suitably can help the creative process itself. The Rajneesh meditation, if you examine it, is a do-be-do-be-do-practice just like in thought but involves vital energy. So, this is the same creative process as mental except you have to involve vital energy movements and be attentive of your energy. For further discussion on this, read my book with the physician Valentina R. Onisor, *Quantum Spirituality*.

CHAPTER 13

# Reincarnation and Evolution: The Purpose of Human Life

The idea that we are born into the world as empty slates—is passé. It is gradually being replaced by the idea that along with genetic inheritance from biological evolution and the contribution of socio-cultural conditioning, we also come with certain propensities from our past lives as part of our standard equipment at birth. Yoga psychology calls this past life inheritance by the Sanskrit word *Karma* (or by another Sanskrit word, *samskara*). These propensities lie dormant within us, until they are triggered as needed by current life circumstances.

I have spoken of the ego/character at length, but it cannot be stressed enough in this work. It consists of the habit patterns and character traits resulting from conditioning. The specifics of how conditioning takes place, is quite amazing.

If we feed back the secondary stimulus to the original quantum equation of movement, the quantum equation of an electron is modified in such a way that the response becomes less quantum and more predictable, somewhat determined as in Newtonian physics; in other words, the response upon feedback tends to be probability weighted a little in favor of the previous response. This is conditioning in psychological terms. In this way, the effect of repeated feedback of an infinite amount of reflection in the mirror of memory, infinite reinforcements of the response, produces total conditioning. Before conditioning, the electron showed up in a variety of places making a bell curve around the most probable position; after infinite conditioning, the probability is 100 percent that it will show up only in that one conditioned position (*Figure14*).

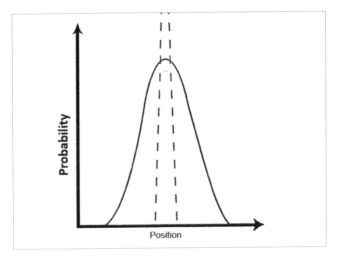

*Figure 14: How an electron gets conditioned before measurement, the electron's probability distribution is a bell curve. After infinite number of measurements with memory reinforcements, the electron's probability distribution hovers around one position.*

It is fair to assume as it is for an electron, so it must be for the quantum vital body and the mind. What is at the root of this change of probability weighting? The root cause is the modification of the quantum mathematics of movement. The law of this modification is part of the potential world of the Truth archetype. These propensities called *Karma* are a law-like inheritance; furthermore, they are stored in the nonlocal domain of reality. If we call them memory, we must qualify this memory as nonlocal memory, memory that is stored outside space and time.

If memory is nonlocal, the question of reincarnation becomes easy to answer. Your nonlocal memory of your Karma related to vital and mental bodies can be inherited by an aborning baby in some other place at a future time. In fact, you may have been privy to nonlocal memory of a past life before you. In other words, you are part of "string of pearls" chain of manifest reincarnations of an ongoing point of accumulating propensities. Let's call this locus *quantum monad* (*Figure15*).

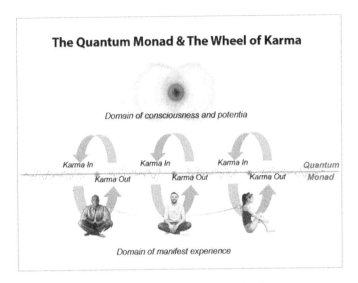

*Figure 15: How the quantum monad reincarnates
as pearls in a string of pearls*

The empirical evidence for reincarnation consists of the data on babies whether they are born as tabula rasa (no built-in mental content) or with an already developed capacity to learn. Research confirms which any parent already knows: babies are born with a considerable number of innate capacities that are triggered soon after the baby encounters the corresponding stimuli. Some of this innate capacity is due to the inheritance of universal software in the collective unconscious; but some of it is personal and undoubtedly has in their origin a reincarnational inheritance.

There is also convincing data on quite a few geniuses, the East Indian mathematician Ramanujan and the German music virtuoso Wolfgang Mozart are two of the most notable examples. These geniuses are born with innate ability (talent) for creativity including ample motivation passed on to them from their previous incarnations.

Along with positive propensities, there are also negative karmic propensities that can be triggered too, for example, when people have a predisposition towards a physical/vital or mental condition. This can be triggered by both external and internal stimuli.

In my (Sunita's) own personal case I believe that I had a predisposition towards developing an eating disorder, which was triggered by a number of events. It is worth noting that negative propensities get triggered very easily because of where we are positioned in the evolutionary curve today. We're born into a society where many people have lost touch with their true natures and hence are operating predominantly from a conditioned mindset dominated by negativity. The actions that evolve in a society from this lack of awareness, act as triggers of past life negative propensities.

The Eastern spiritual traditions discovered that this triggering could be avoided by isolating one from stimuli. In other words, young individuals were taken away from samsara– they were removed from their families and societies, and hence the triggering of past-life *Karma* was avoided. But obviously, nowadays this is not a practical solution, so the question becomes: how do we deal with the triggering of negative propensities, while simultaneously awakening our positive propensities?

Let's first look at awakening our positive propensities. There are some people who are fortunate enough to know what these are from a very young age, such as Mozart in the example given above. There are also cases of people who are born into families that are already engaged in a particular propensity. In India for example, you will come across musical "families" or "houses" known as gharanas. Traditionally, a gharana is defined by a special technique that would be handed down through generations and often within hereditary families, for example, a father passing a technique down to his son. These people have an innate karmic ability in music that is further enhanced by the families that they are born into.

However, not everyone is in such a situation. Some people have to discover or awaken their positive karmic propensities. In fact, I had this issue myself. Growing up I had a number of interests, such as science, writing and teaching. But when the time came to go to university, I was unsure about what I wanted to study. I knew that I wanted to teach in some form, but I didn't know what. I just couldn't find a career path that seemed appealing enough, so I pursued a degree in mathematics, science, and education, followed by a postgraduate certificate in education. I taught for some time, but I knew deep down that teaching in schools wasn't my calling.

A few years later, I stumbled upon counseling by accident (synchronicity?) I had never been open to a career in this area before, but as I started to explore the discipline my positive propensities began to be awakened. I started to understand why I had such broad interests and how I could bring them together.

There are ways in which you can discover your positive propensities. First and foremost, be honest with yourself. What moves and inspires you? What grabs your interest? Look past what you have been programmed to believe and instead turn your attention inward. It may take some time and contemplation to get back in touch with your deeper self, but rest assured your karmic memory is there.

Secondly, allow yourself to explore a range of experiences and disciplines, because as illustrated by my example above, you never know what might awaken your karmic memory. Also, where children are concerned, encourage them to partake in a number of different subjects in school. We don't know what karmic memory they hold, so we need to create a conducive liberal multifaceted environment for this exploration to take place.

Third, do memory recall practices especially recalling childhood memories. You must set your intention first that you want to remember your *Karma* and the information that you can "download" from your younger self.

Now that we have some idea about awakening our positive karmic memory, let's look at dealing with negative karmic memory. In addition to the current cultural triggers mentioned above, we also have to deal what this life presents us with, how we perceive our experiences may be further adding to our negative propensities. Therefore, it is essential that we start to learn how to work through these issues. The material presented in the rest of this book will help you to deal with your negative karmic memory and will equip you with the potential to ensure that you're building positive karmic memory.

An important point to consider. Like the gharanas of musical family, it is gradually becoming well known via family constellation therapy that entire generations of families pass on their negative propensities to future generations via reincarnation. Read the book *Quantum Activation* by Amit Goswami, Carl Blake, and Gary Stuart, for a detailed discussion of how to engage family constellation therapy.

## The Gunas: Balancing and Harmonizing Conditioning and Creativity

One of the big failings of the current practices of psychology in a compartmentalized manner (in the academe and elsewhere) is that the essential importance of creativity in mental health is largely ignored. Remember this Tao of science in the quantum integral view: it is to balance and harmonize the transcendent possibilities and the immanent actualities. In Tai chi, it is a play of yin (stillness) and yang (movement). Yin gives us access to transcendent possibilities; yang brings us the actualities. If we don't engage creativity, our access to the transcendent unconscious is limited to the conditioned past, to the Freudian personal, and at best, the Jungian collective unconscious. And this is not enough for even coping with rapid sociocultural/ environmental challenges prevalent today let alone for making improvements of personal growth.

It is different in quantum psychology. Here from the beginning, we emphasize both creativity and conditioning. Hence, it is important to recognize the qualities of the mind that the Indian spiritual tradition discovered a long time ago as part of yoga psychology—the three *gunas*:

1. The ability to use mind in the service of fundamental creativity which is defined as creative exploration of new meaning in a new archetypal context. We will name this quality by the Sanskrit word *sattva* that means "illumination." This is the quality with which we bring new light (clarity) of the supramental to our immanent repertoire of learning. In this way, we add more and more archetypal contexts to the existing repertoire. This quality is important to make real transformation of ego-character by putting it in the service of the quantum self.

   If this sounds too exalted and high minded— it is—but relax. Normal positive living requires only a modicum of this quality.

2. The ability of using the mind at the service of situational creativity—exploration of new meaning in given archetypal contexts. We will name it by the Sanskrit word *rajas* (meaning kingly). Kings have their kingdom, but it is their prerogative to expand it—empire building. Similarly, with *rajas* we, as today's professionals in the various fields of human activity, build on already known archetypal contexts of living. Having doubts? Name a profession and I will name you the archetype involved. The archetype business people follow is abundance. Scientists follow the archetype of truth. The artist serves the archetype of beauty. For healers, the archetype is wholeness. For the clergy, the archetype is goodness. Lawyers (in principle) should follow the archetype of justice. Politicians pursue the archetype of power.

   This quality of *rajas* is essential to make changes as necessary to adapt to a changing sociocultural environment. It is the most important component in the toolbox for a happy healthy life. This quality expands the ego character, and it also acknowledges the role of the quantum self to a modicum extent.

3. The ability of using the mind in the service of the status quo, as demanded by our conditioning. This quality we will name by the

Sanskrit word tamas that means "darkness, "and is vitally important for maintaining stability as the ego-character-persona of the adult life. With tamas dominance the ego-character-persona rules our lives with hardly any acknowledgement to the quantum self.

We seem to be born with a mixture of these mental qualities or *gunas*. Where do they come from? They are the contributions of our past lives.

The purpose of reincarnation is now clear. It moves the individual to more and more *rajas* first, and then more and more *sattva*. The more the *rajas*, the more is the ability to creatively adapt to environmental changes and take leadership. The more the *sattva*, the more is the capacity for fundamental creativity, the more the flow experience, the more is the happiness of spiritual joy in our lives—the joy of flow.

What determines our place in the happiness spectrum previously mentioned in Chapter 2? Sure, environmental conditioning plays a role, even genetic conditioning may play a limited role (such as being a factor for our physical stamina) but is there one factor that plays a pivotal role?

Quantum psychology agrees with Yoga Psychology that reincarnation is that pivotal factor, and it is determined by the learning we have accumulated through many past lives.

## Reincarnation History: Are You an Old Soul?

Clearly, our place on the spectrum of happiness depends crucially on the mixture of *gunas* we bring with us when we incarnate anew. For most people (even today) and especially for the vast population of underdeveloped countries, the dominant guna is tamas. The more *rajas* we bring, the more we desire to achieve. This is the case in economically developed countries such as the United States. The more *sattva* we bring, the more is our tendency to delve into fundamental creativity, and eventually engage it for emotional wellbeing and positive mental health in search of enlightened living not only for oneself but also for the whole of humanity. How much *sattva* or *rajas* or *tamas* we can bring to bear in this life depends on our reincarnational history. The rule of thumb is this: new souls have more *tamas*, and old souls have more *rajas* and *sattva*.

## The Purposive Universe: Messages from Evolution

How do we bring purpose in the dynamics of our life in a scientific way? Let's be clear on this. The quantum actualization takes place in the tangled hierarchical brain with which consciousness identifies as the quantum self of a subject-object split experience. But the causal source is downward causation, the choice of quantum consciousness.

This quantum consciousness better be objective to save quantum collapse from subjective whimsy. It can be objective if all collapse events are carried out with a universal purpose. We can then assume, that the choice of quantum consciousness, in the old language would be called "God's Will," is purposive, and the purpose at this time of our evolution is to make better and better representations of the archetypes. More love, more beauty, more justice, more goodness, more abundance, more wholeness, in that direction.

How do we know? I wrote a book titled *Creative Evolution*, in which I showed that Darwin's theory is incomplete and must be replaced by a new consciousness-based theory of evolution, that I actually developed in that book. One of the most important data that proves the incompleteness of Darwinism is the one-way-ness of evolution: as the fossil data demonstrates, evolution proceeds from simple organisms to more and more complex organisms. Simple creatures do represent the archetypal biological functions but in very uncomplicated way with primitive software. With evolution, the software gets more sophisticated first through the evolution of the vital (biologists call this kind of evolution development; it follows Lamarckian theory, not Darwin's; read *Creative Evolution*) and then through the evolution of the mental. Anthropological history clearly shows that mind evolves from simple to complex: from physical mind (mind gives meaning to the physical world) to vital mind (mind gives meaning to the vital world of experience) to mental or rational mind (mind gives meaning to the meaning itself—rational abstract thinking). Right now, we are almost at the end of the mental age and the beginning of the era of the intuitive mind. Today, so many people (perhaps a full 15%) are embodying the archetypes more and more, and as a seeker of happiness, you are not alone.

## The Concept of Dharma

We spoke of evolution and purpose in the preceding. Is there a specific form that our purposiveness expresses itself in our lives? Quantum psychology says yes. Each one of us who has been on the reincarnational journey for a while picks up the idea that life is most meaningful when we pursue new meanings in new archetypal contexts. Since exploring an archetype is time consuming, naturally we adapt a specific learning agenda for each incarnation, to explore only a few archetypes. In yoga psychology this learning agenda is called by the Sanskrit word dharma spelled with a lower case 'd.' This is to distinguish dharma from *Dharma* with capital D which stands for the totality—Tao.

In 1973, I had an experience that reminded me of my dharma. I was invited to an American Physical Society meeting to give a talk which was considered quite prestigious. I gave my speech (which I felt went quite well) but the feeling did not last long. As other speakers presented, I felt they were doing a much better job and naturally getting more attention and

I was jealous. The jealousy only increased during the course of the day. In the evening, I went to a party in honor of the speakers and now I was getting jealous because others, not this handsome dude—moi—are getting more attention from the females at the party. At 1 a.m., I noticed that I had exhausted an entire packet of antacids and I still had heartburn; I felt disgusted and went outside. The party was being held at a place called Asilomar on the Monterey Bay. As I stood on the terrace, the ocean air hit my face, and a question (in the form of thought) came out of nowhere: "Why do I live this way?" And at that very moment I knew. The experience told me clearly that the purpose of my life would be better served, if I do "happy physics," integrate how I make a living (doing physics) with how I live. If I knew then what I know now I would have realized that I had discovered the archetypes of my choice in this life and it was wholeness.

For normal functioning, we don't necessarily need to know our dharma but obviously it is useful because it can help to set a purpose to life. And if we are "old" mature souls and are ready to explore archetypes, it definitely helps to know it. The reason is that life becomes joyful if we follow our learning agenda.

## The Reincarnational Journey

In the movie *The Groundhog Day*, the hero is driven by the archetype of love from life to life until he learns love's self-less essence. We all are doing that sort of thing, pursuing one archetype or another through myriad incarnations. Exploring archetypes takes time; it takes developing first *rajas*, then *sattva*.

How do we increase our motivation to move up the happiness spectrum? Following the lead of the mystic philosopher Sri Aurobindo, we can do so only through the gradual purification of first *rajas*, and then *sattva*. Initially, when our *rajas* are impure, tamas dominates, and all that comes up for unconscious processing are the repressed images of the personal unconscious governed by negative emotional brain circuits and our childhood suppression/repression dynamic, even perhaps the suppression/repression dynamic of past lives. Then we struggle with Level 0 and Level 1 of pleasure-based happiness; at most we are capable of creativity Freudian style. Through art and music for example, we can transform our neurotic images to acceptable forms producing some relief from tamas opening the door to *rajas*. Or we transform through the accidental grace of a teacher or mentor.

With *rajas'* dominance, the images of the collective unconscious have allowed us for processing along with the archetypal discoveries of our predecessors, so we engage in creativity situational-style. At this stage our motivation comes mainly from suffering, which serves to create crisis conditions. It is only with further purification, with the development of *sattva* dominance, our motivation toward creativity is so much driven by pure curiosity that we can delve into unconscious processing involving previously uncharted archetypal territory without external prodding.

Using *rajas* when we learn to make positive emotional brain circuits using both mental and vital creativity, the negative tendencies of the brain are balanced, and we develop a modicum of emotional intelligence.

This is happiness Level 3.

When we learn to process our own meaning from somebody else's archetypal exploration, we become an individual. We become "individuated," when we directly have an archetypal experience of fundamental creativity: now we have our very own archetypal context that we embody, we have become originals, we deserve a new term to describe ourselves.

Previous to individuation, with emotional intelligence it is happiness Level 3. Individuation is happiness Level 4 since you can use your own archetypal context for many explorations of situational creativity giving you much happiness of flow.

Progress in these areas, has come at a snail's pace in human civilization and is always maintaining a hierarchy. The lower rungs of the hierarchy are followers; a few become individuals and they lead. Fewer still become truly individuated and they are the great leaders of history like Lincoln and Gandhi, Nelson Mandela, and His Holiness, the 14th Dalai Lama.

Systematic exploration of knowledge through science has now given us quantum psychology and with it the know-how of the purification of *rajas* and *sattva* in a hurry. Today, anyone can be an inner creative for which there is no entrance requirement of talent and move up the ladder of happiness. What is lacking is the quick social acceptance of the quantum worldview and quantum psychology so their lessons can be deployed at a large scale. If you are interested in further research and concepts read my book, *How Quantum Activism Can Save Civilization* where I (Amit) have initiated the movement of quantum activism to that end.

# PART 2

# From Neurosis to Normality to Positive Mental Health

Hints For Quantum Psychotherapy

# Beginning the Journey: A Pedestrian Approach to Internalizing Quantum Psychology's New Contexts of Mental Health and Happiness

Before you begin your journey to increasing levels of happiness and proceed to the upcoming chapters where the journey takes shape, you first need to personalize the new contexts that quantum psychology is giving you for psychological wellbeing.

The following is a short list of aspects of the quantum worldview, that will be your guide:

1. Consciousness is the primary foundation of reality.

2. We are an immanent consciousness—the self—in association with the brain and also a transcendent consciousness—unconscious—beyond the manifest world, including the manifest brain.

3. Consciousness is the ground of all being with four universes of possibilities: physical, mental, vital and supramental; the last three constitute the psyche.

4. For every brain state, there is a corresponding state of the psyche. Non-local consciousness maintains the parallelism between the two.

5. We are literally capable of identifying with two selves: the quantum self is the unity self or the transpersonal self, it is our reminder of our origin in unity. The ego self (more accurately ego-character-persona) brings separateness with some individuality, our own unique character and persona.

6. The quantum self is tangled hierarchical and unconditioned. In this state the subject-object split is always fresh and numinous. The ego/character/persona is conditioned and simple hierarchical and likely inauthentic.

In the rest of this chapter, I (Sunita) will further elaborate some of the aspects above.

## Personalizing the Understanding of the Transcendent

My second book, *The Transcendent Mind* was a result of my own deep yearning to explore the question of

"Who am I?" Over time and through much research, I arrived at clarity: we were individuals, yet we were part of a greater consciousness that transcends us. The transcendent consciousness is the ground of all being. It is our potential interconnectedness that transcends time and space.

I hope by this point, you will agree with me, that quantum physics is convincing—could we be a universal consciousness that gives rise to all, and yet be an individual self-manifest in the brain? Yes; the concept of tangled hierarchy and how consciousness identifies with the brain because of it, is self-evident. But from an emotional perspective what helped me was the following analogy from a spiritual teacher; maybe it will help you, too:

Imagine the ocean to be the transcendent consciousness, and now imagine yourself to be a single droplet of the ocean. Being a single droplet of that ocean, you still possess the qualities of the whole ocean such as being the same consistency and being salty in taste. However, although you possess these qualities, you are not the whole ocean. In this way you are both a manifestation of the transcendent unity, possessing its qualities, but you are also individual and separate immanent consciousness standing independent.

Even in immanence, there is the further problem of reconciling the personal self and the transpersonal. The Upanishads illustrate how these two components, the unity (quantum self) and the separate self (the ego), operate within us:

There are two birds sitting on a tree. One of the birds is eating the fruit off the tree, hopping from branch to branch engaging in the different tastes of the fruit. The sweet fruit brings him joy and the bitter fruit brings discomfort. This bird experiences anxiety and moroseness.

The other bird sits on a higher branch in a state of calm and peace, and silently witnesses what is happening. He is unmoved by the temptation of the fruit on the tree.

One day the fruit-eating bird looks up and sees his friend and is immediately attracted to his peaceful nature. With his attention on and interaction with his peaceful friend, the fruit-eating bird becomes free from his anxieties.

Metaphorically speaking, both birds reside within the human being. The fruit-eating bird represents the ego-character-persona whose happiness is dependent upon the material world and changing circumstances. This part of us experiences stress and anxieties based on what is happening in our external environment.

The peaceful bird represents the quantum self, which is always there in the background of every external experience, unmoved by the changing circumstances that life brings. The quantum self is able to help us transform anxiety and grief if we chose to shift our internal attention toward it. To shift the attention to the quantum self, the easiest way is to pay attention to our intuitions, the harbingers of the archetypes with which to transform and bring new meaning and new contexts of living to adapt and excel in a forever-changing scale of happiness.

Is this the purpose of our life then, exploring the archetypes and be progressively happy? The answer to that question is a resounding—Yes!

## The Five Bodies of the Human Being

At its very core consciousness is undivided (we call this non-local consciousness or simply unconscious). This undivided state manifests as five bodies of human experience. The first is the physical body, with which we navigate through our sensory world. The second is the vital body whose movements/energies we feel. The third is the *mental body* with which we think and process meaning. The fourth is the *supramental body* (sometimes called the soul) that is built from the vital and mental representations of the supramental archetypes that we intuit, explore, and creatively embody. The fifth body is associated with the quantum self (or spirit), the body of *ānanda*—happiness, also called *bliss body* in the spiritual literature.

This last one requires elaboration. Quantum self is the subject; but how can this be a body, an object? The object here is the joy—*ānanda*—that we experience when we are in the quantum self.

The quantum self is not really a self (Buddhists love to remind us of that calling it "no-self"), but a doorway to the unity beyond—the state of *Turiya*, which is unconscious or "imperience" (remember that word from Chapter 6?) and unbounded joy—*Turiyaānanda* in Sanskrit. However, in order to be one with the unity consciousness itself in suchness, without any qualifications, we have to penetrate even this joy. In this sense the Upanishads call the quantum self and the *Turiya* state it leads to *ānandamaya kosha* or bliss body.

In quantum psychology, we work with all these five bodies to optimize happiness. We use our physical senses to experience all the pleasure the neurotransmitter molecules can bring us without becoming addicted. We work to balance our vital energies and release emotions that no longer serve us. We explore new meanings to cultivate the mind. And finally, we strengthen our intuitive capacity so that we are able to better embody the supramental archetypes, which is the evolutionary purpose of our being right now. And we do all the last three with creativity while realigning ourselves with the quantum-self. This expansion of consciousness brings us happiness too.

## The "Iceberg" Nature of Consciousness

In quantum psychology we picture consciousness as a many-faceted iceberg, part of which is hidden below the surface(unconscious). The exposed part of the iceberg is conscious awareness with its three faces of the self; the hidden part is the unconscious with three faces as well: the personal unconscious (subconscious), the collective unconscious and the quantum unconscious.(see *Figure16*).

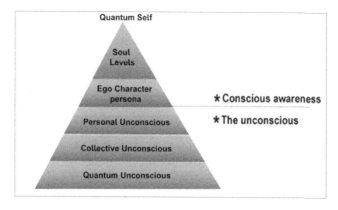

*Figure 16: The iceberg nature of consciousness*

## Non-Local (Un-)Consciousness

Non-local consciousness—or consciousness as the ground zero of all being—is the agent of choice and downward causation. It is the white board upon which everything manifests itself, like vibrant ink from a marker.

Non-local consciousness has two important features. Firstly, it is benevolent in nature, which means that it will align with our choices at the ego level. Ultimately, there are only two choices: conditioning or creativity. In any given moment, we can either express ourselves through past conditioning, or we can open ourselves through creativity that begins with saying "no" to conditioning and surrendering to the unknown. The important thing to remember is that non-local consciousness will support our choice, no matter what we choose. But then, how do we get out of the ego and its choices? When ambiguity enters, that is, the ego is unsure about what to choose, consciousness often helps out with events of synchronicity. Of course, we can always invite nonlocal consciousness in our play by saying "no" to conditioning.

The second important feature about non-local consciousness is connected with creativity. Non-local consciousness is always making a choice conducive to the benefit of the evolution of humanity. We experience this in two ways. Firstly, when we engage in the creative process of (do-be-do-be-do as outer creativity), we open ourselves up to creative insight and manifestation in the outer world.

In the words of the poet Rabindranath Tagore:

> "I have listened
> And I have looked with open eyes.
> I have poured my soul into this world
> Seeking the unknown within the known.
> And I sing out loud in amazement."

This then is how we produce inspired works of art, music, and literature; it is also how we make new discoveries and find fresh new solutions to old problems including scientific ones. We don't know when this creative insight will occur but engaging in the creative process will certainly open us up to receiving creative insight.

Secondly, we can engage in inner creativity, co-creating a new me as we engage with life. We participate in the dance of life, listen to our intuition, engage the creative process for inner exploration, and "go with the flow" when the quantum-self calls. We follow the creative guidance that non-local consciousness is providing for us, and we allow circumstances to unfold without trying to "push the river." However, to do this we have to recognize our conditioned patterns, we have to look beyond the "clouds that cover the sun," and work on making the creative choices that work for us. It takes practice but is well worth the effort.

We often live in a state of fear: fear of not being good enough, fear of not having enough, fear of not being talented enough. Granted, in some cases fear can be transmuted into motivation that pushes us to achieve more. Fear can bring about positive change in some cases; but when fear dominates much of our mental conditioning, and when it begins to infiltrate into our health, education, and financial systems, then we have an issue. And indeed, this is where we stand in evolution today. We are not progressing; we have fallen back a little. We have been conditioned to live in fear when we also have the natural potentiality to love, and this is what creates the deep inner ambiguity: whether to stay within the known and accept the straitjacket it forces upon us or to explore our potentialities.

If we don't recognize this conflicting dynamic playing out within us and if we don't recognize our true nature and true potentiality, how will we recognize the truth in another? If we don't learn how to forgive ourselves, how can we possibly forgive another? So, in order to fully experience and express our transcendent nature, we first need to manage our individual fear-love dynamic appropriately. In other words, we need to examine and change our belief systems as we explore creativity.

Non-local consciousness is benevolent! It will allow whatever choice we make. If we choose to align with our conditioned selves and engage outer creativity, then non-local consciousness will allow us to follow that route. Outer creativity brings us momentary high, but we remain in the same place on the scale of happiness overall. Or we can engage inner creativity in a journey along the ladder of happiness to higher and higher stations. Being able to thus maneuver the benevolent consciousness is the greatest gift we have!

## The Ego-Character and Authenticity

Expressing authenticity means that your personas are in synch with your character. In this way, your dominant persona is always expressing your character. As your character changes, so does your dominant persona over time.

Several years ago, Irene came in for therapy. She had a beautiful vibrant energy and was both very passionate and successful in her corporate career. She was fiery and outspoken and as a result often encountered hostility from people around her. At some point during sessions, we started to explore authenticity, and she said that her fiery nature was her authentic self. She was right. At that particular point in her personal evolution, this was her expression of authenticity, although I suspect it might have been an indicator of her hidden fear.

After working on herself for some time though, she developed a softer nature, love entered, and her expression of authenticity changed.

## The Quantum-Self and the Attractor Principle: Soul-Making

The quantum-self experience is most commonly experienced in our intuitions and is most numinous when we receive a creative insight with an AHA! moment.

So, is there anything you can do help make a quantum-self experience happen? Well, there is that attractor principle that operates to help you: the archetypes are attracted to you. If you pay attention to the archetypes, (that is align yourself with purpose) the quantum self-experiences will be quite frequent although you can never make it happen in a predictable way. And per chance, if you know your archetype, your reincarnational dharma, and explore it, that would be a big help.

As you creatively explore these intuitions and embody the archetypes based on your quantum leap of insight, the self/experiencer of the new elevated vital and mental software is your soul.

## The Unconscious: The Personal Unconscious or Subconscious

The personal unconscious (also known as the sub-conscious) is our personal database and stores the potentialities of every experience we have had. The psychologist Stan Grof has found evidence that we also preserve some of our prenatal and perinatal experiences in our memory and personal unconscious.

The personal unconscious sets up responses to keep us safe, even if these responses do not necessarily serve us in the long-term. Personal unconscious also stores our childhood traumas and all that suppressed/repressed emotions.

## The Collective Unconscious

The next level on the submerged part of the iceberg of consciousness is the collective unconscious. The term 'collective unconscious' was introduced by Carl Jung to describe the reservoir of collective memory that is shared by the whole of humanity. The collective unconscious includes within it both positive and negative Jungian archetypes which are thoughts and images that have universal meanings across cultures and may show up especially in dreams. The collective unconscious has great influence on individual minds. The collective unconscious is also the repository of our universal software, such as those correlated with the negative emotional brain circuits.

## The Quantum Unconscious

The final level, the bottom of the iceberg so to speak, is what we call the quantum unconscious. This is the level of the previously unmanifest; this is where the unconditioned possibilities reside. This is also the home of the pure and non-conditional Platonic archetypes, truth, love, wholeness, and all that.

The quantum unconscious is also what allows us to create a new future, bringing into manifestation the unmanifest possibilities of new meanings and feelings; otherwise, we would create a future the same as the past, which is what we continue to do if we remain predominantly aligned with our ego and the quality of tamas. When we experience AHA! moments, we are intuiting aspects of the quantum unconscious, and we feel inspired.

## The Key to Wholesome Emotional Healing

Why do we suffer emotionally, why do most of us live with a persistent lack of inner peace? We suffer emotionally because of the way in which we perceive and respond to our environment. To shift this perception, we need to shift our belief system; and if we're shifting our belief system, then we need to ensure that we're aligning ourselves with the correct belief system. Again, it takes an awareness of the process and ongoing "inner work" to change our perception and perspectives.

Understand that:

1. Truth is absolute

2. Science is a good way to approach absolute truth having three prongs—theory, supporting experimental data, and technology to help us live the truth.

3. Quantum psychology is the latest science to boot, with creative theory supported by experimental and experiential data and technology of living by it developed for millennia; and it is the only science so far developed for describing the whole human being.

4. In this way, quantum psychology is a reliable belief system to start your journey of happiness. It is based on verified science and yet it allows you the art of creative transformation.

Quantum psychology is an essential guide for us in the journey towards happiness beyond mere material pleasure; for one thing, it is based on the definitive evidence of unity, for another, it upholds absolute truth, but most importantly it enlarges the scope of happy living. Let's face it: pleasure is fairly boring in the medically or socially accepted way and this is a major reason why people become obese or delve into infidelity or even drugs. In the quantum approach, we know that human beings have immense power for manifesting immanent reality when they learn to access the causal power of the unconscious, that when used correctly, namely, the exploration of meaning, feelings, and intuitions, this power can transform individuals to happy people and the world to a much happier place.

## A Sneak Preview of the Journey
## The Lower Mind - Lower Vital, Inner Creativity, and the Higher Mind - Higher Vital (Soul)

Our lower mind-lower vital remains unchanged when we engage in thinking and emoting using our past memories or when we respond to external stimuli using the same old thinking and emoting patterns we are used to. But when we use our situational creativity to make a positive emotional brain circuit, we are engaging with an archetypal context. A known one to be sure, but we are nevertheless making a representation of that archetype in our own brain, and this marks the beginning of what we call a "soul" or "higher mind-higher vital." However, when we intuit and then follow up on our intuition in the exploration of the various archetypes, the higher mind-higher vital starts building up, a process that I call "soul-making." Let's use the word soul for the self/experiencer of the higher mind-higher vital.

In this way, your soul is the result of your repeated encounters with your quantum-self; these encounters provide valuable insights embedded in their manifestations. These insights alter our perception and can become the basis for new conditioning. If we follow through and repeatedly act out these creative insights and their manifestations, positive emotional brain circuits are created, and they become part of our habit pattern; creative quantum leaps make these habit patterns into character traits, creating "new us" and over time, we begin to display soul-behavior. Of course, negative brain circuits do not disappear, and lower mind lower vital tendencies also continue, but there is balance and control. Finally, when we embody the archetypes with fundamental creativity, acting under the guidance of intuitions becomes a part of our character and so does happiness.

The ego-character-persona has higher and lower forms as well. For example, a lower manifestation of the persona would be when a person changes his or her persona to fit into a situation/circumstance in order to be accepted. This action is coming from a place of fear and need—the need to be accepted is okay, but the happiness level remains low.

A higher-mind higher vital or soul manifestation of the persona would be different. People of soul would still change persona, but not out of fear or wanting to be accepted but rather because they are strong within themselves and recognize the need to change persona to make the interaction comfortable for the other person. A good example of this is a coach who works with transforming teenagers. An effective coach would be prone to express a certain persona, or 'get on the same level' with the teens so that he or she could build enough rapport with them to help them. Such people expand their consciousness to include others in the process creating happiness for themselves.

The higher up we climb on the ladder of happiness, the less we need to wear the masks of persona. When intuitions become a trusted guide to us in our lives (more or less) we arrive at a place I call quantum enlightenment. You live and engage in the world, but from a much happier state of being. At the highest stage of happiness—traditional spiritual enlightenment—you are still "in the world" but not as much "of the world" and greater happiness is a result.

You must be curious: how do I work towards attaining a higher level of consciousness that will result in more happiness? Before you take up the challenge of transformation, it is imperative to ask another question: What is it that keeping you from happiness?

# CHAPTER 15

# The Dichotomies: The Fundamental Clouds that Cover the Sun

The three most fundamental barriers of happiness are also our three fundamental dichotomies: transcendent-immanent, inner-outer and male-female. Let's take a deeper look at each of them.

## The Unconscious-Conscious Dichotomy

The first fundamental dichotomy is the unconscious-conscious dichotomy (that spiritual traditions call the transcendent-immanent or above and below dichotomy). In the unconscious, we are one in potentiality; in conscious awareness, we experience the subject-object split, eventually the explicit separateness of the ego. Since most people seldom experience any signature of the unconscious unity (not even the quantum-self glimpse at unity) the separateness of the manifest world dominates them; but real freedom to make a new choice, the key to make changes, is in the unconscious.

*Mulla Nasruddin was looking intensely for something under a streetlight. He was a spiritual teacher in the village and many people knew him. A passerby recognized him and naturally became curious, "Mulla, what are you looking for?"*

*"For the key to my house," said the Mulla. So, the person like a Good Samaritan, started looking for the key as well. After a while, the helper became impatient, "Mulla, are you sure you lost your key here?"*

*"I lost my key in the house," said the Mulla.*

*Now the helper was angry, "Then why are we looking here?" he demanded to know.*

*"Because this is where the light is."*

There is more "light" in conscious awareness, and we often get lost in the issues it raises. So often, the key to change is in the unconscious (the dark "house") and that is where we need to look. When we are acting guided by our conditioning and impulse to avoid unpleasant trauma, we are dominated by the unconscious anyway; we are acting neurotic. So, we need to balance the unconscious and the conscious from both sides—positive and negative—when looking at the situation. The subtitle of the book has the phrase "live quantum." By now, you know what living the quantum way entails.

## The Inner-Outer Dichotomy

The second fundamental dichotomy is the outer-inner dichotomy. We experience material objects outside of us but experience the subtle feeling, meaning, and archetypes as internal objects. Again, the external world dominates us more, especially under the dictates of the current worldview of scientific materialism. But now that the quantum science explains the origin of the internal-external dichotomy and we can measure the internal feelings of vital energy and mental meaning giving them credibility, this could and should change.

Undoubtedly, you live in the psyche more than you live in the external world. Even so, you engage your mind and vital energies to the service of the external. Your internal world is sending intuitions, direct messages from your innermost consciousness, but for the most part, you don't listen to them as you should. You need to pay attention to both the inner and the outer to create happiness. Working with the inner is partly a process of cleaning up and paying attention to internal hygiene; partly it is cultivating the positive via the exploration of the archetypal objects of intuition.

Dreams are purely mental experiences. To be sure, consciousness uses brain noise to make visual images, but it is our mind that gives meaning to these images. Therefore, dreams are all about your meanings in life. So, learn to pay attention to dreams. It might be of value to keep a journal of your dreams, which can become a map of sorts, as to what is going on in your meaning world—of the external and the internal—that you might be missing.

## Dream Psychology

Neurophysiologists make a good case that we make our dream pictures from the Rorschach of white noise that the electromagnetic activities of the brain provide. What we see in a dream is what meaning your mind gives to the white noise.

According to Jung, dreams tell us about the great myths that run through our lives. Many others believe that dreams help formulate and perpetuate personal myths that we create and that we live by (such as the hero's journey).

Consciousness dreams by converting waves of possibility into the actual events of the dreams and in the process of conversion dividing itself into two parts: one part, the dreamer sees itself separate from the objects of its experience, the other part, dream objects.

Some philosophers say that dreams do not have cause-effect continuity; they jump around from episode to episode without any apparent causal continuity whatsoever. In contrast to the apparent fixity of waking awareness where quantum uncertainty is camouflaged, dreams retain their quantum nature to a much larger extent, only yielding somewhat to Newtonian fixity because of ego-conditioning. So, in dreams, we do have some conditioned continuity, and this gives us the story line of a particular dream episode. But when the episode changes, we have the opportunity to experience the causal discontinuity of quantum actualization. In truth, however, very often there is a subtle continuity even in episodic change.

This brings us to the other question that philosophers ask: when we wake up from a dream, we return to the same waking reality (with minor changes), but when we go back to dreaming, seldom do we encounter the same dream reality; so how can dream reality be taken seriously? The answer to this question is that dreams speak to us about the mind—their concerns are meaning, meaning of the physical, the vital, the mental, the supramental, and even wholeness—the quantum self and ultimately consciousness itself. So, we have to look for continuity not in content, but in meaning. When we do that, we can readily see that most often, especially during the same night, we do return to the same dream reality in terms of meaning. The contents and images change, but the associated meanings retain continuity.

So, psychotherapists who encourage their clients to engage in dream work mainly at the meaning level are right on target. The implicit assumption that psychotherapists working with their clients' dreams make is that the meaning that the dreamer sees in the dream symbols is the most significant. The Gestalt psychologist *Fritz Perl* summarizes this attitude best when he says, "All the different parts of the dream are yourself, a projection of yourself." Quantum psychology agrees;

a dream symbol is a projection of yourself to the extent that it represents only the personal meaning that you attribute to that symbol in the overall context of the dream with proper attention given to the feeling and archetypal aspects. Especially important are the other human characters in your dream. For example, if you see your wife (or husband) in a dream, she/he is that part of you which is like your perception of your wife (or husband). Of course, there are also universal contextual symbols (usually the Jungian archetypes of the collective unconscious) representing the universal themes that appear in people's dreams in which case we universally project the same meaning. The themes of archetypal dreams are codified in our mythologies, such themes as the hero's journey.

The meaning level of our life is playing also in our waking events, but we get so sidetracked by the clamor of the fixed meaning of our symbols in waking life, that we seldom pay attention to their present meanings. For instance, suppose one day you have an out-of-the-ordinary number of encounters with stop signs while driving; would you stop to think that this may be some kind of synchronicity! Dreams give you a second chance. The same night you may dream that you are driving your car and then you come across this stop sign! Upon waking up, you may easily realize that the car is representing your ego and the stop sign is attracting your attention to put a stop to your rampant egotism.

## Dreams Give Us an Ongoing Report about the Health of Our Five Bodies

Most dreams can be much better analyzed and understood if dealt with from the quantum science viewpoint of the five bodies of ourselves, that includes the physical, the (vital) energy body, the mental body, the supramental theme body, and the bliss body of wholeness.

1. Physical body dreams: These are the so-called day residue dreams whose dominant concern is the physical body and the physical world, those memories of the waking events which did not arrive at closure.

2. Vital body dreams: nightmares in which the dominant quality is a strong emotion such as fear. The analysis of vital body dreams can teach us about our suppressed traumas.

3. Mental body dreams: dreams in which the meaning of the symbols, rather than the content dominates. Good examples are pregnancy dreams and flying dreams. Many recurring dreams (not counting nightmares) also fall into this category. These dreams tell us about our meaning life, the ongoing saga of our mind.

4. Supramental dreams: dreams that contain objective universal symbols, the Jungian archetypes for example. These dreams tell us

about the ongoing exploration and unfolding of the meaning of archetypal themes of our lives. If you don't know what your dharma— the archetype of your current life—is, pay attention to these dreams.

5. Bliss body dreams—these are rare dreams in which the dreamer wakes up with a deep sense of bliss, grounded in "being."

Consider the following scenarios. First, is an example of a predominantly vital body dream touching also the mental. "Nancy," was a member of a dream group that the psychologist *Laurie Simpkins* on and I (Amit) had created at the Institute of Noetic Sciences, she shared this emotionally charged dream with the group:

*"I was walking up the driveway and my sister said she was leaving, and then I walked into the house, and nobody was there. I looked and looked in every room and nobody was there– they had all left me. And at the same time, it is scary because I feel like there is a ghost or something in the house."*

Driving this dream is the emotion of fear–fear of being left alone, fear of the ghosts, etc. From that perspective we can take the symbolic images to be that of the dreamer's psyche (the house), and she is fearful that she'll be left alone with the "ghosts" there.

The fear of ghosts indicates that being alone in the psyche is a scary experience. Nancy indicated that she did spend a lot of time alone, but with further investigation the time spent alone was still spent doing something whether it be reading a book or cleaning the house. The point here was the lack of time spent doing nothing–just being with oneself. In both her waking life and in this dream, there was fear around this idea. This nightmarish aspect is based in the vital body of feelings, which is also the area of the psyche that was demanding attention.

This dream revealed the need for solitude and calm. Two weeks after this dream Nancy unexpectedly had to find a new living situation and moved into an apartment by herself. However, it wasn't until she came to the next dream group meeting and mentioned her move that she was able to connect the story of the dream to the manifestation of her new physical situation. Although the move into a solitary place was not the entire solution–she still needed to use the space to spend time with herself–it was another important symbol suggesting the need for being alone in her psyche. It is very important to see how both her waking life and her dream life manifested symbols that are relevant in revealing directions for her personal growth.

We have discussed mental hygiene before. In the 1980s, I went through an intense period of cleansing my internal ecosystem. I saw all kinds of purgative dreams in that period; working with a teacher on those dreams really helped me. I still remember the last dream I saw in that series.

In the dream, two characters appeared. One was Ronald Reagan, a very conservative politician, and the other was the actress Jane Fonda, a very liberal person. But what stood out in the dream, is not who the characters were. Here was a president, and a famous actress, and they were literally dancing around piles of garbage and waste. The ground they were walking on was full of excrement. I woke up with the feeling that okay, being liberal or being conservative is all shit. It is following somebody else's opinion. And I was ready to give up somebody else's opinion influencing who I was. My slate was thus clean, so I could get into discovering my own opinion through real creativity—fundamental creativity. After this episode ended, I never experienced another excrement dream.

Finally, I will share with you an example of a bliss body dream that I had. In this dream, I was being doused with joy, and then I saw the source: a radiant man radiating joy. I just kept looking at him, I could not stop looking, I could not get enough of the joy that emanated from him. That was the dream. When I woke up, I excitedly told it to my dream teacher, and he said, "Amit, don't you understand? You were dreaming of your own enlightened self."

## The Male-Female Dichotomy

Finally, the male-female dichotomy. The two sexes process things very differently as author John Gray points out in his book, *Men Are from Mars, Women Are from Venus.*

In spiritual traditions, they refer to the male-female dichotomy as head-heart dichotomy. For the most part, men are more centered in the head while women listen to their heart. There are of course exceptions on both sides of the male/female of the species.

When we were hunters and gatherers, men got the big food items, they certainly were physically more imposing (still are), so they dominated (there is that domination circuit built into the brain). Men are security and survival provider for which the brain (and also the lower chakras) are essential. Naturally, men are brain centered and if they pay any attention to the feelings in the body, they would be more centered for the self at the navel. Women on the other hand, have to nurture children, have to connect with the dictates of the maternity circuit in the brain, and have to be in touch with their heart chakra. Mind you (and this is the sad part) women do, quite naturally, have access to the self of the brain as they must; but when we went from the vital era to the mental era, powerful men (the male aristocracy and the religious oligarchy) forbade women from processing of meaning, and this sad story continues even today although the women's liberation movement in the 1960s did help women to balance the head and the heart to some extent.

In the same way, traditional societies encourage little girls to give love to others to prepare them for eventual maternity to be sure, but it often prevents women to develop identity with the navel self. In contrast, boys are pampered; they are encouraged to be narcissistic. So, men have some awareness of the navel self (many men report gut feeling in creative experiences), but not much awareness of the self of the heart.

When a woman feels both with her heart (other love) and with the navel (self-love), she is balancing the two chakras. When men are engaging in other love, they are balancing their navel with their heart.

My conclusion is that both sexes have a 'head voice' which is the voice of reason, and 'heart voice' which is the voice of positive emotion coming from the body. I think, the reason both men and women in our culture are so ignorant of a feeling-self (men more than women), is that by itself the navel or the heart, cannot compete with the self of the brain, whose dominant voice drowns out the tiny voice of the weak self of the body. So, there is much to be integrated here to get a proper balance of the male-female dichotomy.

Carl Jung theorized that the dichotomy of the sexes has its origin in the collective unconscious. When our ancestors were connected enough (as our illustrious ancestors of the vital mind era of human evolution were) to make the collective memory that Jung calls the collective unconscious, they universalized the human sex difference.

In Jung's system, the male potentialities of self-respect and self-worth appear to the female as the archetype of *animus*; similarly, the female potentiality of other-love appears to the male as the archetype of *anima*. Jung advocated that males integrate their archetype of anima in themselves and females cultivate the archetype of animus.

I intuit that anima is the suppressed female heart self in men; similarly, animus is the suppressed male navel self in women. Not only does this makes sense, but it also jives with an *anima* dream I once had.

As a male, at a certain period of my life in the 1990s, I was feeling emotionally all dried up, very intellectual and very brain centered. Then one night I had a dream, in which I was looking for water, searching, searching, and then I found this stream, but as I got closer, I found that the stream was all dried up. I was very disappointed, and then a voice said, "Look behind you." When I did, I was surprised; it was raining. I ran into the rain enjoying it falling all over my body, and then I discovered a young woman had joined me, a delightfully pretty woman. We walked together for a while, thoroughly enjoying the rain and each other's company. But then we arrived at what appeared to be the place she lived, and she said goodbye. Seeing the disappointment in my face, she added, "I am going to London for a while. I will be back."

When I woke up, I immediately recognized the young woman as the archetype of my anima and felt excited about the prospect of finding emotional fluidity once again in my life. But of course, it did not come immediately. "She went to London." But she did come back into my life later and I was able to integrate my anima. I have told that story in a book with Valentina R. Onisor, *The Quantum Science of Love and Relationships*, in press.

Interesting that anima showed up as a young woman in my dream. Apparently, many men see anima dream and it is a young woman that fits the image of suppressed self perfectly. Same for animus in women; it shows up a handsome young man.

## Morality and Ethics:
## Good Vs. Evil Dichotomy of the Collective Unconscious

The efforts of our ancestors of the vital mind era on making representations of the Platonic archetypes in general gave us the Jungian archetypes of the collective unconscious, often split in dichotomies. In this way, via the collective unconscious, we also experience dichotomy in other archetypal areas of our life and not understanding how to manage this also creates an inner conflict.

A major such dichotomy is the good vs. evil dichotomy: We have both a "dark side" as well as a "light side" to our personality. This is why seemingly "good" people sometimes do "bad" things.

Religions, as I stated in Chapter 11, introduce the concept of morality as the solution of the good vs. evil dichotomy: Be good because it is the moral thing to do. But of course, given the Jungian split in the collective unconscious and the negative emotional brain circuits, we cannot be good just by wishing it. We have to study the archetype of goodness creatively and directly discover the truth of ethics. In this way, via creativity we can override the universal software of negative emotions that the collective unconscious has in it.

And, if our educational system encourages you to check out ethics via your own creativity, even going through the preparation stage, you will be better for it. For it is a fact, that when eventually you take a quantum leap to the truth of ethics, the goodness circuit of positive emotion that you build in your brain will be quite adequate to overrule your evolutionarily inherited negativity, evil; although it may take a while, it is worthy of your efforts.

## Other Archetypal Dichotomies

Here is another way in which we experience archetypal dichotomy: the true or false dichotomy. In Platonic terms, truth is absolute, false is simply ignorance of truth. But because of the true or false dichotomy of our collective unconscious, we tend to give "false" a lot more importance than it deserves. The news media, for example, sometimes become obsessed to maintain balance between true and false news instead of just emphasizing the truth.

We are naturally gifted with the potentiality to be authentic and truthful in our behavior, but we are evolutionarily and socially programmed to ignore this potentiality. Instead, we are encouraged to behave in a certain way in order to "fit in" with society, to take on different personalities to fit different situations.

Another dichotomy of the collective unconscious

is the one between beauty and ugly that may have a lot to contribute to racism. To arrive at wholeness, we need to integrate all these dichotomies as well as others.

Balancing the archetypal dichotomies consists eventually of exploring all the different major archetypes and bring them down to manifestation.

Is integrating these dichotomies worth it? The great Swami Vivekananda used to boast about his guru Ramakrishna, "My guru has the most beautiful eyes." His challengers would say, "You are biased. His eyes are just like ordinary eyes." And Vivekananda would smirk, "Where we see ugly and beauty, my guru only sees beauty. That's why he has the most beautiful eyes that do not discern with such dichotomies."

Indeed, Ramakrishna treated everyone the same, rich, and poor, untouchables and high caste, prostitutes, and Brahmins. We all have the same potential to see the world with "beautiful eyes" and thus bring forth a sense of heaven on earth, and a greater depth of peace and happiness within ourselves.

# CHAPTER 16

# The Brain Game: Handling Your Emotions

The many habits we use to deal with our emotions, are due to our sociocultural conditioning and genetic and reincarnational inheritance of traits. Knowing these habits and being aware of which habits you are prone to abuse will help you to be more aware of who you tend to be in terms of your emotional being.

The science of Ayurvedic medicine is based on the following idea: unbalanced application of the *gunas* (qualities) at the vital level gives rise to *doshas* (defects)—kapha, vatta, pitta—in the software representations of the vital morphogenetic liturgical fields correlated with the physical organs. Thus, we should look for the analogs of the vital-physical doshas created in the brain behavior by the defect of the mental software via the excessive childhood use of mental qualities or *gunas*. Let's call them mind-brain doshas.

Overactive unbalanced use of mental *sattva* creates the intellectual-one who discovers new contexts only for more thinking, not balanced living in both mind and body. In other words, an intellectual can become detached from the body.

*Mulla Nasruddin, a boatman in this story, is taking a pundit in his boat to a certain destination. As soon as they started their journey, the pundit started giving Nasruddin a sample of his knowledge, in this case grammar. But Nasruddin was bored and did not try to hide it. The pundit got irritated and retorted, "If you don't know grammar, half of your life is wasted." Nasruddin let the comment pass. After a while, the boat developed a problem and began to capsize. Nasruddin asked the pundit if he knew how to swim—to which the pundit replied that he did not and added that the idea that physical exercise bored him. Now it was the Mulla's turn. Said he, "In that case all of your life is wasted. The boat is sinking."*

Overactive mental *rajas* gives rise to hyperactivity at the physical brain level. Hyperactive people have short attention span; they like to solve one problem after another in quick succession. They also live a do-do-do lifestyle being always tuned to mental accomplishment. In the current information age, mental accomplishment for these people consists of processing information—other people's meanings as opposed to intellectuals who at least process their own meaning. Since situational creativity's demand for attention is considerably less than that of fundamental creativity, this works out, but the collateral damage is mind-brain hyperactivity. Attention deficit hyperactive disorder is an extreme case of this brain dosha.

Overactive mental inertia or tamas gives rise to mental apathy of the brain, a basic lethargy of the brain to engage in mental learning. This may happen due to parental neglect or lack of proper stimulation in the environment for the child to engage with. It may also happen due to a mismatch of past life propensities with the stimulations available in the child's environment. A deficiency in the genes may contribute to this as well.

Although these mind-brain doshas reside in the brain, they also govern our attitude toward all emotions. Of all the three doshas, only the mentally apathetic may avoid the mind-brain duo and live in the body, and not only in the three lower chakras, but also in the heart. Persons of the other two doshas excessively "mentalize" their feelings, often giving wrong meaning through imagination creating additional negative emotional software than we already have.

People of predominant intellectuality will suppress emotions and would suffer from chronic depression as a result. On the other hand, people of dominant *rajas*ic dosha—hyperactivity—are of the expressive kind; they are easily irritable and will be prone to quick anger and hostility in their reaction to emotional stress. Hyperactivity is also closely associated with anxiety.

In India, there is always a long wait at airports, because planes are seldom on schedule. To fill time, I often watch people and it is interesting how very quickly I find verification for the three-fold classification of their mind-brain doshas. Some of the people look stoic, but if you give them an opportunity, they will immediately start grumbling. These are the intellectuals. Then there are those whose anxiety readily shows, they are impatient and restless, very prone to outbursts of anger. These are the hyper-actives. But some people are quite content with the situation and appear to be quite stable. However, we cannot assume that they have arrived at the much-coveted state of emotional equanimity. It's quite possible that these people are just mentally slow to process things.

The general rule of thumb is this. Excess intellectualism has the tendency to suppress emotions. Excess hyperactivity leads to the tendency to express emotions.

Know your dosha as part of your education and awareness about yourself. How do you handle emotions? The following sections will be of further assistance with regard to that question.

## Expression of Emotions and Mind-Body Disease

For men in the West, (especially in America) there is strong cultural conditioning against expressing emotions, which is often considered a sign of weakness and hence, almost universally, Western men learn to suppress their emotions. For women who have often been categorized as the "weaker sex," the cultural conditioning against expressing emotions is not as deep. However, this is now changing-due in great-part to the "women's liberation movement" that emerged in the late 1960s.

Nevertheless, not all Western men engage in suppressing emotions. For example, if one has an exaggerated notion of self-importance, one can and does indulge in expressing emotions, not needing the usual social constraint of defending one's persona. Under emotional stress, these people have well-recognized responses of short-temper or irritability. Thus, the dosha of hyperactivity, when in excess, can easily result in expression when confronted with emotional stress.

Something else to consider. If one is fortunate enough that there is someone to whom they can "vent their emotions", this other person can help to dissipate the negative impact of the emotional expressions. In traditional societies this used to be the general rule, so the health impact of emotive expression was relatively minor. But now it is all changing.

The powerful impact that unsupported expressions of emotions under mental and emotional stress has on us, is now fairly well understood. Response to stress is a function of the autonomic nervous system that has two components, sympathetic and para-sympathetic. As its name implies, the sympathetic nervous system sympathizes with us and brings to bear the change in physiology that we need to "survive" the stimulus responsible for the stress. The parasympathetic system controls the "relaxation response" designed to bring the body back to equilibrium. So, if you handle prolonged exposure to stress by expressing emotions as you will if you have an excess of the mind-brain dosha of hyperactivity, this will produce an imbalance in the activities of the sympathetic and parasympathetic nervous system. The end result is that the system is left in a permanent state of sympathetic arousal.

What happens then? Chronic irritability and nervous tension can lead to sleeplessness, (and this is only the beginning) as the chronic irritability, which comes from hurriedness, combined with competitiveness—an instinctual negative emotion—gives rise to downright hostility. Eventually, what was previously mental hyperactivity expressed through conditioned programs of the brain, becomes manifest in the physical organs, which all begin to function at an increased level producing disease of organs in the body. Often, the disease will settle in a specific organ.

In this way, chronic arousal due to the expressiveness of the emotional response has been associated with especially heart disease, hypertension etc. But heart disease is not the only result of expression.

When irritability gives way to hostility as when combined with competitiveness, an advanced response of people with excess brain-mind hyperactivity, where is the vital energy felt? Hostility is looking at the world as an enemy, as not me. When this happens vital energy in the heart chakra—love energy—is depleted. Thus, hostile reaction inevitably will lead to disease of all organs in the heart chakra, not just the heart.

If you direct the hostile reaction at people that you are in an intimate relationship with, you will become abusive in those heated moments. But of course, just because you are abusive in those moments you don't quit on love, so your immune system function is not affected; but eventually, the organ affected is the heart. Heart disease can be the result.

If the hostile reaction is directed toward the environment and people around you because you don't have an intimate relationship, you are in effect quitting on love. The organ that becomes affected is the immune system and a compromised, damaged immune system malfunction can lead to various forms of cancer.

## Suppression of Emotions and Other Mind-Body Diseases

What does the suppression of the emotional response do to us? Seeing the role of consciousness in decision-making and the role of the vital body in the choice of the location of the psychosomatic reaction in emotion, answers the question. Every emotion has a vital body counterpart, and a feeling, associated with its move-ment. The physical effects of the vital movements that we feel at the chakras involve the corresponding organ(s) and the muscles in which the organs are embedded. When consciousness suppresses the emo-tion through the intermediary of the mind-brain and its connection to the physical organs through nerves and neuropeptides, the vital body movements in the corresponding chakra are suppressed along with the programs that run the functions of the physical representations, the organs. This is what is responsible for the somatic effect, the experience of illness at a specific organ site because of actual change in physiology there.

This emotional repression with the aid of the mind, by mentalization-giving meaning to a feeling-and in this case, making it into something to be avoided, when chronic, becomes malfunction of organs at the chakra corresponding to that feeling.

In particular, if the emotion of love is suppressed, the immune system does not get the needed rest, and malfunctions. This makes one cancer prone. The suppression of the throat and the brow chakra deprives you of satisfaction with your life and contributes to depression.

However, repression most commonly is memorized in the muscles. This is because when we are defensive, we tend to tense our muscles. As we repress the mental-emotional experience, we also repress the muscle tension and never fully relax them. In this way repression of the emotions translates as the repression of muscular activity. The muscles retain a "body memory," so to speak of the emotional trauma repressed. It is fair to say, that a muscle holds a memory when the muscle is fixated in a certain position and cannot relax that position.

What does repeated repression of an emotional response mean then in terms of muscular tension memory? Quantum psychology says this: in subsequent experiences of that stimulus, since consciousness is not allowed to actualize certain mental/vital states of awareness of the emotional response, the particular muscle memory is never released. So, this particular muscle is not reactivated by subsequent emotional experiences if always the mental/vital defense mechanism is aroused.

It is very likely that repressed emotions all over the body gives rise to serious diseases such as fibromyalgia-diagnosed as a state of widespread muscle pain and chronic fatigue syndrome for which the main physical body symptom is total fatigue. If feelings are repressed in all the body chakras, practically all the corresponding vital body movements will be repressed. This may manifest as a general lack of vitality explaining chronic fatigue. If the feeling suppression involves more the structural parts of the body in which the organs are embedded, but not the organs themselves, the lack of vital energy may be felt as pain all over the body as fibromyalgia.

The presence of pain is interesting, because as a feeling, it must have a vital energy connection. And yet, the role of the nerves is also undeniable, since by numbing them (local anesthesia), we can in turn lessen the symptoms of pain. Also, the role of neuropeptides must be acknowledged. So, pain is a mentalized feeling, a feeling connected with the suppression of vital energy at any structural part of the body and interpreted by the mind as pain, because it is undesirable. This is a very persistent mentalization, obviously millions of years old, and it has much value as a survival tool.

## This Too Shall Pass

The suffering that comes to us via the mishandling of emotions is sad, often difficult and debilitating, but I hope you will see the opportunity to transform it into motivation, a springboard to jump into the ocean of happiness. We do not have much control as children how we grow up. So, there will always be people of various brain doshas unless we drastically change as whole societies. We can however, as grown-ups make lifestyle changes.

Is there an alternative way to handle emotions rather than suppression and expression? Without question, meditation is an effective prescription.

Instinctual emotions are automatic responses involving the amygdala bypassing the neo-cortex. These are guided by universal software and difficult to change.

But there are also mentalized emotional software that we create through imagination based on an erroneous belief system. One of the major virtues of meditation is that it slows down the psyche. This buys us time to watch the response to the stimulus arising as we act. In this way, we gradually, with practice, can realize that the response, suppression or expression, passes; we don't have to be stuck on a conditioned "knee-jerk "response. In other words, we engage our freedom to say no to continuing in the state of conditioned choices for taking action. In time, we build brain circuits involving the hippocampus and the anterior cingulate cortex, bypassing the amygdala—positive emotional brain circuits—using the creative process. This makes the time of returning to equilibrium after an emotional upset, even of the instinctual kind, faster.

This way of dealing with stressors can vastly eliminate a major source of your unhappiness in today's individualistic societies, and thus contribute to your happiness.

There was a time when I was an intellectual but having grown up in Indian culture where expressing emotions is encouraged, I too, was expressive to a fault under stress. I had a temper. And then in my mid-forties, I learned the Sufi meditation—this too shall pass. Now, if something is upsetting me, and I feel my anger is rising, and I engage in Japa,—this too shall pass—becomes my mantra, and more often than not, it works.

Slowing down the mind enables us to examine more clearly how we give meaning to a particular feeling and realize after some practice that we do not have to give the conditioned meaning. We do not have to fear the boss the way we need to fear a Bengal tiger.

Also, generally, there are more stressors in our lives because of the materialist style of living in high standards having to have jobs that do not satisfy us. Many of you have come in this incarnation in an economically advanced society or an economically advanced class of society that requires a lot of *rajas*. This shows that you are an "old" hand in reincarnation, you have a soul waiting in potentiality that needs to awaken. You most likely also have a dharma—a preferred archetype—that you chose to explore in this life. But the sociocultural environment encourages you to take on jobs that do not satisfy. If this rings true, try to become aware of your dharma. And if you find your dharma—the archetype of your choice—try to follow it, find another job if necessary; that will bring you a greater measure of happiness and positive mental health.

Even if all this effort of seriously exploring an archetype does not fit with your lifestyle, do consider the issue of congruence and your ability to synchronize your life with your livelihood.

If you contract a mind-body disease anyway, how do you heal it? You cannot heal it by doing anything at the purely mental/emotional level; you have to resort to creative quantum healing, quantum leaping to the supramental/archetypal to change the context of your mentalization. In my book, *The Quantum Doctor*, I address this in greater detail.

A final important point for parents—be aware. The concept of "Surfing the Internet" that in a previous time encouraged our children to learn, has now become a main contributor to increasing hyperactivity in children and dumbing them down. The same holds true for adults as well.

## The Journey Towards Happiness

This then completes the preparation for what follows in this book. The next two chapters are about people who fluctuate between Level 1 and 2; in other words, people who have mental health issues that need to be addressed. Then, we'll discuss tool sets of positive psychology and the phenomenon of mid-life transition as preparation for the journey forward in happiness. Mid-life is an important period of our life when we have the opportunity to give adult personal growth a second chance. The final five chapters of this work are about growing past positive mental health in the journey towards new heights of happiness.

# CHAPTER 17

# Emotional Trauma, the Subconscious and Belief Systems

There are two critically important aspects of our life experiences:

1. Those that we collapse with attention and intention and therefore with full conscious control.

2. Those that our unconscious generates on a statistical basis from the external and internal environmental stimuli, and we are only superficially aware. It is the latter on which we do not have complete conscious control.

A couple of examples to illustrate these two aspects. You're behind the wheel of a car but have transferred control of the vehicle to autopilot mode. As a good driver, your intention is clear: not to have accidents and to reach a certain destination. We are usually able to do this, so there is some conscious control.

But suppose we have suppressed trauma that we consciously avoid as to not "deal with it" (unfortunately, that never works in the long run). In the unconscious, possibilities interact with possibilities producing a possibility that passes our sensors and actuality manifests an experience that from a conscious perspective is irrational. Such is the way of manifestation of the symptoms of PTSD. When that happens, the loss of conscious control is far more spectacular (and devastating) than when driving a car on "auto-pilot" and the results can cause chaos on many levels.

## Conscious Psyche

The conscious ego is primarily correlated with the pre-frontal cortex in the brain and is responsible for our higher cognitive functions, such as planning, decision-making, things like that. The conscious self can imaginatively visualize the future or the past. In its most creative form, the ego self operates in synchrony with the quantum self–our point of real free choice.

The theater of operation controlled by the conscious self is small though in comparison to that under the control of the subconscious, and accounts for only 5% of all that goes on in the psyche's total theater.

## The Subconscious

The subconscious is correlated with the limbic system in the brain and accounts for 95% of our psyche's theatrical play. It processes everything in the eternal present. This means that if we experience a trauma in the past, that memory stays alive forever in our subconscious as possibilities most likely to influence the choice of experience when we are inattentive, and on some level may still affect us and influence our behavior years down the line.

Although our conscious ego-self may not be able to remember everything that we have ever experienced on demand or intention, our subconscious domain of potentiality does retain all as possibilities to choose from. For example, if as a child, we were given a cookie each time we fell over and hurt ourselves, and if this cookie made us feel better, then the subconscious may prompt us to eat a cookie as a self-soothing action in the future because of the associated memory of feeling better after experiencing pain. Over time and many reinforcements this can develop into emotional eating because it becomes a habit, so each time the experiencing self perceives some form of physical or emotional pain, it resorts to eating to soothe the pain. It becomes an endless subconscious self-fulfilling cycle.

The subconscious is the reservoir of the instinctual memories including the survival instinct. If it processes a stimulus that is a threat or danger to our survival—our Bengal tiger in the visual field for example—it processes the threat immediately putting us into fight, flight or freeze mode, all unconscious, of course. While the fight, flight or freeze mode can be lifesaving in certain situations; it can at times be triggered by everyday (seemingly non-threatening) situations if there is an unresolved trauma within the psyche. Many of the psychological responses that we display are a result of the subconscious trying to keep us protected.

In the discussion above we are talking a lot about unconscious brain actions. This may be a little confusing. Isn't everything in the unconscious only potentialities? Yes, they are. However, you have to remember that for the macro-physical, quantum movement gives way to virtually Newtonian determined movement. So the unconscious brain actions, (in principle are potentialities for consciousness to choose from) and for all practical purposes they are much like actualities because whenever consciousness does actualize them (via delayed choice, for example) as when conscious awareness takes place, or when conscious awareness returns as in waking up from deep sleep, what is actualized would be virtually identical to what we expect from Newtonian deterministic predictions.

In other words, the macro-world of matter goes on as materialists expect it except that it goes on in potentiality as if actual. There is no manifest macro-world out there independent of our experiencing it.

## How Belief Systems are Formed

The first six years of our life are critically important. During this phase, we are in highly suggestible state, absorbing information from our surroundings that set the foundation for our life-long belief systems. We take in massive amounts of information about our environment and how the world works while at the same time, simultaneously developing complex motor programs such as speech.

At this stage our conscious faculties have not fully developed hence we do not have sufficient knowledge or know-how for rejecting an idea when it enters our conscious awareness; therefore, we learn behaviors from the people in our immediate environment and we take these onboard without question—even if they are wrong or are negative. The more a thought or action is repeated the stronger the programming becomes, hence forming a habit or automated response. The perceptions acquired during the first six years of life become our fundamental subconscious programming from which we operate for years to come.

If for example, we are told continuously that we are stupid, this becomes one of our fundamental beliefs and may manifest as low self-esteem. If on the other hand, our minds are carefully cultivated as children, then we are more likely to have a higher self-esteem that will reflect in our actions.

James was a shy child, softly spoken and very well behaved. At the age of six, his parents separated. His father moved out leaving his mother distraught and struggling financially. Unable to cope, James' mother started drinking alcohol regularly at home and while socializing leaving James home alone. James quickly learned how to look after himself and over time he would often have to look after his mother too.

While James was shy, he was also a gifted artist. When his father left home, not only did James witness his mother's emotional pain, but he also had to grow up very quickly. He was forced to leave school at sixteen, as he had to work for a living. As the years went by James remained the shy type, finding it difficult to make friends and entertain romantic relationships.

In his mid-twenties James' mother passed away which led him to drinking heavily. James found that the drinking helped him to become more social, but he also found that he would sometimes behave abusively while drunk. James would wake up each morning vowing to cut down on his alcohol intake, but each day he found himself in the same situation by the evening, hating himself a little more each time.

There was an aspect of James that learned how to survive and look after himself. He was hard working and was prepared to do whatever it took in order to take charge of a situation. However, there was also a side of James that felt bitterness and resentment towards his mother. He was angry that he had to give up his childhood in order to become the adult in their relationship. He had not learned how to process his emotions effectively and felt that he couldn't integrate very well socially.

When James started therapy, he said that he could not understand how a shy, gentle child had become an alcoholic, especially since alcoholism was the one thing that he detested. The analysis is straightforward, however. The messages that James received during his childhood had set the foundation for his adult experience, and when his mother passed away James turned to drinking—the only behavior that he believed would lessen his pain momentarily.

Our beliefs run deep and are intricately connected, influencing our behavior in a complex manner. We continue to form beliefs throughout our life, often through our own interpretation of experience or by listening to experts. Continuous negative beliefs about ourselves as well as traumatic experiences that have become internalized very often cause us to become emotionally wounded. Furthermore, the more we re-think these thoughts and experiences, the more we strengthen the negative programming.

A vast majority of people will experience some form of emotional wounding during their lifetime. Even if they have had a positive upbringing, their personality and karmic propensities may make them naturally sensitive and hence they may sometimes perceive things in a negative manner.

Hence the conclusion: in order to lead happier lives, we need to change our programming and heal the emotional wounding that has taken place. This in turn will change our perception.

## More about Trauma

A trauma is an unexpected emotional experience that we encounter for which we have no strategy to deal with. The experience may be dramatic for us, and we may be left feeling isolated.

There are two categories of traumas. Firstly, there isa "Small-t" trauma, which, although not life threatening, may significantly affect our sense of security—for example, the separation of parents or failing a test at school. In some cases, it may be a small action that someone carries out unintentionally, but yet affects the victim significantly.

Small-t traumas can be particularly damaging to us in our younger years. While frequent enough occurrences that in some cases may not appear dramatic to anyone else, but still have a significant traumatic effect on a child, as the child has not yet developed the strategies to deal with and manage such experiences effectively.

The second category of trauma is a "Big-T" trauma. Unless we live in a life-threatening environment, this type of trauma will be experienced infrequently. Big-T traumas are considered to be life threatening, such as experiencing terrorist attacks, sexual assaults or being personally attacked in a violent manner.

We won't go into the details of the brain mechanism of trauma here, but the essential points are these: 1.) The midbrain organ amygdala is the main actor; the neocortex and our usual conscious awareness with proper memory-making capacity enters the fray a little later after the amygdala has done its job. 2.) As a result, the memory made of a traumatic event are "fuzzy"; in particular, they lack proper sequencing. 3.) The upshot is that a replay of even a little aspect of the trauma-causing stimuli will trigger the amygdala into a full-fledged repeat of the trauma response.

For example, let's assume that somebody is violently attacked, and the attacker is wearing a red shirt. Because the victim is under the fight or fight response, the memory-making is not working properly and hence the brain isn't able to record everything that happens consciously in sequence. A few weeks later, the victim is out shopping and experiences a severe panic attack, which has been triggered by someone wearing a red top. In this case, the amygdala has been set off and has gone into fight-flight mode as soon as it senses the red top, and because the memory-making hippocampus was not able to store the memory in the full context, the amygdala precipitates action albeit there is no real threat—it only associates the red top with danger and hence responds.

The crucial thing to note here is that all this may happen outside of the victim's conscious awareness, which means that the victim may not even know what the trigger is, but yet experiences significant psychological symptoms because the limbic system has responded superfast and unconsciously.

In some cases, trauma can bring on the freeze response where the person "freezes" instead of fighting or running away. Interestingly enough *Dr. Robert Scaer* has researched the freeze response in wild animals and has found that some wild animals experience the freeze response frequently, when they fall to the ground and freeze while being chased by a predator. If the predator loses interest, then the surviving animal will literally shake off the trauma by experiencing seizure-like symptoms.

Often, we humans however do not shake off the trauma, but rather hold on and internalize it. This unresolved trauma may then manifest itself in the form of mental or physical illness. Also, brain scans of trauma survivors have shown that the pathway between the left and right hemispheres of the brain, the corpus callosum, may be eroded by trauma. In this case an individual will have difficulty in integrating the left and right brain processes. Therapies such as the aforementioned Emotional Freedom Techniques (EFT), Eye Movement Desensitization and Reprocessing (EMDR), as well as practices such as mindfulness meditation can help individuals with these issues.

## What Does All This Mean for You?

Although the above is a very simplified summary of what happens in the brain when we undergo an event of trauma, it helps to explain why we experience certain psychological conditions later. Some people need specific guidance as to how to heal from such issues, and quantum psychology allows us to look outside of the box and blend a range of techniques together to make this happen.

Not everyone reading this book will have experienced major trauma that requires healing. However, everyone reading this book will have some belief systems that do not serve him or her very well. As quantum science works across the happiness spectrum of consciousness, exploring this part of yourself is a crucial element. It is just as important as understanding the bigger picture of who you are.

A good place to start is to build a timeline of your life and highlight significant events (both positive and negative) that have impacted you. Ask yourself what beliefs or decisions you made after experiencing these events. This exercise will give you a good indication of what belief programs are running you.

It's important to remember there are four worlds of quantum possibilities that you need to address within you: physical, mental, vital, and intuitive. Using tools and techniques across these four levels will help you to begin to break free from your belief systems.

## Trauma and Quantum Physics: A Dialogue

Sunita: "Do you think I overdid it on that section of trauma. After all, we are writing about happiness and trauma talk is a bit depressing."

Amit: "It is depressing. On the other hand, you are right on target, and it needs to be included in the happiness conversation. Childhood traumas are very common. So, it is of great benefit to know about it and understand the role it plays in our lives, so we can deal with it if we have any lingering effect."

Sunita: "I remember an incident as a seven-year-old child of being in a temple kitchen and wanting to help in preparing the meal. I accidently dropped some chapatti flour on the floor and a lady nearby shouted at me very loudly, leaving me shocked, confused and feeling rather stupid. That event for me was unexpected, dramatic, made me feel isolated and being a seven-year-old child, I had no strategy to deal with it. It affected the way I felt about myself subconsciously for years to come."

Amit: "Allow me to share my own experience of a small t-trauma which had a big effect on my committed relationships with women until I became aware of it and worked it out. When I was six years old, my whole family decided to go to a movie, but not to the movie of my choice. I tried to manipulate them, but an elder brother vetoed all my clever efforts. When I tried my last weapon, "I won't go," he called my bluff. "But if you stay alone, for your own safety, we have to lock you up in your room," he said sternly. So angry was I that I did not bother to respond.

So, they locked me up and left. Even my mother. Just like that. Of course, I panicked. Imagine staying confined for two hours like that. I thought my mother had abandoned me!

A few years later, the big Hindu-Moslem riot took place in a nearby town and again for my own safety my mother sent me away, and again that panic of being abandoned came to the surface.

Two years later, when my mother came to visit me, I did not recognize her. I had pushed back all my memory of her deep in the cavern of my unconscious to cope with the panic."

Sunita: "I'm curious. You said, you worked out your problem with the fear of abandonment. Would you mind sharing how you accomplished this? I think our readers would find great value in your process."

Amit: "Not at all. In the 1970s, I met a London psychologist who asked me if the past can be changed. I said I was pretty sure it can't and then asked her why she wanted to know. She claimed that she successfully treats her patient's problems with neurosis by changing their past.

When my wife made me aware that I have an issue with abandonment, I remembered what that psychologist claimed about changing the past. By then I was a bit wiser; I knew about delayed choice and that there is nothing in concrete about the past unless the event is memorized.

Neuroscientists say children cannot properly memorize an event of trauma because their hippocampus is not fully ready yet. As a quantum aficionado of delayed choice, I saw many un-actualized possibilities. So, I carefully actualized the sequence of events via visual imagination that clearly absolved my mother of any abandonment via delayed choice.

I was able to go back, in order to move forward and 'clear my memory' so to speak, which was a very effective process in terms of dealing with and resolving my abandonment issues."

CHAPTER 18

# The Four Fundamental Aspects of Emotional Healing

What is it that motivates people to seek out healing and happiness beyond the molecular variety? There are people for whom the desire for transformation starts because they have connected with something inspirational that someone has said, or through a movie that they have watched, or a spiritual book they have read, or even through witnessing great suffering firsthand. The call to healing and growth comes in many forms.

Some of the people that I have worked with have experienced the desire to heal through their religion, whereas for others the process has started through therapy itself. A Course in Miracles states that psychotherapy and religion are both sources for these experiences, and at their highest levels they merge into a oneness of sorts, a singular journey.

In general, there are two motivational paths toward healing: one is positive, through willingness and curiosity; the other is negative, through suffering.

## Willingness And Curiosity

Being willing and committed means that you know real change takes dedication and patience and you are ready to put in some serious work. It means that you are ready, willing, and available to "go deep" and question the validity of your current beliefs.

Willingness opens the doors to curiosity. Rather than judging the pros and cons of your actions, you have chosen to just become curious. Curiosity opens the doors to creative exploration. This is the positive route to transformation.

There is also the negative way, via suffering, the deterioration of mental health and feeling unhappy, desperate to seek healing. This is usually when people seek out a therapist, when their pain can no longer be avoided, and becomes debilitating on many levels.

## Suffering: Via Negativa

My clients often question why they experience emotional suffering, and they ask why life presents them with so many challenging circumstances. My answer is simply this: These challenging circumstances give us the opportunity to grow in happiness as individuals, and to choose to express different *gunas* as they are needed. When life forces us into a corner, it is like being hit by a two-by-four; we eventually have no other option other than to change our perception and learn more about ourselves. These "gifts of chaos" are really about learning that we have possibilities and choices that enable us to create something new of our suffering life.

However, when we make a choice to change, we do so with an understanding that we will continue to face challenges throughout our journey of happiness. This is why quantum psychology is so important because without the understanding of the quantum principles, we would lack the necessary framework to implement real change.

Deep change requires that we observe, question, and strip away our masks and look at ourselves for who we really are, find our authentic self. The process requires you to be ok with vulnerability as it may be the first time that you are really exploring your innermost thoughts, feelings, actions, and fears. Quite simply, it may be the first time that you are getting to know yourself—and more than likely– uncomfortable in parts. Getting out of your comfort zone is essential for growth, but it's also why most people stay stuck where they are, because it's not easy.

I also tell my clients that their journey does not stop with the end of therapy, but rather continues as they begin to experience life through a renewed perception of who they are and who they want to be. I ask them to remember what they need to do in order to take care of themselves physically and emotionally; and most important of all, I ask them to continue exploring and creatively engaging in quantum psychology as it will continue to help propel them forward to increasing levels of happiness.

## Four Aspects of Healing and the Creative Process

There are four aspects of personal growth in emotional healing: inner exploration and education; trauma and belief system clearing; acquiring a taste for the flow experience; and developing a new skillset.

These four aspects of healing provide the practical tools within which the creative process of quantum psychology is applied.

## The Healing Journey

What does the process of healing look like? For most people, emotional healing is an on-going process that occurs gradually over time, going through a process of recognizing and removing layers of suffering-causing programming and false beliefs that have built up over the years, interspersed with moments of realization– quantum leaps– discontinuity at play! And then the follow up: restructuring a new belief system geared toward exploring higher meaning, noble feeling, and happiness.

Emotional healing is in fact creative healing in the style of creative problem solving. Our emotional wounds have an effect on our behavior (the ego-character); when we experience creative insights, glimpses of the truth, they can shift our perception in a moment, heal the wounds, and change our character.

1. **Inner exploration and education.**

The inner exploration is about you becoming aware of and paying attention to your internal world, "your story." You begin to explore your thoughts, feelings, and actions and how poorly these are serving you. At this stage when I work with a client, they talk, and I listen, with occasional feedback.

Alongside this my clients and I also engage in some education. Together we discuss more about how human beings function, contemplate the nature of our reality through knowledge already available such as transpersonal psychology, neuroscience, and quantum physics.

This book is designed to fulfill some of this educational aspect of emotional healing, to provide the self-help-oriented reader with a pair of good conceptual lenses.

I would inspire my clients to understand why they do what they do. Together, we would then explore the quantum psychology of the whole thing—how the self in us works the way it does. This activates their intention and that is a game changer. The client's own healing power is awakened- or in the words of chiropractor-author Dr. Joe Dispenza, "You are the placebo."

The *Placebo Effect* is often misunderstood. Doctors give sugar pills and patients think it is medicine; as they take the sugar pills it is said that they are healed because of placebo—a mental belief of the patient that he or she is getting real medicine. In truth, placebo is your own personal power, your ability to intend healing for which your body-vital body-mind already has the needed wisdom. Your wrong beliefs rob you of your confidence in your personal power; this is what a doctor or a therapist helps you restore.

Indeed, many of my clients have experienced shifts in consciousness (psychological insights of mini quantum leaps or "AHA!" moments) just by engaging in this way with simultaneous inner exploration and education.

## 2.  Trauma and belief system clearing.

Here you actually work to clear any trauma and belief systems that are not serving you. These tools of clearing have to be put to work on a physical, mental, emotional and transcendent level—the aim is to release emotional wounding.

There are many tools and techniques. For my clients, I usually use a combination of hypnotherapy, Emotional Freedom Techniques (EFT) and Matrix Reimprinting—which I find is a powerful combination.

## 3.  Cultivating a taste for the flow experience.

You can develop and acquire a taste for flow experiences by practicing acts of outer creativity such as painting, singing, and dancing, writing or by inner creativity and intense creative interaction in relationship with another including your own quantum self.

Both methods give you invaluable familiarity with flow to help you with the real stuff of therapeutic heal-

ing—intense flow interaction with a therapist. You
see how it works! A good therapist (or a guru) is an
excellent substitute for your quantum self! And the
best part of the deal is that a therapist is not abstract.

4. **Developing a new skillset that enables positive
   behavior.**

You need to engage in new positive behavior, you need
to find different rituals and routines for yourself. So,
you build skills that enhance your quality of living
experience and inspire you toward further exploration
of happiness. In your me-centered condition, you are
hanging by your teeth barely to the happiness of Level
2; you begin to use these skills; the skills stabilize you
in the normal happiness Level 2 and act as springboard
for gradually growing to 2+, positive mental health.
At this level, you will see that it is possible to control
your negative tendencies and even transcend them
with situational creativity. That's when your journey
to happiness levels of positive mental health begins.

The skillset according to quantum psychology consists of developing the ability to look at your story and
even laugh about it, so you can set boundaries; developing the ability to see all situations as both danger
and opportunity and be open to new perspectives of
looking; the ability to relax; and the ability to focus.

This skillset above not only helps you with the
healing process but also enables you to remain stable
and content at the particular station of happiness you

reach. A second group of skillsets in the next chapter will propel you in exploring the ladder of happiness further, they will help you build groundwork for positive emotional brain circuits.

## Skills for Emotional Healing

### Skill #1: Develop the Ability to Observe and Question Your Beliefs

What many of us do not realize is that most of the time, we are engaged in an internal dialogue. We are constantly interpreting situations and telling ourselves stories based on what we perceive, stories that can keep us from joy. If we wish to experience a state of inner joy, then we must question the validity of our stories. We must see that our beliefs are not serving us and we must learn to say no to conditioning whenever the situation calls for it.

Here are some tools that will help you develop the skill to observe your inner dialogue:

1.) Be objective. When it comes to relationships and an "other" is involved, we may not see the other clearly, so lost we get in our own internal world of thoughts. I often ask clients to imagine that they are watching a movie of the situation with actors playing out the different roles. I ask them to consider each actor's feelings and reasons behind their actions. This exercise allows the clients to practice objectivity and empathy—it invites them to try to step into someone else's shoes (allowing nonlocality) and try and understand their point of view, and also to see whether they, the clients themselves, are perceiving the situation accurately. I then ask them to reflect upon their internal dialogue. What have they been telling themselves about the situation? And most importantly, is it true?

2.) Every day, spend time in being silent and observing your thoughts. The ability to introspect is a powerful one. Consider this: we are able to both think a thought and watch ourselves thinking that thought. Anyone who has experienced breaking free from an addiction will know that at times, our inner dialogue can be very convincing in its quest to take us back to the negative behavior. Part of breaking free is recognizing this inner dialogue and choosing not to engage in it, choosing saying "no" to conditioning.

### Skill #2: Flexibility and Openness: Develop Different Contexts of Perception

A change in perception equals a change in the way in which we experience life. A few years ago, my brother graduated from a university and attended a job interview arranged by a family member. The interview did not go too well and left him feeling disheartened. The experience impacted his confidence significantly and he seriously doubted his ability to secure a good job.

A few weeks later, much to my surprise, he accepted a ticket to a motivational seminar that I was attending, as it turned out that seminar changed his perception completely as he experienced a creative insight—an

"AHA!" moment. To this day he is not sure exactly how the change occurred, but by the evening of that day he had decided that he was good enough and smart enough to get a job. And he did—within a week. He has gone on to do tremendously well in his professional pursuit.

Working on different contexts of perception can transform your fear into courage and allow you to become comfortable stepping into the unknown, as you begin to recognize that you cannot control everything. Eventually you come to realize that the greatest, most mind-blowing, knock-your-socks-off type of experiences usually occur in an unexplainable, discontinuous way.

Make no mistake about it: therapy helps. As individuals begin to talk through their issues with their therapist and observe their thoughts and behaviors under the therapist's guidance, they begin to see things from different perspectives and these reflections often bring about an openness.

In order to institute an even deeper shift you have to begin to inquire about the grander spiritual purpose of life: who are we, where have we come from and where will we go, once we die? You can look to those who have been here before and found happiness via integrating spirituality in life and also to those who have experienced near-death states or miraculous healing. Not with skepticism but with confidence now that these once miraculous phenomena have found scientific explanation. I find that reading about real life miracles is a powerful perception-changer because for a short period of time it takes us away from our daily routine and feeds our unconscious with material that upon further processing and expanding in possibility has the potential to propel an aha moment.

You need to understand that human beings are not merely individuals to whom things happen, but rather they have some personal power to make things happen. Although you cannot control all outcomes, you can always be on alert and align yourself with the movement of consciousness.

Watching, reading, or spending time with people (here is where you let quantum nonlocality do its magic) that inspire you also helps to create a change in perception. In India, they call this Satsang.

Service is another way by which you can work to change your perception. Making a difference in someone's life, no matter how small, can help you to shift your own perceptions in a big way. Serve someone from a place of love and not just obligation; love enables nonlocality, even tangled hierarchy to come into the picture; this not only helps the other but also helps you, because you have actualized your potential oneness and expanded your consciousness.

Changing perception is about recognizing that every situation can be viewed in both a positive and a negative way. Every experience, no matter how challenging offers you the opportunity of personal growth and gives you a choice of how to respond. You can choose to stay where you are—this would be non-quantum behavior; or you can opt for quantum behavior and change. In any given moment and circumstance, you can choose forgiveness over revenge, kindness over hostility, and love over hate if you allow the shift of perception.

It is the new perspective of perception that allows us to transform the darkest times in our lives into the greatest gifts that we can receive. And remember this: all deep shifts of the perspective of perception comes discontinuously to us, they are mini quantum leaps of situational creativity.

### Skill # 3: Humility: Develop a Sense of Humor and Humility

When we completely identify with our conditioned ego at any level of archetypal accomplishment, we are identifying with one aspect of the archetype, the one that we have cultivated, ignoring other possibilities. We are taking our so-cultivated "I," (and the head honcho of our simple hierarchy) too seriously. How to break up this simple hierarchy of this accomplished "I?" To undermine the swelled up "I" we bring humor to the game, we learn to laugh at ourselves, we play around our ideas and make fun. This is why Einstein said, "Creativity is intelligence having fun." Fun effectively breaks down the simple hierarchy of the ego/character/persona.

Learning self-deprecating humor also helps us deal with failures which it is said correctly are the "pillars of success." This is why the late English anthropologist Gregory Bateson said, "Humor is halfway toward creativity."

Humor, especially self-deprecating humor is also halfway to wholeness. This is why in the Chinese and Japanese cultures, you see laughing Buddhas everywhere.

To reemphasize. One of the big problems that happen in the spiritual journey of happiness is that as we go through the levels, and we may develop a sense of accomplishment. The good part of this is that it gives us self-respect and a strong ego to travel further. Unfortunately, with accomplishment, our ego tends to swell up. Not good. It's always worth realigning with humility.

### Skill #4: Your Meditation Practice will lead to skills of Attention, Awareness, and Relaxation

Recall the story taken from the Upanishads of two birds sitting in a tree. One sits peacefully and the other moves from branch to branch sampling the fruits. The branch hopping bird is a metaphor for our ego level of mentation. We need to work on reducing our mental chatter as this becomes the cause of some of our inner suffering. Meditation is a key component in this process as it helps to slow the mind down. This creates mental space which allows a higher level of awareness to penetrate through, and indeed it becomes easier to "think before you act."

Many people believe that meditation is a complicated technique to be done for hours on end, but this needn't be the case. If you're new to learn meditation, start off easy-five minutes a day of a simple technique is enough in the beginning.

Find a place where you can sit comfortably and ensure that you are wearing comfortable clothing. Close your eyes and relax your body. Start off by paying attention to your jaw, we can often hold tension in this area, so place your attention on relaxing this area. Relax the muscles around your eyes and allow your shoulders to drop. Now, place your attention on your breathing, and notice each in-breath and each out-breath. Focus on staying present and noticing your breathing. If you find that thoughts, come into your mind, allow them to be, but bring your attention back to your breathing every time you get distracted.

This meditation is called concentration meditation; it is meditation on an object. You can use not only breath for your object of concentration but also a mantra (one syllable word such as om), or a candle flame.

If you want to climb the scale of happiness, meditation is going to be your lifelong friend. So, let me caution you what the journey of meditation is like. When I first started to practice meditation, I thought that it would be a linear journey and that each practice would be better than the last. However, this was not my experience. Some days my mind would be very quiet and yet on other days the mind chatter would be so loud that I would have difficulty focusing on my breath. (Some of my clients also report this to be the case and often feel that they are going backwards instead of making progress.) Although my day-to-day experience would differ, with time I found that there was more space in my mind, my mind did slow down. The following Zen story illustrates this lesson well.

> A student went to his meditation teacher and said, "My meditation is horrible! I feel so distracted, or my legs ache, or I'm constantly falling asleep. It's just horrible!"
>
> "It will pass," the teacher said matter-of-factly.
>
> A week later, the student came back to his teacher. "My meditation is wonderful! I feel so aware, so peaceful, so alive! It's just wonderful!'
>
> "It will pass," the teacher replied matter-of-factly.

As you become good and stable in concentration meditation, you can graduate to awareness meditation, see Chapter 19. Concentration meditation teaches you the skills of focusing and paying attention; awareness meditation teaches you mindfulness, awareness, and relaxation.

## The Vital Body and Energy Psychology

For a long time in my psychotherapy practice, I used various tools and techniques that covered the aspects of education and awareness and building a new skillset. However, even though some of my clients worked hard at changing their thinking and building new skillsets, they still struggled with managing strong emotions.

Bringing energy psychology into my practice changed this. Through the aforementioned Emotional Freedom Techniques (EFT) and Matrix Reimprinting for the vital, my clients were able to better address their vital bodies.

These techniques are very effective at swiftly releasing traumatic events that are frozen in the mind-body system. There are vital energy manifestations in every living being. This energy is quantum, but approximately we can visualize it to circulate along pathways that Traditional Chinese Medicine (TCM) calls meridians. When the energy is flowing freely through the meridians, health is maintained. However, if a blockage occurs in the system (for example through trauma), then physical or psychological illness occurs. EFT is a psychological acupressure technique that involves tapping on certain points around the body. The mechanics have evolved from acupuncture, which uses needles to stimulate the meridian pathways. Instead of using needles, EFT combines stimulating these points through tapping whilst focusing on a specific issue or problems. In the language of quantum psychology, what acupuncture or acupressure does is to introduce new vial possibilities for unconscious processing so that consciousness can permute and recombine that with existing possibilities to choose a healing gestalt of possibilities. This works to release these blockages allowing the energy to flow freely and restore health.

Although EFT is used to restore flow in the meridian system, it also works to rebalance chakras too.

Most people feel strong emotions in their head, throat, chest, or stomach. Notice that these points coincide with the chakras, hence when we follow the EFT protocol, we are working on rebalancing our chakras too.

Working on the vital body is extremely important because if we are able to manage strong emotions and reduce the emotional charge from painful memories, then building new positive emotional brain circuits becomes easier. Therefore, energy and chakra psychology are an essential element of the creative healing process.

## The Aspects of Emotional Healing are Non-Sequential

Each of these four aspects of healing works together to create wholesome healing-however- working across these four aspects may not be a linear process. The four aspects can be implemented simultaneously or in different orders depending on what a person is experiencing at the time.

Michelle came to see me when she was experiencing some of her darkest days. She was struggling with very low self-esteem and had just come out of a long-term relationship in which she had experienced significant emotional and physical abuse. Although it was clear that Michelle needed to work on clearing these traumatic memories, she expressed that she first just wanted to talk. She needed time and space to process her feelings, and hence we started to work with aspect one. As sessions progressed, she felt drawn towards learning how to meditate (skill#4) and hence we started to work on that too. It wasn't until a little while later that she felt ready to work on clearing the trauma she had experienced. Over a few months, Michelle's self-esteem improved considerably, and she began to make peace with her traumatic past.

## Fundamental Healing

Fundamental healing can be defined as healing with fundamental archetypal creativity in action. This means that emotional healing comes about as a result of a spontaneous direct encounter with the archetype in the quantum unconscious, hence we experience a brand-new facet of the archetypal potentiality. An example of fundamental healing would be a spontaneous recovery from cancer, as was seen in the famous case of Anita Moorjani who healed very quickly from terminal cancer after having had a near-death experience (NDE).

Indeed, a near-death experience is one way in which a fundamental healing can occur, and this is because an individual has had a direct encounter with the fundamental archetypes of love, beauty, justice, wholeness etc. albeit in the Jungian representation. Some who have had a near-death experience have, reported feeling a sense of deep love and acceptance (which is what we refer to as an archetypal encounter), as well as gaining a deeper understanding about the purpose of life and the way in which we function. These direct archetypal encounters produce a profound shift in the person's perception, hence resulting in physical and emotional healing.

Does one have to have an encounter with death to have a fundamental healing experience? No worries. There are other ways of experiencing fundamental healing as well. Some people encounter this healing spontaneously just when they are in the midst of a rock-bottom emotional low—deep depression; the author Eckhart Tolle, is a good example of this. We recommend reading his book, *The Power of Now*. What are these people going through? They are taking a spontaneous quantum leap to a fundamental creative insight.

These reports then give us the idea: if such spontaneous healing can take place, then why not try the creative process to precipitate the quantum leap? Clearly then, the general and pragmatic way to fundamental healing would be to engage the creative process. The perceptual shift itself is a quantum leap—it is discontinuity in action, so it will happen in its own time. Until then, we do-be-do-be-do.

## Quantum Psychology in the Healing of Clinical Neurosis and Psychosis

Can we heal clinical neurosis or psychosis via therapy? This amazingly is a viable option; however, it requires a therapist stably situated in higher consciousness. The reason is that there are such things as mirror neurons and "induction." Our mirror neurons enable us to mimic somebody else's experience. This produces what we call sympathy when we are in the presence of person in distress.

Induction is a phenomenon of magnetism. If you put a nail in contact with a magnet, temporarily the nail acquires the ability to attract iron as in other nails. For people of higher consciousness, such induction takes place through quantum nonlocality. The effect is empathy—a nonlocal connection between you and another that enables you to be "in the other's shoes."

Back in the 1980s, there was a time in my life when I (Amit) was very unhappy, and my unhappiness was affecting my marriage. In short, my wife and I fought a lot. Circumstances sent us both for a month to the ashram of an American enlightened mystic named Franklin Merrell Wolff situated in the small town of Lone Pine in California high up in the Eastern Sierra. Franklin was ninety-seven years old at the time. When I tried talking quantum physics with him, he refused. "It gives me headaches," he said. Since I liked him, and there was nothing else for me to do to spend the long summer afternoons (my wife was not available), I just sat with Franklin in his garden. Franklin napped while I vegetated. This went on for a while.

Then I started hearing people talk about a "delightful physicist" on the grounds and became curious. "I'd like to meet him," I said, and everybody laughed. Then I realized I was that physicist! A little internal checking showed that indeed I have been happy lately! My wife and I have since found harmony together.

What produced the transformation? I am convinced that it was the local proximity of Franklin that triggered in me a quantum nonlocal consciousness whose wholeness made me happy—magnetic induction effect—and incidentally, as soon as wife and I left the campus, within a few minutes, we started fighting, right in the car proving that the effect was a temporary induction indeed!

# CHAPTER 19

# Keys to Unlocking Happiness for the Me-Centered You

The previous chapters have shown you how to effectively remove clouds that cover the sun of happiness for you. You are in Level 2 of happiness; you still fluctuate between 2- and 2+. This chapter is about practices that will stabilize you at the happiness Level 2+, a preparatory stage for going further in the journey of happiness. You can think of these tools as positive psychology—quantum style.

How do you leave behind your normal homeostasis and go for higher levels of happiness? There are tools you can practice and learn new habits. Here I will discuss many tools that I teach my clients and that are consistent with quantum psychology. These are tools designed to help you out of the me-centeredness that still constricts your consciousness and additionally create a springboard for you so you can attend to the part of you that still indulges in negative emotions and needs to balance those with positive emotions.

### Tool #1: Build and Express Your Authenticity

Authenticity, bringing your personae in congruence with your character, is very important for creativity, for both listening to intuitions and to play with the quantum self. It brings you in synch with the purposive movement of consciousness.

At the age of twenty-three, Bella, a bright ambitious girl, secured herself an excellent position working in a city bank. Born into the Indian culture, and with a family that followed strict tradition, she was expected to marry in her early twenties. Her parents had already found a suitable boy. Not wanting to go against her culture or her family, Bella married within the year.

Although Bella's parents were happy to let her study and work, her in-laws followed a particularly traditional belief system. They demanded that she leave her job and manage the household duties instead.

Although Bella tried to protest, she knew how difficult it would be for her parents if this union failed to work, and so complied with the demands. Bella felt resentment about her situation. Over time, this manifested as overeating, anger, and irritation.

Once her children had left home, Bella found herself deeply unhappy, without any purpose. She had spent so much time looking after other people that she had forgotten to nourish herself both physically and emotionally in the process. In therapy, she soon recognized that she had to reconnect with herself again, and so started off by taking out time for herself to do the small things that she really enjoyed. At first, her family wasn't pleased with this change because it meant that their normal routine was being disturbed. However, after some time, Bella's husband started to see the positive impact that these steps were having on her and began to understand and accept the change.

To be authentic is to express who you genuinely are in terms of your character traits. It means to live your propensities and repertoire of expertise and character traits that you have developed and to be the author of your life.

One of the main challenges that we face with authenticity is, as children we are not encouraged to find and follow our dharma and see ourselves as the hero of a journey. From a young age we learn about the roles that we are expected to play and quite often we do not question these expectations. We look around us and find that others seem to be doing the same thing too; hence we study I.T. instead of music, or we take a job in a bank instead of pursuing art and we "choose" to do what is practical over what inherently feels right, (obviously there is nothing wrong with studying I.T. or working in a bank if that is really what you want to do, if that resonates with the archetype of your heart).

However, when we become so accustomed to wearing masks of persona that hide who we truly are, we lose connection with our authentic selves.

Done in the right way (that is when we recognize the archetypal content of it) authentic living is a process that includes others. It asks us to be aware of our thoughts and feelings and enables us to have more compassion and understanding for others at the same time because of the subtle awareness that they too need to follow their archetype. We come to accept others (nonlocality again) for who they are and allow them also to just 'be.' In addition, our authenticity, silently gives permission for others to do the same.

If we were to teach children how to live authentically, we would not teach it either as a stand-alone topic or in a simple hierarchical authoritative way, but rather we would teach it alongside kindness, compassion, empathy and understanding. We would teach how to achieve a balance between self-love and love for others, allowing the power of tangled hierarchy to guide us.

Here are some tools using which you will begin to connect with your authenticity:

### 1.   Ask Yourself: What is My True character?

Spend some time reflecting upon the unique qualities that make up your character. What are your core values and beliefs and are they congruent with your actions? For example, let's say you think that you are a good natured, patient, and compassionate person. Now, step back for a moment and reflect upon your behavior. How do you treat others around you? What do your personal relationships look like? Sometimes it can help to close your eyes and imagine that you are watching a movie of your interactions with people. This will give you an outsider's perspective on actions, and you get to observe your behavior objectively.

Reflect upon the different areas of your life such as work, health, family, and leisure time. How authentic is your expression in these different areas? Is your work fulfilling, or do you feel that you were born to do something else? How well do you relate to your family? Also, do you take time out to do things that nourish you on every level—when was the last time you engaged in a hobby that you really enjoy?

As you begin your journey of transformation, there may be family members, friends, colleagues, and acquaintances that will find your change difficult to handle. Think carefully about how you communicate with them and try to come from a place of love as you begin to be more the authentic 'you'.

## 2.  Become More Self-aware.

Start to observe your behavior frequently and pay attention to when you act non-authentically. Each time you recognize that you are behaving in such a manner, realize that it is an opportunity for you to learn more about yourself. In a very non-judgmental, gentle manner, ask yourself: in what way is wearing a mask serving you? Why do you feel the need to eat unhealthily under social pressure, or not express your opinion fully, instead going along with political correctness?

Also, it is important to recognize that your expression of authenticity will change as you learn more about yourself. The more you connect and understand about yourself, the more authenticity you will express.

3. **Follow Your Intuition.**

Intuition is communication from the non-local quantum unconscious, and it may be subtle. Therefore, pay attention to your gut feelings or feelings in the heart and begin to honor them. Ask yourself how you feel about certain people and situations and begin to express yourself in a way that is coherent with your core values.

4. **Be Prepared to Handle Vulnerability.**

You have to be willing to feel vulnerable. Living authentically means that we explore and express our deepest feelings, and this may make us feel vulnerable at times. It takes courage to be both open about how we really feel, and then communicating these feelings to others—especially if we are new to expressing this side of us.

*Tool #2: Awareness meditation and do-be-do-be-do*

One form of meditation is concentration, the first form to learn, mediation on objects. In another form of meditation, we watch our thoughts without interfering as if we are watching passing clouds in the sky. If we find we got fixated on a particular thought, we firmly stop doing that and come back to witnessing ourselves watching our thoughts. This awareness meditation, also called mindfulness is a meditation on the subject, the watcher or witness.

Our waking life is full of tasks, and in between tasks we tend to vegetate in our ego. If we are not mindful, consciousness actualizes our experience in response to a stimulus statistically according to our conditioning. This gives rise to entropy—disorder—in all our worlds of experience, an overall general decay. Learning to prevent that is a basic ingredient of promoting the positive in our life.

Concentration meditation enable you the ability for focusing on a task. One effect of the awareness meditation is to produce a slow and relaxed mind—the ability of being. Some people though seriously expect that if you meditate a long time, your mind will become totally empty. On that note, let me share this story.

Subhūti, a disciple of Buddha, has been asked to speak about meditation and emptiness. He is thinking: "I have meditated so long, but never have I experienced an empty mind. How can I speak of emptiness?" So, he kept quiet. Unexpectedly, flowers began to shower upon him, and distended voices said, "We are rewarding you for your speech." *Subhūti* said in surprise, "But I haven't spoken." And the voices responded, "You have not spoken, and we have not heard. That is true emptiness." Upon hearing this *Subhūti* was enlightened, and once more the flowers showered on him.

Some very good news from the empirical front. Neuroscientists have found that long-term awareness meditation does increase our levels of happiness. In the 1970s, researchers Richard Davidson and Daniel Goleman consolidated earlier work to point out one measure of happiness. Brain structures usually exist on both sides of the brain; both left and right hemispheres have a prefrontal cortex. And here is the signature: leftward activity, activity in prefrontal cortex in the left hemisphere LPFC is correlated with positive affect—happiness; and shift of activity to the right RPFC signifies negative affect—unhappiness. Indeed, research shows that long-term meditators pass this happiness test hands down.

In one of Davidson's experiments, the behaviors of volunteers with predominant activity in left prefrontal cortex were compared with those who have predominant activity in the right prefrontal cortex. Indeed, the former was found to be sociable and cheerful, enjoying themselves, full of the joy of life. In contrast, the latter with RPFC dominance behaved like the characters the comedian Woody Allen plays, moody and melancholy.

What does this prove? The right brain is unconscious, no quantum collapse takes place there. It is the left brain where the possibilities actualize and the self-arises. So, this shift of activity signifies a shift from unconscious to conscious, implying that you have regained more control over the brain. As I have been saying all the time, the more you get control back on your experiences, the happier you can become.

But of course, this may not give us a scale, neuroscientists maintain. We cannot say the more positive we are, the more happiness we experience, there will be more and more shift of activity in the brain leftward. I think we can. Remember the brain is five times more negative than it is positive. So, getting control back from the brain certainly indicates more positivity and less negativity. And the more the better.

Much recent neuroscience research has focused on Dr. Matthieu Ricard, a biologist who became a Buddhist monk in the Tibetan tradition and then was dubbed as "the happiest man" in the world. Indeed, his brain shows much increased brain activity in the left prefrontal cortex.

The neuroscientist Owen Flanagan says, "Suppose that Donald Trump's, Rupert Murdoch's, and Hugh Hefner's LPFC (Hefner was alive when this comment was made) light up just as (the Tibetan Buddhism meditator) Mathieu's did, with the ratio of LPFC and RPFC activity the same. We know that the causes and constituents of those people's 'happiness' are different from Mathieu's and thus it seems one ought to say that the happiness itself is different in kind." That is the point. The happiness of Donald Trump and company comes from the molecular rush that pleasure and domination give them; their happiness in pleasure would show up as a lot of dopamine in their brain and that's it. No shift in brain activity from right to left! Whereas Mathieu's happiness, being due to expansion of consciousness due to positive emotions, is measured correctly via the ratio of LPFC and RPFC activities.

This way of measuring happiness may apply only up to Level 3 of happiness though. The higher grades of happiness—Level 4 and beyond—must have other neurophysiological signature; to find these signatures is a challenge to neuroscientists.

I also suspect it is not just the mindfulness meditation that does the trick of enhancing happiness in Davidson's study; in all these studies, the practitioners focus on loving kindness and that maybe the key. What these practitioners actually do is to practice do-be-do-be-do, the meditation of mindfulness—be-in service of loving kindness—do-in tandem. In other words, do-be-do-be-do is the perfect recipe for occasional quantum leaps to the quantum self, and in turn a measurable increase in happiness.

### Tool # 3: Balancing the Vital Movements

Balancing the vital body is extremely important for wellbeing. While the trauma release work may need specific guidance, there are vital energy exercises that you can all do that will help to rebalance our energies at the chakras.

1.  **Sacred Meditation with a partner.**

Start off by rubbing your palms together and then bring them apart about half an inch (rather like the 'namaste' style of greeting.) You will be able to feel a tingling sensation in and about the hands, which is the movement of prana (vital energy) in correlation with the skin. Now, outstretch your arms so that your palms are facing the sky, and invite all of the healing energy that the universe is willing to send you. This will energize your palms further and you are now ready to give a pranic healing to a friend.

Ask your partner to lie down in a comfortable position and to remain receptive to the process. Now bring your energized palms close to each of your friend's major chakras in turn, with the intention of healing. Start with the crown chakra and move across all the chakras in turn (crown, third-eye, throat, heart, solar plexus, navel, and root). Please take note: no physical touch is required.

2.  **Pranayama: Alternate Nostril Breathing.**

This is a great exercise for activating the parasympathetic nervous system which helps with relaxation and regeneration. It also helps to balance the body's energy systems.

Ensure that you are sitting comfortably, take time to relax and focus on normal breathing. You will be using your right hand, specifically the thumb and you ring-finger for this exercise. Gently close your right nostril with your thumb, and exhale slowly through your left nostril. Using your ring-finger, close the left nostril, and then gently exhale through your right nostril. Keeping the left nostril closed, inhale through the right nostril. Now, close the right nostril with your thumb and exhale through the left nostril. This is one cycle. Repeat this five times and then return to normal breathing.

### Tool #4: Acceptance

This was the fourth time that Andy had to change house in three years. Tired of having to pack and uproot himself again, Andy could feel that the frustration was beginning to build. Still living at home with his family (which he considered to be rather dys-functional) he felt angry at the way in which life had presented him with challenging circumstances. Not knowing how to handle the shift, Andy became angry, distant, and snappy with those around him. Andy was stuck once again with the challenge of 'change'—something that he did not like.

Acceptance is the willingness to tolerate a situation. It is about understanding that sometimes there is nothing that we can do about a particular occurrence, and if we choose to hold on to the negative perception that we have formed about it, we will experience emotional and physiological suffering.

Acceptance is also a very useful concept to apply to other people as well. We need to accept that we cannot change another, and that we need to let people be. At the very core we're all potentially connected via non-local consciousness, we all operate on the same potentiality; but years of conditioning and layers of emotional wounding cause us to behave differently. Acceptance is a tool that will help us to reduce our emotional suffering in relating to someone who is "different."

Before we go any further, few words of caution. Understand that acceptance does not mean that we drop our values and boundaries, as there may be situations that require us to put forward our point and to stand up for what we believe in. Certain groups of people throughout history have had to fight for positive change—women's voting rights being one such example.

I like the Serenity Prayer (penned by the late Reinhold Niebuhr) and used by Alcoholics Anonymous, that is as follows, "God, grant me the serenity to accept the things I cannot change, the courage to change the things I can, and wisdom to know the difference."

### Tool #5: Watch Synchronicities, Expect the Unexpected

It is very important that you keep yourself open for synchronicities to guide you whenever ambiguities arise. Synchronicities are movements of consciousness designed to help you in such situations. By the same token, if you have taken a path and no synchronicities seem to be happening, it may a sign that you have to change your path. Take a new path and if it's right synchronicities will begin to show up and confirm your decision.

The meditation teacher *Jack Kornfield* gives a wonderful example of synchronicity. At a meditation retreat that Kornfield was teaching, a woman was struggling with wounds and emotions arising from childhood abuse inflicted upon her by a man. At this retreat, she finally found forgiveness in her heart for this man. When she went home from the retreat, she found a letter in her mailbox from the man, her abuser, with whom she had had no contact for fifteen years. In the letter, the man asked for her forgiveness. When was the letter written? The very same day the woman had completed her act of forgiveness, an act of inner creativity. Such is the power of synchronicity.

### Tool #6: Forgiveness

Forgiveness is letting go of negative, bitter, and resentful thoughts and feelings that we harbor against others or even ourselves. When we forgive someone, we let go of the need for revenge and we make the decision to no longer hurt ourselves. You may have heard the phrase, "hanging onto anger is like drinking poison and expecting the other person to die." Ill thoughts and feelings towards another person do not harm them, but rather, harm you because they create non-conducive physiological reactions in your body. They also create an emotional suffering that may for example, manifest as depression or anxiety.

Here is a list of things to consider:

1. Forgiveness does not make hurtful behavior acceptable, but rather is a tool for you to use to lessen or stop your own emotional suffering. We need to be able to make the distinction between the person who has hurt us and the actions that they have taken. We must recognize that we are all human beings fundamentally seeking the same thing—happiness; even those people that inflict great pain and suffering upon others are in search of happiness albeit in the form of pleasure, and their actions serve them in some way.

2. Forgiveness and tolerance are signs of strength, not weakness. When we take the step to forgive someone, not only are we taking responsibility

for our own health and healing, but we are also acknowledging the potentiality of Unity consciousness in others.

3. Consider the following trio: empathy, compassion, and forgiveness. Empathy is the ability to understand another person's circumstances, feelings and motives using nonlocality. It is a powerful tool that we can use in the process of forgiveness because it allows us to gain a glimpse of why the person did what they did. Understanding through empathy allows nonlocal oneness in the relationship; this is what leads to compassion and compassion is what leads to forgiveness. Perhaps the most important thing to remember is that forgiveness may take time. The process of empathy, compassion and forgiveness may not be a straightforward process—especially if the action has caused you immense pain—and the process may well be a case of taking two steps forward, followed by one step backwards. It may be a good idea to talk to a trusted person or go for some counseling in order to work through the thoughts and feelings that you are experiencing.

4. Forgiveness may not necessarily mean reconciliation with the person. If the person continues to behave in a negative manner, then it is perfectly ok (and safe) to distance yourself from him or her. Forgiving somebody is not about allowing them to continually hurt you, instead it is about

recognizing what is going on within you; and realizing that the person's actions are coming from a
wounded place. Both these factors will help you
to find inner peace.

5.  Forgiveness and trauma. Sometimes when we experience what we perceive to be a traumatic event
caused by another, we can remain stuck there. Years
may pass, but yet the pain may be as fresh as it was
when we first experienced the event. I strongly
recommend that you engage in some energy psychology techniques to release any trauma first. Also,
while on the journey to forgiveness, it is important
to remind yourself that each moment is a new
moment and is an opportunity to experience life
differently than you have in the past.

### Tool # 7: Giving

Why does giving gets high billing in dealing with the
predicament of constricted consciousness? Because we
have mirror neurons built in our brain which almost
helplessly get us to mimic behavior that other people
are displaying in our environment. If somebody is
crying in your presence, you will notice an irresist-
ible urge to cry within yourself. It is called sympathy,
right? If you are reading this book, you are surely
familiar with it.

Sympathy makes a lot of people altruistic; they
will offer help even to strangers in distress. If I have
a flat tire while driving on the freeway, I never worry,

because sooner or later one of these altruistic people will magically appear and offer help. If you are altruistic, you already know that giving help to somebody makes you feel better.

Neuroscientist have been studying the effect of giving on the brain using neuroimaging techniques for some time. The initial studies all concerned the receiver; indeed, if you give somebody money, the receiver's brain's reward circuit will be activated. We all would expect that. Receiving money is a reward!

But imagine the surprise when researchers found that the giver's brain's reward circuit is also activated in the giving process, the same reward circuit that is activated in the receiver!

More recent clinical studies have shown that giving relieves people from severe depression albeit temporarily, even better than Prozac!

What does giving do experientially? Watch yourself next time when you give money to a homeless person without judgment. You will feel energy in your heart chakra, as your heart will seem to have expanded.

This is a good recipe for bringing us out of the contracted consciousness in which everything we do is geared to serving only myself-and I have been there. Once, a teacher told me to always carry a bunch of coins in my pocket when I took a walk, and the instruction was to empty my pocket to the very first homeless person that would ask without judging how they would spend that money and to do it with as much of an open heart as I could muster. I did this for years and it always helped to open my heart a little more.

### Tool # 8: Practice Gratitude

The counterpart of giving is of course, receiving. When we are me-centered, our attitude toward receiving is, "I deserve it." This attitude does not acknowledge any relationship to the giver. If, however, if a giver comes with the right attitude of "opening the heart" through giving, this is an opportunity to open your heart from the receiving end as well. This is what gratitude is about.

Studies have shown that if you just make a habit of writing down a few instances of gratefulness every day, it will make you healthier and optimistic. A brain study in 2015 has shown that efforts at expressing gratitude, thank you notes for example, leads to neuronal changes that lasts. This is the beginning of the making of a positive emotional brain circuit.

### Tool # 9: Practices for Inner and Outer Creativity in Tandem

A pedestrian on a busy street in Manhattan asked a passer-by, "Excuse me, how do I get to Carnegie Hall?" He was looking for the famous concert hall. The passer-by happened to be a musical maestro. He took the meaning of the question quite differently and replied, "Practice, practice, practice."

If creativity is the way to higher levels of happiness, can we practice creativity? Yes, of course we can and throughout the book you have already been doing it. There are of course many manuals of creativity with easy recipes to follow and some of them are even useful in the beginning steps; mostly the kind of popular practices are intended for help with problem solving. Are there practices that are guaranteed to contribute to your engagement in the creative process for both situational and fundamental creativity? Are there practices that can enhance your inner motivation? Absolutely.

Here is a list of seven practices I recommended in my book, *Quantum Creativity: Think Quantum, Be Creative*.

1. The practice of intention setting.

2. The practice of slowing down-openness, awareness, and sensitivity.

3. The practice of concentration or focusing and awareness or mindfulness meditation.

4. The practice of do-be-do-be-do.

5. Working with dreams and Jungian archetypes.

6. The practice of outer and inner creativity in tandem.

7. The practice for remembering your dharma.

In the preceding you have received initiation into items 1-5. Now we will complete the list with a discussion of items 6 and 7.

Although it is convenient to classify creativity as outer and inner, you are a whole—outer and inner creativity are not necessarily separate networks of enterprises—in fact, each can help the other. When the novelist Natalie Goldberg had writer's block, her Zen master told her, "Make writing your Zen practice."

In outer creativity, we take a momentary leap to the quantum self beyond the ordinary thinking ego. Since the ultimate objective of inner creativity is to always act from the quantum self, a state we reach in happiness Levels 5 and 6, you can see why engaging in outer creativity is good practice for the inner creative. Can engaging in inner creativity be a similarly useful practice in outer creativity? The answer is a resounding yes.

Both inner and outer creativity are about freedom. Engaging in inner creativity and happiness is the way to access greater and greater freedom through its emphasis on cleaning up your inner being outer creativity is the expression in the outer world of your inner happiness and freedom.

The problem of creativity, both outer and inner, is the paradoxical role that the ego plays. You cannot be creative without a strong ego to handle the anxiety of creative uncertainty. You also need a huge repertoire of learned contexts and contents for manifesting outer products from creative insights. Outer creativity helps. At the same time, creativity requires that you continually take the risk of changing the character of the ego. You become afraid: what if changing my ego affects that very strength that makes me creative! Some of us don't even want to transform our negative emotions! Dedication to inner creativity is a tremendous help.

Until now– with notable exceptions such as William Blake, Walt Whitman, Rabindranath Tagore, Mahatma Gandhi,Carl Jung, Sri Aurobindo , Bishop Tutu– inner creativity has been used primarily toward the journey to God or spiritual liberation from the world. But spirituality does not have to be world negating; we are in the world, so why negate it? And since the world evolves toward spirituality, why not be tuned with that movement of consciousness? Let me propose that your practice of inner creativity be redirected toward a spirituality of joy in which your spiritual transformation is used in creative service, including outer creativity, to the world.

### Tool # 10: Exploring Your Archetype, Your dharma

Giving expands your consciousness and brings you happiness. Expansion of consciousness means that you are closer to the quantum self in the process, but why? We give out of goodness; by giving we cultivate the archetype of goodness.

If goodness is your dharma, your chosen archetype for this life, the first time you practice it will precipitate a crystallization experience. If that does not happen, no sweat. There are other archetypes and ways to find the one that is your dharma.

One of these ways is dream analysis which I emphasize in my workshops. In Chapter 15, I shared my anima dream of a beautiful young woman sharing raindrops with me right when I was suffering (emotional) drought in real life. That is an archetypal dream for the archetype of wholeness which is my dharma for this life.

The archetypal dream I shared in Chapter 15 about seeing a radiant man is a dream of the self-archetype. Not the Platonic self, mind you; they don't come to us in dreams. The image can be interpreted as the Jungian archetype of the self; however, it also has the flavor of the archetype of wholeness, my dharma.

So, rest assured; these archetypal dreams do come and tell us about our dharma. Just make an intention and then pay attention to dreams, write them down if need be.

There are other quite specialized ways to look for your archetype and professionals are available to help you with that. One is astrology. It is now well established that the planets in your astrological birth chart signifies archetypes. Your sun sign and all that is determined by the time of your birth gives the influence of the archetypes in various aspects of your life (depending on which planet occupies which "house" in your chart in the astrological lingo). From that you can infer which archetype has the most influence on you that you need to cultivate.

Another method is the enneagrams discovered by the mystic Gurdjieff and further elaborated on by the spiritual teacher A. H. Almas. There are nine enneagrams each corresponds to one of the nine major archetypes. Empirical studies reveal the persona(s) of a subject corresponding to each enneagram; usually each of these personas will be antagonistic to one of the important archetypes—abundance, power, goodness, love, truth, beauty, justice, wholeness, and self. Read any good book on enneagrams, compare with your patterns, and you can find your archetype.

It is a fact that every professional is already in an occupation which is about a particular archetype. So, for you, if you are happy in your profession, you have already found your archetype and now all you have to do is to engage inner creativity and embody your chosen archetype.

For others it is a bit of work. The Sufi mystic Hafez wrote:

> *"Ever since Happiness heard your name,*
> *It has been running through the streets*
> *Trying to find you."*

Aren't you also running the streets trying to find happiness? Why then do you keep missing each other? Can it be because you are not acting in your dharma?

Finally, I suggest a simple exercise for remembering your dharma. The trick is to realize that the moment you know what propensities you brought with you when you reincarnated this time, you would have a crystallizing experience telling you crystal-clear what your dharma is. So, the key to knowing your dharma is hidden in your childhood memories that are no longer under your conscious recall.

### Step 1
Lie down comfortably on a mat on the floor. Do a body muscle awareness exercise. Breathe deeply a few times, then first become aware of your head, then your torso, your limbs, and finally, your whole body. Then recall a recent memory of an experience with a strong feeling and meaning tone. Visualize the characters in your memory experience vividly. Activate your chakras so the energies you feel now are the same as in your memory. Visualize the environment, the flora and fauna with as much details as you can. Stay with the memory for a bit and then let it go.

This practice is to get the hang of what an authentic memory recall feels like. Now on to "The real McCoy."

### Step 2
Begin with an intention exercise: Intend for quantum consciousness to gift you with a childhood memory recall that will reveal your dharma. Promise to yourself that once you discover your dharma, you will follow it wherever it takes you, no matter what. Assert that this intention of yours is also for the greater good and is in attunement with the evolutionary movement of consciousness. Gradually, let the intention become a prayer, then end in silence for a minute or so.

Now choose the time of your childhood that you want to retrieve your memory from (anywhere between age 3 and age 8). Create the most likely ambience where the incident you are trying to recall is most likely to have occurred. Was there anybody else than you likely to be present? If so, create them in your imagination. Now wait passively for your intended memory like a fisherman waits for his fish to take his bait. Just like the fisherman, if you get a nibble, if a little bit of memory surfaces, amplify it to help along the entire memory to come alive in your imagination.

The entire exercise should take you about half an hour. If you do this for a period of two weeks or so, you should expect some results. Once you know your dharma, and if, (as is likely) it is not the path of your dharma that you are on, make the transition that your present life is asking you to make. Choose the archetypal path of your dharma for beginning the exploration of happiness, and synchronicities will help your choice. Once you find your dharma, stay in it and explore it, and happiness will most assuredly find you.

# PART 3

# Happiness and Enlightenment

# CHAPTER 20

# The Mid-Life Transition

It's long been established that we are torn between our two selves; however, psychologists say that we have certain "drives" towards unity as well. The transpersonal psychologist Stan Grof calls the human drive towards unity as *holotropy* and the drive toward separateness as *hylotropy*. The philosopher Ken Wilber calls the two drives by more Freudian names: Thanatos and Eros. (Eros is God of sex which gives life. Thanatos is death God. Why invoke death god here? Because holotropy carried out to its traditional goal of self-realization leads to death of the ego.) In quantum psychology, we recognize these drives, but we also recognize that the transition from ego/character to ego/character/persona is designed to partly respond to the call from unity as well. The development of ego/character/persona is the result of our interaction with others as an individual embedded in societal local unity.

Yoga psychology enunciated four stages of life: in the first phase of young adulthood you experiment with your developing ego; for example, you explore your new found sexuality including the idea of celibacy; the second phase consists of life with a partner in which you explore all the pleasures and pains of living in *Samsāra*; in the third phase, you gradually say farewell to desires and accomplishments; in the fourth phase you practice renunciation of the world of *Samsāra*. Obviously, the first two are hylotropic; ideally, the second two, yoga psychology urges, should be more and more holotropy oriented.

The term "mid-life crisis" was coined in 1965 by Canadian psychoanalyst and social scientist, the late Elliot Jaques, who described the time in life between ages 40-64, as a "psychological crisis" brought about by events and experiences that reflect on a person's ageing and mortality, along with missed opportunities and lack of accomplishments in life. The concept of this in-between "mid-life transition" is good strategy from a quantum psychology point of view.

If young people heed the call of the unity (some do) while at the same time the call of Eros, sexuality is also very strong, this can set up a conflicted dynamic. As many psychologists (such as Otto Rank and Rollo May) point out, such conflicts can lead to psychopathology, even schizophrenia. Indeed, there is evidence of schizophrenia outbreak for young adults. The other dangerous age for adult schizophrenia is found to be during mid-life transition, and here the strategy of yoga psychology can be one of the triggers for schizophrenia. So, there is potential danger here, and one has to proceed with caution.

Abraham Maslow's hierarchy of needs is of great value in this situation. Maslow distinguished between ego's survival needs and higher needs. We don't go for personal growth and higher needs until our survival needs are under control. However, most of us go through imperfect childhood and develop certain deficiencies. So, paying attention and fulfilling our deficiency needs should be a prerequisite to turning around toward personal growth.

Recall the discussion of inauthenticity. Not having grown up with unmixed unconditional love, in order to get love we try to please the "other," even lie in the process, and become inauthentic. Any time we cater to any one of our personas that is not congruent with our character, we are catering to inauthenticity. To live in society, we may need our persona, but we need to be aware that they are potentially a source of inauthenticity and conflict. Developing this awareness is another prerequisite for growth and happiness.

If in our *Samsāra* phase, we live a life of pleasure-pain and information dynamics, during midlife transition it is important to discover subtler ways to be happy: in other words, discover happiness in feelings, meaning, and explorations of purposeful archetypes. In this preparation, we balance the inner life with the outer life. We do this with paying attention to synchronicity, paying attention to dream life, paying attention to feelings in the body, engaging with the chakras, paying attention to our intuitions.

How do we respond to the call of unity, the call of our deepest intuitions except through creativity? What is needed is what I call inner creativity devoted toward personal transformation in which the product will be a new you with more quantum self-identity. This is to be contrasted with outer creativity devoted to creating products in the outer arena—art, music, science, etc. The problem is adequate preparation or readiness for inner creativity. If one is not familiar with the creative process which involves frequent encounters with the quantum self, the encounter can be very threatening to the ego.

In quantum psychology, in the first and second stages above—young adult and normal adult life—we encourage not only enjoying the sweet and bitter fruits of *Samsāra* but also venturing forward with outer creativity. Outer creativity is needed to make the psyche dynamic, not static. To engage in outer creativity is to find meaning and purpose in adult life. Instead of drifting in a life centered around pleasure and pain, you then will have found other more refined ways to explore happiness.

Outer creativity also helps balance the above and below, yang and yin, conditioning, and creativity for the psychologically normal person.

Additionally, outer creativity is a preparation for inner creativity; in this role, it satisfies in part the call of holotropy; it is also then, preparation for engaging with holotropy.

This many-fold strategy during phase 1 and 2 ensures adequate preparation for a life of inner exploration for the older adult, for those who hear the call of unity during mid-life transition.

However, let me emphasize once more. Quantum psychology differs from yoga psychology in a major way. It is good to respond to the call of holotropy, even of Thanatos if that is the way you hear it—a call for self-realization. But regardless, quantum psychology suggests you do it in the spirit of hero's journey; you remember that there will be a "hero's return" to *Samsāra*, after you successfully complete your goal.

So, to recap once again. The journey in happiness begins with an intuition that life can be joy. As we explore, grow up, acquire knowledge, explore the world, we are a little disappointed in what we find and finally figure out that life is about service. We become inner creatives and convert knowledge into wisdom, and we serve with more and more wisdom. Guess what? When we discover that service is joy, and that joy is a critical component of happiness, our lives shift for the better.

In the words of Rabindranath Tagore:

*I dreamed and felt that life was joy*
*I woke and found that life was service*
*I served and grasped that service was joy.*

# CHAPTER 21

# Inner Creativity and Positive Mental Health

Inner creativity is creative energy directed to and intended as a process of transformation of the experiencer; the intention of which, is a new you.

After emotional healing, comes inner creativity. The best way to transit from happiness Level 1 (frequent bouts of neurosis requiring therapy) is to take a quantum leap of healing, (when you manifest the healing insight) and you are then transported on to Level 2 or stable normality; otherwise, neurosis will continue to be an ongoing (but manageable) problem in your journey to Level 3.

The first objective of inner creativity is to make positive emotional brain circuits of behavior, in order to balance particular negative emotional tendencies on one hand (for example controlling the violence circuit by developing a compassion circuit) and then developing proactive positive emotional circuits, such as those of giving and altruism. The developing of tool sets (Chapters 18-19) is akin to practices of discipline (Sanskrit - niyama) to keep away from the negative on one hand and positive action (Sanskrit - yama) to promote positivity on the other hand as it applies in yoga psychology and other religious psychologies. No doubt that these practices build brain circuits of positivity, but unless you fall into your quantum self, they do not become part of your character. So, we use the creative process—situational creativity to gain faith in our practices enough so we employ them without thinking, without new resistance. Balancing the negative emotional brain circuits with positive ones engages us in emotional stability and management as well as the beginning of emotional intelligence that are the tale-tell signs of Level 3 happiness.

However, you take only half a step toward archetypal transformation if you engage in inner creativity within a traditionally defined path, within somebody else's definitions, understandings, and representation of the archetype, however rational and exalted the path may seem. "Truth," said the mystic *Jiddu Krishnamurti*, "is a pathless land." Only when you pursue inner fundamental creativity and explore the archetypes leaving all preconceptions behind, can your discoveries lead to an upgraded version of your present self—a new you, a soul who is "individuated"—and a fully original individual.

Socio-cultural conditioning does not make your brain software identical to others who grow up in the same society and culture. This is what neuroscientists are telling us with powerful measurements with fMRI. So, some heterogeneity is automatic even for people of the base-level human condition; you don't have to do anything to earn it. It's your ego-essence where the problem is: even with the individual heterogeneous brain, you essentially feel, think, and behave in similar ways on the average as others under the same socio-cultural conditioning in response to the usual environmental stimuli. Like everyone, you, too, think and feel guided by other people's opinions via information processing, very machine like. Materialist scientists love you because you fit their theory that human beings are hu-machines, an individual but deterministic. Marketing analysts love you because they can predict your shopping proclivities. You suffer pain and enjoy pleasure—downs and ups—but your experiences are just predictable plays of molecular movements; they have no discernible causal effect on the world.

With emotional healing and following up with (and engaging in) situational creativity and forming your own opinions reflected from your own understanding and performing behavior based on your own brain circuits that manifest your own creative meanings, you transcend your machine tendencies and become a human person, a human individual. When you begin to take quantum leaps, your experiences bring new meaning to the world—casual effects that at once disturb and shift the society and help transform and evolve it toward positivity.

By engaging inner fundamental creativity and exploring an archetype directly and embodying it based on your own insight, you become an original.

This is what quantum psychology of happiness defines as individuation—becoming an original human individual of happiness at Level 4. Not only will your actions bring happiness to the world but also your own original brand of happiness. You now have your individual mark on the disturbance of your society and culture.

The poet John Keats wrote to a friend:

*See the world as a*
*Vale for soul-making.*

If you do, he said to his friend, you will see the purpose of the world. The soul is our supramental/archetypal body, the body that we cannot manifest yet except through mental and vital representations. But so long as we are creative, we are okay, we are embodying archetypes albeit indirectly, we are into soul-making. The word soul here connotes what we earlier called higher mind—a mind where knowledge has given way to wisdom.

Soul-making this way can keep you busy indefinitely; the journey in wisdom never has to end. And as you cultivate wisdom, as you integrate and transcend all the fundamental and archetypal dichotomies dealt us, you increasingly embody the archetype of wholeness. You live in a state of more or less continuous flow; you not only become a "lamp unto yourself" but also a guiding light for others. This then, is Level 5 of happiness, quantum enlightenment.

The final goal of personal growth work is to discover consciousness in its state of being. This is often called self-realization; it is arrived at through the creative investigation of the self-archetype. This also takes you to ultimate happiness, Level 6, touted as enlightenment and the ultimate goal of human life as per yoga psychology.

At Level 6, after manifestation of the self-realization insight, one spends much of one's time in the ultimate state of consciousness, Oneness—called God-realization in the West and called *Turiya* in Sanskrit. This claim is interesting from a scientific point of view: is one awake (which is rationally impossible) or asleep or awake while asleep (paradox)? I have already answered this question in Chapter 6. The answer is: awake (in the sense of delayed choice) while asleep.

As we climb higher on the ladder of happiness, some of these vitally important concepts bear repeating. In Chapter 25, we'll take a look at this issue one more time.

# CHAPTER 22

# Balancing the Negative with Positive Emotions

Once you have worked through your predominant emotional issues using situational healing with the help of your therapist, and furthermore developed the tool set discussed in Chapter 19, when you are stably situated in happiness Level 2+, you are ready to take on personal growth and focus on building positive emotional brain circuits using situational creativity and achieve happiness Level 3 and what is also the beginning of genuine emotional intelligence. At this stage of your journey, the following guidance will be easier to implement because you are comfortable using the tools of energy psychology and skill set of transpersonal living.

In the first stage of the creative process—preparation—you imagine some possible answers to your problem via conclusions gained from your reading and engaging with other people's existing work; you can use imagination perhaps for thinking even some semi-original possible answers. But you can only go so far. All this divergent thinking on your part is nothing compared to what the unconscious can do for you.

Consider that your thoughts, as soon as you are not thinking them, become possibility. Each thought of divergent thinking becomes a seed for an expanding quantum possibility wave of meaning in the unconscious. As the waves continue to expand, they become bigger and bigger pools of possibilities. The waves of possibility interact with other waves of possibility producing even more possibilities. In this way, unconscious processing in no time produces a huge pool of quantum possibilities for consciousness to choose from. The probability of success in finding the right answer obviously is much bigger in this two-stage quantum thinking than it would be with simply one stage conscious Newtonian thinking.

## Do-Be-Do-Be-Do: Making Positive Emotional Brain Circuits

Which archetype should you choose for exploration in your quest for making positive emotional response as a part of your character, an important step toward happiness Level 3? It is best to choose an archetype that brings you out of me-centeredness as well as helps you make a positive emotional brain circuit that balances those negative ones—goodness or love.

Let's say you choose goodness. You explore this archetype in relationship. Choose you subject carefully: the best choice is a friend or former friend.

There are many books that give you known contexts for developing good relationship with a friend.

Say you choose the teachings of Jesus from the New Testament. If a friend wants a ride from you, not only do you give him the ride to his or her current destination, you make sure he/she has a ride back home. Now watch. What's happening in your mind? Is there resistance? Conflict between the demand of goodness and the demand of accomplishments? Is there a tendency to bargain? What can I extract from him in return? And pay attention to anything else that is keeping you from enjoying the expansion of consciousness that should come when we offer a helping hand to a friend. Work on removing the obstacles and keep on practicing goodness this way until there is no resistance, and you feel expanded when you help someone.

Helping someone is also about the ability to receive help with gratitude; not to take the helper for granted. Perhaps your child is sick, and you are needed at the office, and you cannot find a babysitter; so, you call your retired stay-at-home mother for help, and she babysits for you. Watch yourself! Is there an expansion of consciousness because you feel gratitude? If not, what is obstructing it? Try to clear the obstacle, practice, practice, practice.

Progressively, make your practice more difficult. Jesus challenges you: "Love your enemy for anybody can love a friend." You can interpret this in many ways, some very deep (see Chapter 23). One obvious meaning is to bring on the ability to forgive if your friend does you wrong and acts like an enemy in a certain transaction. Be mindful. Do you feel expanded when you forgive? If not, find out what is obstructing you and try to clear up the blocked energy in the heart.

However, it won't be so easy this time. You are missing something about the creative process. What you have engaged so far is all doing; how do you make this into a creative practice, do-be-do-be-do? By learning to relax; nothing needs to be done immediately. You don't have to feel good immediately! Let the unconscious process what you begin at the conscious level.

Nothing is happening? Start another round of doing with another idea keeping the same theme—love your enemy. It is hard to see that intellectually. You have to engage feelings.

That's basically it: do-be-do-be-do with variations of ideas and subjects on a challenging theme that posits a thesis and an antithesis, such as being good to a perceived enemy with two barrels—thinking as well as feeling.

## Insight

When insight comes, you will have clarity of what blocks you and now you seriously begin unblocking and actively embodying goodness by effortlessly practicing the same things as before and enjoying the positivity. Your brain and heart will remember your positivity and will come to your rescue every time negative emotions hit you. You have made you positive emotional brain circuits of goodness involving your heart chakra and your brain. Additionally, you have developed a trait of some conviction in your positivity, a character trait.

About conviction. When consciousness chooses a new answer, you get a surprise of sorts which makes it quite clear that the choice is discontinuous; it is then you know that you have taken a quantum leap. In situational creativity, you are working within the archetypal context already established by earlier researchers (Jesus in your case), the paradigm you are using. You get a surprise, (new meaning) but the quantum leap involved does not necessarily take you to the pure quantum self-experience; a close enough state of the preconscious works just fine. This compromises the surprise element. Also, there is no archetypal encounter in situational creativity, no truth value per se in the experience, and the conviction that the new meaning is right for you depends on your faith from whom you borrowed the paradigm you are using. However, with all the fake news floating around today, it is hard to have that kind of faith in anything.

Moreover, as a situational creativity explorer, you are likely a little hyperactive, with a do-do-do lifestyle. So, it is in your pattern to be impatient and force your unconscious to make an actualization even though the required gestalt of possibilities to solve the problem is not there yet. In this way, in all likelihood, the choice that comes to you is erroneous. Being human, you are going to make such mistakes in gauging your ideas for their surprise and truth values—but don't be dismayed—failures are in fact, the foundational pillars of future success.

In outer creativity what people do is to use the scientific method at this stage: try it and see. And most scientists work within a paradigm, and indeed they use the scientific method routinely, and this is one reason why they have been so unreceptive to acknowledge the importance of unconscious processing or the importance of quantum in creativity.

## Placebos, Doctors, Gurus and Psychotherapists

What do you do after a situational insight of inner creativity if doubt keeps creeping up? You can try a behavior change and see if it works. But how many behavioral changes can you try? The "trial and error" methods are not a very practical use of your time and resources. This is why spiritual traditions emphasize a guru when exploring situational creativity; they say only a guru can tell you if your insight of new meaning is the right one for you to implement.

How does the guru tell you? In the Indian tradition, sadgurus are supposed to be people who are transformed, who live by intuition, and so they can tell you by that keen power of intuition.

But finding such gurus in today's world is difficult. Well, you can use your own intuition; that is one choice. But I suggest you use a transpersonal or Jungian psychotherapist for a reason. It is the aforementioned placebo effect.

I have already discussed how placebo works. If you go a psychotherapist you trust, it can work the same way as the placebo effect with medicines. This is how the guru system has worked in India, Japan, and other places (such as the shamanic cultures) so well in the past.

One more point before we close. Exploration of happiness beyond Level 3 will take fundamental creativity, no less. And you must appreciate the difference in depth between the two brands of creativity.

## Difference between Situational and Fundamental Creativity

As you know, archetypes are the objects we intuit. When we learn to pay attention to our intuitive thoughts, archetypes pay attention to us—the attractor principle. In our exploration of fundamental creativity for inner transformation, we begin with paying attention to intuition; we end with embracing intuition as our new way to cognize and live.

In situational creativity, even in inner creativity, our purpose is to serve ourselves—our egos, please ourselves, fulfill our selfish desire for happiness. In fundamental creativity, our own happiness is only part of our motivation. We do it also to please the quantum self, God if you will. In other words, the object of fundamental creativity is to serve both the ego and the quantum self in balance and harmony.

Emperor Akbar of medieval India had a court

singer named Tansen; so great was he that even now his name is legendary in the Indian culture. Akbar loved to listen to Tansen's music.

*One day as he was heaping praise on Tansen, he asked, "tell me Tansen. Is there anyone in the world who is even better than you?"*

*Tansen said without hesitation. "Yes, your majesty. My music guru."*

*The emperor was surprised. And curious too. "Can I summon him? Will he sing for me?"*

*"Your majesty, he is a renunciate and recluse. Does not see anybody. Please. We have to leave him alone."*

*But Akbar was persistent. Tansen agreed to take Akbar to his guru but only on the condition that the emperor would listen to the music from the background without intruding. The emperor consented.*

*So, one morning, very early, they rode to the suburb of Delhi and hid in a bush near the abode of Tansen's guru. Tansen whispered, "When the first light of dawn appears, he will come to the terrace and sing."*

*It happened. The guru sang and sang. The emperor listened and listened, totally mesmerized by the joy of the expansion he felt. The performance ended; the guru went back inside. Akbar and Tansen commenced to turn back toward Delhi. After a while Akbar spoke.*

*"Tansen, you are his student. Why can't you sing like him?"*

*Tansen gave his famous replay, "Your majesty! I sing to please you. My guru sings to please God."*

# CHAPTER 23

# Exploring the Archetype of Love

Direct exploration of an archetype takes engaging in fundamental creativity-however- the creative process of fundamental creativity is a little different from that of situational creativity; there is no more need for any consultation with a guru after your insight or any "try it and see." Fundamental creativity comes with certain knowledge. You know.

In the manifestation stage, YOU manifest the insight TO MAKE A NEW YOU, a transformed you. That makes knowledge into wisdom—lived knowledge—and that deep "knowing" is light years beyond a simplified belief system that gets handed down to us in our formative years.

When it comes to a specific archetype, I have personal experience of fulfillment with only one archetype—the archetype of love. So, the rest of this chapter will be dedicated to an exploration of my style of love. This is a summary of a similar exposition in my book with physician Valentina R. Onisor, *Quantum Spirituality*.

## Preparation: From Sex and Romance to Commitment

Because of the instinctual brain circuits, our sexuality is aroused easily and often by a variety of stimuli. When we are teenagers and these feelings are unfamiliar, we often become confused about our sexuality. Most societies have a taboo against educating the young about sexuality and in some spiritual societies, the idea of celibacy is introduced for the young. Unfortunately, this is often done without much guidance as to why or how. The original idea could have been good: remain celibate until you discover romantic love when you will no longer be confused about the creative potential of your sexuality (beyond procreation). But without any avenue for such education, how is the confusion going to go away?

If a teenager goes into sex without understanding the creative potential and purpose of sex (we are not referencing "the birds and the bees" reproductive aspect of sex, that is generally taught in schools as sex education), he or she will blindly respond to the brain circuits and body hormones and look upon sexuality as a gratification, as a vehicle for a unique kind of intense pleasure. Since the fulfillment of sexual pleasure for a male with a partner can raise vital energy to the third chakra associated with the ego identity with the physical body, a sense of personal power may enter the equation as well. For many males, it is common to think of "sexual conquests" in connection with sex that is not associated with romantic love. In the Western world, the pattern that has developed over the last few decades, at least for men, is this early conditioning of sex as a power.

Women, thanks to some protective ("conservative") parents, are somewhat exempt from this trend although that is rapidly changing, as social media often indicates.

What happens when we eventually discover a partner with whom our heart chakra resonates? Sex in romantic love raises the energy from the sex chakra to the heart chakra to collapse. We enter the romantic love relationship, but our habit of conquest remains, just temporarily abated. The romance eventually runs out; it does that sooner or later because of our brain's tendency to habituate every new experience, the sex-hormone oxytocin (popularly called the love-hormone) becomes scarce in the bloodstream. Then the sex-for-power tendency returns-but then-we have a choice. We can look for another romantic partner or go deep in the existing relationship to explore its creative potential. Can we love without being driven by the love-hormone? Can we love unconditionally?

Marriage is a commitment at the vital level to make love, not war (or conquest). Unfortunately, this vital body agreement concurrently has to find agreements between the mental bodies of the partners as well. For mental bodies of a couple, the individual ego conditionings are very deep; in the arenas of overlap of mutual ego activity there will be territoriality, and competitiveness and domination will emerge and bring the energy down from the heart chakra to the navel chakra once again resulting in a return to narcissism. A man might say to his wife when she expresses dissatisfaction with their marriage: "I don't get it. Your job is to make me happy. I am perfectly happy. So, what's the problem?"

Where are women in all this? Unless their navel chakra is strong (and more often than not it isn't), they are at the receiving end of all these male tendencies to be dominated from their male partner. As a result, they also become unhappy and resentful, unable to maintain steady heart energy.

The competitiveness, domination, resent, hate, and other negative emotions will relent only when both partners begin to intuitively glimpse that it is possible to surrender the negative emotions within the positive energy of love.

It is then that we are serious about engaging the creative process of discovering love; we have passed the entrance requirement, motivation. The next step is preparation, unconscious processing of the do-be-do-be-do formula, which is the same as situational creativity except that we don't restrict ourselves to one teaching or another in exploring love; we research all known paths to generate divergent thinking, and then engage in unconscious processing and do-be-do-be-do following that.

## Double-Slit Processing in the Exploration of Love

Our conditioning does not allow incoming stimuli to evoke all possible responses in our mind-brain-vital body-body organs complex, however, our conditioning acts like a slit that permits us to process the stimulus in the same conditioned perspectives that we have seen before. It is very much like the case of the electron passing through a single slit before falling on a fluorescent screen. It appears right behind the slit, only a little blurring of its image due to diffraction gives away that the electron is still a wave of possibility and not an entity of complete fixity of a point.

But if we pass the electron through both slits of a double-slit screen (see *Figure9*), every electron wave becomes two waves of possibility that interfere. If we put a photographic plate to catch them, they will arrive at some place adding constructively; at in-between places, they will arrive in opposite phase and destroy each other. The net effect is what physicists call an interference pattern. Notice how the possibility pool of the electrons is enhanced enormously; the electron is able to arrive at so many more for places on the photographic film now.

So, this is the magic of having an intimate relationship whom you want so much to love and cherish that every stimulus-response you not only allow your belief system to sift it through but your partner's as well making her/him into a double slit for unconscious processing.

In this way, having a committed intimate relationship is like having a double slit to sift all your incoming stimuli-responses through in this way enhancing your possibility pool for unconscious processing. The truth is, you may not yet consciously recognize your partner's contexts for looking at things; but responding to your intention, your unconscious is already considering them, hence the change. Your possibility pool to choose from is now much bigger, and chances are better that new possibilities for creativity are already there for the quantum consciousness to enter the picture and choose.

Is there any other way to enhance the possibility pool to choose from even further? Is there any way to guarantee that there will be new possibilities in the pool?

## Using Quantum Consciousness to Resolve Conflicts in Intimate Relationships

At this stage, your relationship has to take a turn toward transforming from simple hierarchy to a tangled hierarchy.

Look at the Escher picture of the Drawing Hands (see *Figure 17*).

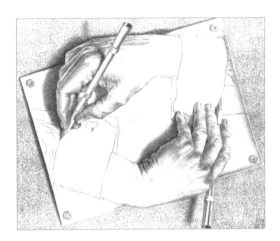

*Figure 17: Drawing Hands by M. C. Escher*
*(artist's rendition)*

In this picture the tangled hierarchy is created because the left hand is drawing the right, and the right hand is drawing the left, but you can plainly see that this is an illusion. Behind the scenes, Escher is drawing them both. When from your study of the quantum measurement you truly have taken the quantum leap of understanding that the reality of your manifest consciousness, the subject-hood of the subject-object partnership arises from the quantum choice and actualization from an undivided quantum consciousness, you also have identified the source of your tangled hierarchy you are trying to emulate-the unmanifest quantum consciousness. You have to relegate authority to that one. But how do you shift your authority from the manifest to the unmanifest, even temporarily?

It is in this process of discovery that if your love partner is also your intimate enemy can become a huge boon. This "love your enemy" is also the best strategy for situational creativity, for settling external differences that cause the enmity (see Chapter 22). Here the challenge is deeper—a transformation in our mode of living.

There is an intense fight scene in the movie *The Wedding Date*, between a romantic couple, the hero says to the heroine something to the effect of, "I want to marry you, because I'd rather fight with you than make love with another person." To practice unconditional love, it is important to recognize your love partner shamelessly as "the intimate enemy." The behavioral advice is to use reason to settle the differences that cause fighting ("renegotiating your contract") but unfortunately, this usually amounts only to suppressing emotions. Or if emotions break out anyway, the behavioral advice is to leave the scene, to not to let things "get out of hand," or "to kiss and make up," which is usually a pretension until sexual instinct takes over. This is perhaps good advice for people who are not ready to explore unconditional love but for you—the inner fundamental creative—your challenge is to love your partner in spite of your differences. And when these differences cause a fight, then so be it, remain in the fight explicitly or implicitly until a quantum leap takes place or until the situation become unbearable at your present stage of personal emotional maturity. Conflicts are guaranteed to bring new possibilities in your pool for processing and who can process the new but quantum consciousness/God? Gradually, we become capable of waiting out unresolved conflicts for longer and longer time.

With this strategy, sooner or later, you will fall into a creative "AHA!" which is a quantum leap and discovery of unconditional love.

Once we can love unconditionally, sex is a choice. We do not need it to make love. The manifestation of true unconditional love demands that you act from your intuition and quantum self in every interaction with your partner. This means that although you will make a brain circuit of every such interaction and behavior, you are behooved not to use a brain circuit for your future interactions. Anything coming from a brain circuit is a conditioned pattern, (liberating as it may be). Instead, you make every attempt to live a tangled hierarchy with your love-partner.

The by-product of all this is that eventually you will be able to engage in this sort of relationship with anyone that comes in your sphere of living simply because you find that you cannot do otherwise. This is the legendary love of Krishna and his gopis (Sanskrit for consorts) celebrated in the Hindu *Vaishnavite* tradition. On special full moon nights, Krishna dances with his ten thousand gopis, all at once. Can Krishna duplicate himself in ten thousand bodies? If you think of Krishna's love as love in space and time as in a brain circuit, you will be puzzled by this legend. Certainly, this must be a metaphor—IT IS!—The unconditional love of Krishna is always celebrated outside of space and time, nonlocally, as relationships with the potentiality of tangled hierarchy that can be manifest with anyone that comes in your sphere of living.

Finally, as previously stated in this book, it is worthy your efforts and energy to learn to live at least one archetype via embodiment in a tangled hierarchical relationship (mental manifestation) which elevates you to happiness of Level 4.

# CHAPTER 24

# The Archetype of Wholeness: A Pathway to Total Healing

After reaching individuation, you explore Level 5 happiness through the examination of the archetype of wholeness with fundamental creativity. This is the healing path to spirituality, healing all sources of conflicts, especially the dichotomies.

Actually, you have been reading about the healing path throughout much of this book. When you heal a disease via situational or fundamental creativity—physical or mental—you are exploring the archetype of wholeness. Whenever you engage in creativity, you balance the transcendent and the immanent, and when you pay attention to your internal experiences—feeling, meaning, and intuition—and approach happiness through them you balance the outer and the inner.

What remains are the male-female dichotomy and the archetypal dichotomies that our ancestors created as part of our collective unconscious. Chakra psychology sheds light on both items.

## Creativity and Chakra Psychology

If you are an average Westerner, you might know little about the chakras and not pay much attention to your visceral feelings. But your brain circuits are active; they and your environmental upbringing determine your behavior. So, like most people, you grow up being guided by the mind and finding security anyway from your physical situation: a good house, a good job, lot of money, and oh yes, a great car. If you have these things, your mind says you are "superior," you feel sanguine that this is true even in others' eyes; after all you all belong to the same culture. If you don't have physical security, of course, you might often feel "inferior" based solely on possessions, status, and lack of wealth.

The main reason to explore the root chakra with creativity is straightforward: realize that your real sense of security comes from your capacity to maintain attentive feeling of vital energy at the root chakra. The mental/cultural superiority/inferiority dynamic no longer applies. When potential danger approaches, pay positive attention to the root chakra. The root chakra energy will then collapse at the navel chakra where there is a tangled hierarchy transformed as courage.

How is it that Gandhi succeeded in his non-violence movement? Because he was rooted. He neither had to fight nor resort to flight, instead he had creative control over his root chakra; he knew to watch his energy. To avoid the automatic fight-flight brain directed response to the adrenal glands, being able to pay attention to your root chakra is a powerful, viable option.

Finally, how do you apply creativity to open a chakra fully, to activate new organ function at the chakra? This is creativity in the vital arena whose job, spiritual traditions say, is to raise the kundalini (see Chapter 12). The creative process used is the same however, do-be-do-be-do. For a starter you can try the four stage Rajneesh meditation: 1.) Shake while standing paying attention to vital movements; 2.) Standing meditation on the movement at the chakras; 3.) Closed eye slow dancing; and 4.) Sitting meditation on the chakras.

The techniques of pranayama and Tai Chi are also do-be-do-be-do practices and carried out diligently with the three I's—Inspiration, Intention, and Intuition—will lead to the fourth I—Insight—which in this case is the rising of kundalini. The optimal functioning of all three highest chakras—throat, brow, and crown, has to do with vital creativity.

There is also *Kapalavati*—the pranayama of radiant forehead that deserves special mention. This one is specifically for opening the brow chakra.

Sit comfortably and start by taking in a small inhalation, and then practice forced exhalation of breath, using only your stomach muscles. Practice this between 20-40 times a minute. When this exercise is done properly, you will experience a few moments of breathlessness when you stop. Take your time to return to normal breathing. Notice that when you are without breath, you are also without thought. This thoughtless state makes way for quantum-self experiences, and you may find a heightened sense of intuition.

### Throat Chakra

This is the chakra of expression. Chakra psychology links the throat chakra with the sex chakra. Indeed, who has not noticed that during the creative flow during the manifestation stage in which the throat chakra is a major actor, there is a tendency of sexual stimulation-but we sublimate and maintain attention on the throat chakra regardless.

As you will recall, I had a very telling experience of kundalini rising (see Chapter 12). In retrospect, the kundalini rise did transform my sexuality enough to include the ability to sublimate! This was crucial for further creative explorations, once again—outer and inner.

Our culture innately knows that freedom of speech is probably the most cherished freedom; and ultimately freedom is about the freedom to create. Where is free speech located? At the throat. When you feel restrained to speak your mind, you inadvertently cover your mouth. Body language comes into play when constrained in such a way as to not speak freely.

Note: the throat chakra energy cannot collapse at the throat chakra; the energy must collapse either at the navel, or the heart, or the brow wherever there is a tangled hierarchy.

### Brow Chakra

The brow is the chakra of rational thinking, but it becomes the chakra of intuitive thought when fully awakened. The feelings are confusion and clarity.

In the Gospel of Thomas, Jesus is quoted as saying, "Those who seek should not stop seeking until they find. When they find, they will be disturbed. When they are disturbed, they will marvel, and will rule overall." When we explore an archetype, the archetype responds with an intuition and indeed, we are troubled, confused; we sense the truth-value, feel it in our gut or heart, but cannot engage rational thinking to fully understand it. However, as we engage the creative process and have an insight, a clarity comes upon us. And then, we can express the creative insight via further descent of consciousness to the throat chakra—the chakra of expression.

Our body language can tell us part of the story. When we try to understand something what are we doing? We are trying to remove our confusion. And where do we feel the concentration? You will notice the muscles between your eyebrows are tense. Only when clarity comes, do those muscles relax.

How do you use your new knowledge to help the creative process? During the phase of do-be-do-be-do, you will notice that the brow chakra warms up. In Hindu mythology, there is the story of the great creative, Siva, deep in practice. A sweet girl Parvati, seeks Siva's attention, but to no avail. Then Cupid, (the God of Love) takes pity on the girl and shoots the arrow of

Eros on Siva. It is said that Siva's brow—the third eye—becomes so hot that it burns not only the arrow but Cupid himself! Much later, in modern times, Freud had an inkling of this aspect of the creative process, and he called it sublimation—a defense mechanism of sorts, in which socially unacceptable impulses are transformed into socially acceptable actions or behaviors. Sublimation helps to keep attention on the brow and vice versa.

However, I think it goes much deeper than mere sublimation. In my book with the physician Valentina R. Onisor, *The Quantum Brain*, we have speculated that there may be a chakra and a "self "at our mid-brain of which we have become unconscious of over time. The brain's hypothalamus in the midbrain which controls the pituitary gland that controls our hormonal system in the body, is also an organ of this chakra. The kundalini awakening of this chakra may help us gain control over the hypothalamus and thus over the hormones and even mood swings. There is some evidence of this in the kundalini literature.

This is the key why the legend goes that a full kundalini awakening opens our intuitive facility to the optimum. With mood swings under control, our capacity to be creative takes a serious quantum leap.

Only when the sixth chakra fully opens, are we capable of creatively engaging with more than one archetype to fruition within the span of one life, and as we do that, we integrate the archetypal dichotomies. Now we are ready for exploring the archetype of wholeness in earnest.

One positive feeling associated with creative opening of the higher chakras is satisfaction. Whenever we open our heart or the throat or the brow, the chakra descent of consciousness has met with success and a deep satisfaction arises. These episodes of satisfaction are fundamentally important for all human beings at every level. If we go through a prolonged period of little or no satisfaction in life, we become depressed.

Psychologists worry that there is now such a rampant outbreak of depression, that it has become the third most prevalent chronic disease. The way quantum psychology looks at it, Prozac is only short-term fix if that. The long-term healing remedy of depression is satisfaction—readily obtainable through engagement of the creative process to cultivate the embodiment of the archetypes in us, especially the archetype of wholeness. No matter what economic level we live on, be it rich, poor, or middle class, everybody in society is entitled to this important feeling of wellness from within.

### Crown Chakra

The biological function that has been realized up to this point, is to produce a body image including and integrating all the vital feelings. The organ is in the posterior superior parietal lobe. When energy moves into this chakra producing excess, we feel okay and connected to our physical body; if energy moves out, we feel distraught, disjointed, and often drained.

The spiritual literature speaks very highly of the potentialities of this chakra. When this chakra further opens, one develops an integrated identity with all of one's bodies—both gross and subtle. This is in part what realizing and embodying the archetype of wholeness is about.

The job of the vital body and mental body creativity is to integrate the physical body identity with the identities of rest of our bodies—vital, mental, and soul! When we learn to do that and combine the force of both mental and vital creativity, we open the door to what Aurobindo would call supramental intelligence. Is humankind ready for that? The next few decades will tell if we evolve and move in a really higher direction that includes transformation, or as a species remain where we are.

As a side benefit, as the crown chakra opens, one also develops the ability to dis-identify with the physical body producing the out-of-the-body experience, a capacity now much documented in some people. But don't be misled; people who have out-of-the-body experience do not necessarily develop the supramental intelligence about wholeness as a result of the experience.

## Integrating Male-Female Dichotomy

The summary of our discussions so far is this: men have more developed body identity at the third navel chakra, but a weakly developed heart chakra identity; women have the opposite tendency, weak navel chakra and strong heart. So, the male-female behavioral difference: most men are more self-oriented; they don't know how to love another. However, women are more other-love oriented and while they know how to love another, often they do not know how to love themselves. The cause of the male-female difference is partly sociocultural and partly brain-built.

When we develop sensitivity to our feelings at the chakras, we take the most important first step toward the integration. As men discover their heart chakra by direct experience even in non-romantic relationships, they are surprised to find that they don't really have to be the "iron men" they try to be. Similarly, when women discover their navel chakra and self-worth, they find they don't have to join the lonely-hearts club if they don't have some man to love.

In this way, emotional intelligence that begins with the making of positive emotional brain circuits becomes mature with the integration of male-female dichotomy of chakra-identity.

Some time ago, I saw a play named *Cloud Nine*. One of its episodes is about a lonely older woman who never masturbated. In the last quite touching scene, this woman learns to do it; this is depicted on the stage as the woman dancing with herself and waking up to self-love and emotional intelligence.

## Inner Fundamental Creativity: Exploring the Archetype of Wholeness

Integration of the three major dichotomies of the human condition is a major step of the preparation stage of the creative process for the exploration of wholeness. In all those integrations so far, you have employed situational creativity. Now you want to explore the archetype itself in its suchness. So, the creative process here is that of fundamental creativity.

To recap, the basic process here is do-be-do-be-do. The purpose of "do" is to create new ideas of imagination—divergent thinking—as seeds for expansion into full-blown possibility pools via the "be" phase of unconscious processing for consciousness to choose from. Ideas may come, integrative ideas, so you must be on the lookout for the element of surprise as well as the element of conviction.

If you are ill with one of those diseases that are chronic conditions—cancer, heart disease, clinical depression—you should approach the healing path and the exploration of wholeness, with the help and collaboration of a medical professional. Since our interest is more in healing the mental/emotional, let's discuss depression as an example. You may wonder if this is appropriate since we are discussing positive mental health. I submit to you that it is very appropriate and make no mistake, it fits the bill. Many mystics talk about the "dark night of the soul." They are talking about depression of a specific kind (and it can last much longer than just one night!) In the search for wholeness, depression (which is an intensely felt lack of wholeness) is often the result. You have actually found the problem: what is the worth of human life if we are not whole?

How does a therapist help? All mental health practitioners are interested in their own wholeness; that is why they have chosen their profession (we teach what most need to learn) So, a trusted therapist can give additional help by providing fodder for unconscious processing. It is like allowing a double slit arrangement for the unconscious processing of your thoughts-and can be very effective. If in the course of therapy, your therapist becomes what you call an "intimate relationship," you two can even disagree setting up a conflicted dynamic as illustrated by Picasso's drawing, *The Minotaur* (*Figure18*).

*Figure 18: The Minotaur by Pablo Picasso*
*(artist's rendition)*

This thesis and antithesis set up even more possibilities for consciousness to choose from, new possibilities. Then the creative insight comes, the much-anticipated quantum leap.

How do you manifest the archetype of wholeness so discovered in fundamental creativity? You live the discovered truth about wholeness in your relationships. Your relationships then become a tangled hierarchical incorporating the newly discovered meaning.

## Level 5 Happiness: Quantum Enlightenment

Are you curious if it is possible to live in a state of continuous flow? When we manifest the creative insight in the manifestation stage, a playful encounter takes place between the ego and the quantum self-the flow experience. Every time we engage in fundamental creativity to discover new meaning in a new archetypal context, we can either further explore the new context by many investigations of situational creativity or alternatively, we can investigate a different archetype and go through the same process creating more ongoing experiences of flow.

In fact, we can set up a life with a network of creative enterprises in which each enterprise picks up the slack when we are resting from another. In this effort, outer creativity is equally effective as inner. In this way, our life becomes an ongoing flow experience. This is one way of joyful living with the ongoing touch of the quantum self. What is it like? The words of Walt Whitman describe it as such:

> *"To me, every hour of the light and dark is a miracle*
> *Every inch of space is miracle*

*Every square yard of the surface of the earth*
*is spread with the same*
*Every cubic foot of the interior swarms with*
*the same."*

(Whitman, *The Leaves of Grass*, p. 165.)

This is the sort of quantum living that is very appropriate for the transformation-oriented people of quantum worldview in the 21st century: living with one foot firmly on the ground—strong authentic ego and all—and the other foot in the fluidity of the miraculous quantum self. I call this state the *bodhisattva* state of quantum enlightenment, a joyful state of consciousness full of what Indians call *ānanda*.

This would be considered a Level 5 state of happiness.

# CHAPTER 25

# Perfect Happiness: The Final Stage of Traditional Enlightenment

As the Buddha said, nothing is permanent. So, it is conceivable that for some people, even the *bodhisattva* state eventually becomes boring, a condition that is called *vairagya* (in Sanskrit). The closest concept I can find in English was coined by the late mystic Franklin Merrell-Wolff, a term he called- high indifference.

I once asked Franklin how he solved the problem with sexuality that plagues so many spiritual aspirants. He said, "I don't know. I had sex only once in my life. That was enough." Naturally he himself developed high indifference pretty early on and achieved enlightenment in the traditional style at the age of 49 and would go on to devote his 98 years on the planet, to transcending human consciousness.

When high indifference hits us, even the creative exploration of archetypes does not satisfy, and there is only one thing to do: to get out of the game of birth-death-rebirth altogether. Hindus call this liberation and Buddhists have a similar concept of nirvana—a cessation of desire. The strategy consists of the exploration of the self-archetype.

When we creatively discover the primary nature of the self, that I am the quantum self, we are called *self-realized*: we know we are the quantum self, that the ego is a secondary epiphenomenon. Why identify with the epiphenomenon when you know reality? Thus, begins the journey of manifestation of the unmitigated quantum way of living.

There are many subtleties of this journey, so let me share this analogy. Imagine you in your ego-identity are a salt figurine and taking a swim in the ocean. Your ego-identity will dissolve, right?

So, after the dissolution of the ego-identity, who are you? Some people today bypass high indifference and explore self-realization without proper preparation. They follow the creative process and will have the "AHA!" insight. What then? They are not ready to give up the fruit of their insight which requires a strong ego! So, they do all kinds of egotistic things beginning with writing a book at once proclaiming their enlightenment.

When instead, you first earn your right to investigate the self-archetype—detachment from accomplishments, and you go through the manifestation stage of creativity and identify with the quantum self, you have no place to stand on; quantum self is forever dynamic. Your ego is dissolved in the ocean of oneness, so you need to learn to spend much of your time in the wholeness of the ocean. This is part of the manifestation process. Is that possible? Isn't that living in the unconscious? How is it different from deep sleep then?

## The Fourth State of Consciousness and the Highest Level of Happiness

I have previously discussed an enigmatic kind of Samadhi, called Nirvikalpa Samadhi (see Chapter 6). Nirvikalpa means "without split," without subject-object separation. There are two kinds of Nirvikalpa. The lower kind signifies a state of consciousness called *Turiya*.

To understand this concept, consider deep sleep, in which there is no subject-object split and there is no experience. Yet we have no problem accepting that we all sleep. It is an accepted state of consciousness. Nirvikalpa Samadhi or *Turiya* has to be understood as a deeper sleep in which some special unconscious processing takes place, which is cognized as memory only at the moment of waking via delayed choice.

Clearly *Turiya* is the ultimate state of unconscious processing possible to discuss within quantum psychology. While in the state of *Turiya*, consciousness processes the entire world of quantum possibilities, including the archetypes.

A Christian mystic,Brother Lawrence, correctly calls this *Turiya* state "Living in the presence of God." Some people call this a separate stage of personal growth—God realization.

So, what does this say about transformation? There

is a claim in the spiritual literature of India that people of Nirvikalpa capacity of achieving *Turiya* are totally transformed; their identity completely shifts to the quantum self, except when the ego is needed for everyday chores, for ego-functions.

This also means that the unconscious now processes more or less only new quantum possibilities. Quantum leaping to the archetypes and making mental representations of them would now require little effort—*Sahaja* (Sanskrit word meaning *easy*) Samadhi. Archetypal wisdom now would become easy without much effort. You don't really need to go through the rigor of all those creative investigation of the individual archetypes as discussed in the last chapter. This is why sometimes this level of enlightenment is defined as a state knowing which allows you to know everything.

This state of *Turiya* is also a most joyful state of consciousness, the highest state of happiness conceivable. Indians call the joy in this state as *Turiyananda*—to distinguish it from the ānanda—the joy of flow consciousness. This then, is the true perfection of happiness—Level 6.

There is a state of consciousness, a "higher" Nirvikalpa that a few mystics claim, and they call it consciousness in its suchness, no attributes. So, nobody can talk about it. It is also beyond all quantum science. The great philosopher Ludwig Wittgenstein said, "Whereof one cannot speak, thereof one must be silent."

Good advice.

# The Quantum Eight-Fold Way: Your Path to Happiness

Finally, the time has arrived to give you a comprehensive, eight-point summary, of what you need to do on your journey, to go from a pleasure-centered mechanical life (with added emotional roller coaster rides to keep it interesting) to a happiness centered human life. But first, this reminder. In the Bhagavad Gita which is written as a dialog between the quantum self and the ego, Krishna (representing quantum self) tells Arjuna (representing authentic human seeker) at the end of the discourse, "Arjuna, I have told you everything about how to arrive at psychological and spiritual wholeness; now you act as dictated by your own free will." This list is given with the same appeal and needless to repeat, we have given you all the reasoning and scientific data behind these final "do's" enough to enable you to make up your own mind. There are eight steps in your journey; so, you could also call it a quantum version of the eightfold way that the illustrious Buddha gave to humanity millennia ago:

1.  Work simultaneously on five fronts.

    a.  Get a grip on right thinking and that means the quantum worldview, make it your own. Consult this book whenever necessary.

    b.  Begin the journey from information processing to meaning processing. Try to understand it your way what somebody is saying before you tuck it away as relevant information.

    c.  Clean up the subconscious of memories of emotional trauma and replace your expression/suppression habit to handle emotion with meditation.

    d.  Develop sensitivity to feelings in the body and the chakras.

    e.  Start working toward acquiring all the skill sets discussed in Chapter 19. If you started with happiness Level 1, take a quantum leap of healing. At the end of this step, you will have graduated from a hu-machine to become a hu-person of not only IQ machine intelligence but also real mental intelligence. Your happiness is a steady Level 2.

6.  Use the tool kit of healing from this book as necessary in living situations. This will help you construct a healthy belief system, different perspectives to look at things, build and express authenticity, healing of your emotional wounds,

etc. Happiness Level is 2+ what Maslow called positive mental health and steadily progressing.

7. Use the creative process of situational creativity (Chapter 23) to build positive emotional brain circuits. This will endow you with emotional intelligence so you can thrive in your relationships with yourself and others. You can even begin to integrate reason and emotion. Your happiness is now at Level 3.

8. Use inner fundamental creativity to explore and embody one of the major archetypes except the wholeness and the self-archetype. Again, these are: truth, love, beauty, abundance, goodness, justice, power. You are now individuated and reached happiness Level 4.

9. Start earnestly working on balancing what remains unbalanced of the three fundamental dichotomies: the transcendent/immanent, inner/outer, and the male/female. You mainly work with your chakras trying to make them wide open. You are now an all-around intelligent individual. Fundamental conflicts are getting resolved, you now can make huge progress in your work on being authentic in your ego—making your personas fully congruent with your character. You can also work more on integrating reason and emotions. So far, the process is non-linear, meaning that you do not have to take the order above very seriously. Your

happiness is now Level 4+ and you are getting ready for the final plunge into happiness Level 5, and from here on the order is linear.

10. Integrate, integrate, integrate. Integrate all the dichotomies completely—male-female, inner-outer, transcendent-immanent. Explore, realize, and begin to embody the realized aspects of all of the above major archetypes integrating all their dichotomies. You now have the capacity of living in flow via continuing the journey of embodiment of these archetypes, and you do this for many incarnations. You have achieved a modern form of enlightenment appropriate for our age— quantum enlightenment—living in perpetual flow. Your happiness is at Level 5 and you have the capacity of living an enchanted life in flow with your quantum self. To increase your enchantment, you can explore other minor archetypes, too and go on for even more incarnations. Our recommendation is for you to stay here at this station of happiness level 5 till the end of time and help others to be more human, happy, and intelligent until all of humanity achieves all the happiness they need. Traditionally, people would then call you a *bodhisattva*.

11. If anytime in happiness Level5, you pass the entrance requirement of high indifference towards worldly accomplishments, you can opt to explore and embody the self-archetype and achieve Nir-

vikalpa state of Samadhi without subject-object split. You have the ability of knowing all that is important for you to know with little or no effort. In other words, you have easy access to all potentialities of the quantum universe. The irony of course, is why would you want to access them? You have achieved happiness Level 6. You are now enlightened in the traditional way.

12. Explore going beyond all attributes and qualifications, beyond the potentialities of the quantum universe when you are in Nirvikalpa Samadhi of the *Turiya* state. When you reach the state beyond all qualifications such as the quantum laws of physics, you go beyond happiness, beyond all labeling. For you, the game is essentially over. We'll know for sure if anyone ever reaches this level, as this bloom of consciousness has no happiness or other index, no name, only fragrance.

# RECOMMENDED READING

Aurobindo, Sri. *The Essentials of Yoga*. Pondicherry, India: Aurobindo Ashram

Aurobindo, S. (1996). *The Life Divine*. Pondicherry, India: Sri Aurobindo Ashram

Briggs, J. (1990). *Fire in the Crucible*. L.A.: Tarcher/Penguin

Chopra, D. (2000). *Perfect Health*. N. Y.: Three Rivers Press

Goswami, A. (1993). *The Self-Aware Universe: How Consciousness Creates the Material World*. N.Y.: Tarcher/Putnam.

Goswami, A. (1994). *Science Within Consciousness: a Monograph*. Petaluma, CA: Institute of Noetic Sciences.

Goswami, A. (2000). *The Visionary Window: A Quantum Physicist's Guide to Enlightenment*. Wheaton, IL: Quest Books.

Goswami, A. (2001). *Physics of the Soul*. Charlottesville, VA: Hampton Roads.

Goswami, A. (2004). *The Quantum Doctor*. Charlottesville, VA: Hampton Roads.

Goswami, A. (2008). *God is not Dead*. Charlottesville, VA: Hampton Roads.

Goswami, A. (2008). *Creative Evolution*. Wheaton, IL: Theosophical Publishing House.

Goswami, A. (2014). *Quantum Creativity: Think Quantum, Be Creative*. N. Y.: Hay House.

Goswami, A. (2019) and Onisor, R. V. (2019. *Quantum Spirituality*. Delhi, India: Blue Rose.

Goswami, A. and Onisor, R. V. (2021). *The Quantum*

*Brain*. Delhi, India: Blue Rose.

Grof, S. *The Cosmic Game*.

Jung, C. J. (1971). *The Portable Jung*.

Pattani, S. (2015). *The Transcended Mind*.

Penrose, R. (1991). *The Emperor's New Mind*. N.Y.: Penguin.

Pert, C. (1997). *Molecules of Emotion*. N.Y.: Scribner.

Radin, D. (2009). *The Noetic Universe*. London: Transworld Publishers.

Searle, J. (1994). *The Rediscovery of the Mind*. Cambridge, MA: MIT Press.

Sheldrake, R. (1981). *A New Science of Life*. L.A.: Tarcher.

Teilhard de Chardin, P. (1961). *The Phenomenon of Man*. N.Y.: Harper & Row.

Wilber, K. *The Atman Project*. Boulder, CO: Shambhal

**AMIT GOSWAMI, PHD** is a retired professor of physics from the University of Oregon where he served from 1968-1997. In 1985, he discovered the solution to the quantum measurement problem and developed a science of experience explicating how consciousness splits into subject and object. Subsequently, he developed a theory of reincarnation and integrated conventional and alternative medicine within the new quantum science of health. Among his discoveries are the quantum theory of the creative process, the theory of quantum evolution, the science of love and happiness, the theory of *quantum economics* that extends Adam's Smith's capitalism into a workable paradigm for the 21st century, and the theory of *quantum spirituality* based on the exploration of wholeness.

In 1999, Amit started a movement called quantum activism, now gaining ground in North and South America, Europe, and India. In 2018, he and his collaborators established Quantum Activism Vishwa-layam, an institution of transformative education in India, based on quantum science and the primacy of consciousness.

Amit is the author of numerous books, most notably: *The Self- Aware Universe, Physics of the Soul, The Quantum Brain* (with Valentina Onisor), *The Quantum Doctor, God is Not Dead, Quantum Creativity, The Everything Answer Book, Quantum Spirituality* (with Valentina Onisor), *Quantum Activation* (with Carl Blake and Gary Stuart). He was featured in the movie *What the Bleep Do We Know!?* and the documentaries *Dalai Lama Renaissance* and *The Quantum Activist.*

Amit is a spiritual practitioner and calls himself a quantum activist in search of Wholeness.

**SUNITA PATTANI, M. SC.** is a psychotherapist based in the UK. She is particularly interested in how the quantum worldview informs psychotherapeutic practice, and currently specializes in using energy psychology to treat psychological trauma. Sunita is a graduate of the University of Birmingham, where she obtained a degree in Mathematics, Science and Education in 2003, followed by a Postgraduate Certificate in Education (PGCE) in 2004.

She taught for five years before studying an advanced Diploma in Hypnotherapy and Psychotherapeutic Counselling. She has since studied a number of additional energy psychology healing modalities and has recently obtained her MSc. in Consciousness, Spirituality and Transpersonal Psychology. Sunita is currently studying a doctorate in psychological trauma.

Sunita is also the author of: *My Secret Affairs with Chocolate Cake, The Transcendent Mind.*

# INDEX

## A

abundance 25, 27, 40, 53, 208, 211, 321, 375
acupuncture 293
addiction 3, 10, 42, 44, 45, 47, 51, 68, 73, 286
AHA! 126
AHA! experiences 198
Albert Einstein 83, 133
Alzheimer 128
amygdala 155, 156, 261, 262, 272, 273
ānanda 9, 59, 223, 368, 372
ānandamaya kosha 224
anima 46, 47, 247, 248, 249, 320
animus 46, 247, 248, 249
anterior cingulate cortex 262
archetype 40, 43, 45, 47, 52, 53, 64, 116, 136, 138, 167, 168,
        170, 171, 172, 176, 195, 196, 201, 208, 212, 213, 229, 233,
        243, 247, 248, 249, 263, 289, 295, 301, 302, 319, 320, 321,
        333, 334, 335, 336, 338, 346, 355, 356, 360, 361, 362, 363,
        365, 367, 370, 375, 376
attention 3, 44, 46, 50, 70, 72, 75, 77, 98, 100, 120, 145, 146,
        147, 148, 149, 153, 158, 163, 183, 189, 205, 212, 222, 229,
        238, 241, 243, 244, 246, 253, 265, 282, 291, 292, 303, 304,
        320, 329, 339, 343, 356, 357, 358, 359, 360
Aurobindo 167, 168, 214, 319, 363, 379

## B

Benjamin Libet 186
Berkeley 60, 92, 93, 95
Bhagavad Gita 373
Bishop 319
Brahman 105
brain 1, 10, 11, 14, 15, 16, 17, 18, 23, 26, 27, 28, 29, 31, 32, 33,
        34, 35, 36, 38, 39, 40, 41, 42, 43, 44, 46, 47, 51, 52, 57, 64,
        89, 91, 93, 94, 95, 96, 97, 98, 99, 100, 101, 106, 112, 113,
        114, 122, 124, 127, 130, 135, 137, 138, 146, 147, 148, 150,

151, 154, 155, 156, 159, 164, 165, 167, 170, 174, 175, 177,
186, 187, 192, 210, 214, 215, 219, 220, 221, 230, 233, 234,
238, 239, 246, 247, 248, 249, 250, 252, 253, 254, 256, 257,
258, 261, 266, 268, 272, 273, 274, 285, 294, 305, 306, 307,
314, 315, 316, 332, 333, 334, 337, 338, 340, 347, 348, 350,
354, 357, 358, 361, 364, 375
BRAIN WAVES  33
brow chakra  153, 157, 259, 358, 360
Buddha  305, 369, 373

# C

Carl Blake  206, 382
chakras  47, 63, 120, 141, 142, 143, 144, 145, 152, 153, 154, 156,
159, 168, 185, 198, 246, 247, 254, 258, 260, 293, 308, 309,
322, 329, 357, 358, 362, 364, 374, 375
Chinese Medicine  173, 293
cognitive neuroscience  23
collapse  93, 95, 98, 131, 167, 192, 211, 265, 306, 348, 357, 359
corpus callosum  274
creative process  77, 103, 131, 188, 194, 198, 226, 227, 262, 281,
296, 317, 330, 333, 337, 340, 346, 349, 358, 360, 362, 365,
370, 375, 381
Crown Chakra  362

# D

Daniel Goleman  305
delayed choice  106, 108, 109, 268, 277, 336, 371
dependent co-arising  95
DHARMA  212
DICHOTOMIES  45, 236, 250
discontinuity  126, 188, 191, 193, 240, 281, 296
do-be-do  103, 189, 191, 198, 226, 304, 308, 317, 340, 349, 358,
360, 365
do-be-do-be-do  296, 308, 349
Doug Hofstadter  97
downward causation  28, 100, 102, 103, 122, 210, 225
Drawing Hands  351, 352

## E

ego character 208

emotional intelligence 3, 52, 53, 76, 141, 161, 215, 333, 337, 364, 375

enlightenment 3, 4, 7, 48, 53, 54, 63, 64, 133, 134, 172, 235, 335, 336, 368, 369, 370, 372, 376

entanglement 32, 113

evolution 90, 121, 137, 146, 154, 157, 159, 164, 199, 211, 212, 226, 227, 229, 247, 381

## F

fight-flight 273, 358

fight or fight 273

five bodies 223, 224, 242

flow experience 104, 184, 194, 209, 281, 283, 367

fMRI 333

Franklin Merrell Wolff 297

Fred Alan Wolf 102

free will 2, 18, 76, 185, 187, 373

fundamental creativity 53, 207, 209, 210, 215, 234, 245, 253, 317, 333, 334, 343, 346, 356, 365, 367, 375

## G

Gandhi 215, 319, 357

genes 129, 138, 139, 254

gunas 207, 209, 210, 252, 279

## H

hippocampus 261, 273, 277

homeostasis 299

hyperactivity 253, 254, 255, 256, 257, 263

hypothalamus 361

## I

imbalance 257

immanent 22, 23, 43, 45, 47, 52, 79, 90, 103, 206, 207, 219, 221,

232, 236, 356, 375, 376
immune system  150, 157, 158, 165, 258, 259
incubation  188, 191
information processing  27, 43, 48, 163, 334, 374
inner creativity  51, 65, 183, 226, 228, 283, 311, 317, 318, 319,
        321, 329, 330, 332, 333, 342, 343
INNER-OUTER DICHOTOMY  238
insight  8, 71, 96, 126, 188, 191, 192, 193, 226, 229, 286, 296,
        332, 334, 336, 340, 342, 346, 360, 366, 367, 370
Inspiration, Intention  3, 194, 358
intellectualism  255
intimate relationship  52, 148, 257, 258, 350, 351, 366
intuition  25, 26, 27, 28, 40, 70, 97, 111, 112, 116, 118, 120, 122,
        136, 167, 168, 181, 187, 189, 226, 233, 238, 331, 342, 343,
        354, 356, 359, 360

## J

Jacobo Grinberg  32, 34, 195
Jesus  44, 94, 173, 339, 341, 360
Jiddu Krishnamurti  333
John Searle  39, 125
John von Neumann  91

## K

Kabbala  9
Kali  108
Karma  199, 201, 203, 205
kundalini awakening  197, 361

## L

left brain  306
limbic brain  154
Lisa Miller  14

## M

mantra  58, 262, 291
Mario Beauregard  154

material body  16, 24
maya  16, 28
M. C. Escher  352
me-centeredness  10, 42, 299, 338
mental body  223, 242, 363
mental intelligence  374
metaphysics  10, 60, 61, 68, 91, 106, 109, 120, 129
midbrain  146, 272, 361
mind-brain  252, 253, 254
mindfulness  189, 274, 292, 304, 307, 317
miracle  367
miracles  288
morality  174, 175, 249
movement of consciousness  56, 171, 194, 195, 196, 288, 300,
        319, 322
mystic  60, 93, 105, 108, 214, 297, 321, 333, 369, 371

## N

navel chakra  148, 149, 157, 159, 349, 357, 363, 364
near-death experience  109, 295
negative emotional brain circuits  10, 164, 333
Nelson Mandela  215
neuroscience  12, 33, 34, 101, 158, 282, 307
neurosis  10, 11, 13, 31, 49, 50, 78, 81, 118, 120, 147, 162, 163,
        183, 189, 277, 296, 332
Niels Bohr  21, 84, 191
NirvikalpaSamādhi  54
nonlocality  21, 23, 33, 34, 41, 61, 84, 90, 94, 126, 139, 154, 286,
        288, 297, 302, 313

## O

outer creativity  51, 193, 226, 228, 283, 318, 319, 330, 342, 367

## P

parietal lobe  154, 362
Penrose, R.  380
perception  34, 35, 72, 99, 100, 101, 116, 117, 127, 231, 233,

241, 271, 279, 280, 281, 286, 287, 288, 289, 296, 310
persona  42, 174, 178, 179, 180, 181, 183, 185, 209, 220, 222, 228, 234, 235, 256, 289, 301, 321, 327, 329
Physics of the Soul  ii, 63, 379, 382
pituitary gland  361
pleasure circuits  10, 38, 42, 47
Pranayama  309
preconscious  109, 180, 341
prefrontal cortex  153, 305, 306, 307

# Q

Quantum Activation  ii, 206, 382
Quantum Activism  ii, 216, 382
quantum healing  263
quantum leap  21, 22, 191, 198, 229, 250, 296, 332, 341, 352, 353, 354, 361, 366, 374
quantum self  29, 30, 33, 34, 36, 40, 41, 42, 43, 48, 53, 55, 101, 105, 168, 173, 177, 178, 179, 180, 181, 183, 184, 185, 186, 192, 193, 195, 207, 208, 209, 210, 220, 221, 222, 223, 229, 240, 266, 283, 284, 300, 308, 318, 319, 330, 333, 341, 343, 354, 367, 368, 370, 372, 373, 376
Quantum Spirituality  ii, 198, 346, 382
quantum thinking  338
quantum worldview  1, 2, 8, 12, 46, 47, 55, 71, 72, 106, 134, 172, 174, 194, 216, 219, 368, 374, 383
quantum yoga  64, 65

# R

rajas  208, 209, 210, 214, 215, 262
Ramakrishna  108, 251
Recall  184, 290, 329
reincarnation  62, 136, 201, 202, 206, 209, 262, 381
retrieval  iv, 127, 128
reward circuit  315
Richard Davidson  305
Richard Moss  143
right brain  274
root chakra  145, 146, 147, 357

Rupert Sheldrake 138

## S

sattva 207, 209, 210, 214, 215, 252
Savikalpa Samadhi 105
scale of happiness 48, 223, 228, 291
See the World as a Five Layered Cake ii
sex chakra 147, 348, 359
Shiva 161
simple hierarchy 97, 98, 289, 351
situational creativity 52, 208, 215, 233, 253, 284, 289, 333, 334, 337, 341, 342, 343, 346, 349, 353, 365, 367, 375
slow food 172
spontaneous healing 296
Stan Grof 230, 327
stomach 294, 358
subject-object split 45, 101, 105, 172, 210, 220, 236, 371, 377
supramental body 135, 223
supramental intelligence 363
Susan Blackmore 99
Swami Vivekananda 13, 251
synchronicity 62, 120, 131, 133, 204, 226, 241, 311, 329

## T

Tai Chi 172, 358
tamas 209, 210, 214, 231, 254
tangled hierarchy 97, 98, 99, 100, 118, 137, 145, 157, 158, 159, 167, 221, 288, 302, 351, 352, 354, 355, 357, 359
thalamus 156
the quantum science of happiness 39, 41, 45, 54, 104
third eye 361
throat chakra 153, 359, 360
transcendent 21, 22, 43, 45, 47, 52, 79, 81, 82, 88, 89, 90, 102, 103, 170, 206, 219, 221, 228, 236, 283, 356, 375, 376
transferred potential 33, 34, 195
transpersonal 1, 9, 13, 16, 20, 22, 27, 31, 37, 38, 40, 61, 74, 101, 120, 220, 221, 282, 327, 337, 342
transpersonal psychology 9, 13, 16, 20, 22, 61, 74, 282

trauma  3, 41, 71, 189, 237, 259, 265, 266, 267, 271, 272, 273,
     274, 275, 276, 277, 281, 283, 293, 295, 308, 314, 374, 383
Turiya  108, 223, 336, 371, 372, 377

## U

unconscious  8, 22, 23, 27, 28, 30, 31, 34, 45, 47, 67, 73, 76, 78,
     81, 82, 89, 90, 99, 100, 102, 105, 108, 109, 127, 132, 146,
     148, 151, 155, 161, 162, 164, 165, 166, 171, 172, 174, 186,
     190, 191, 193, 196, 202, 206, 214, 219, 223, 224, 230, 231,
     233, 236, 237, 241, 247, 249, 250, 265, 266, 267, 268, 276,
     288, 293, 295, 304, 306, 337, 338, 340, 341, 342, 349, 350,
     351, 356, 361, 365, 366, 371, 372
unconscious processing  172, 190, 191, 214, 215, 293, 338, 342,
     349, 350, 351, 365, 366, 371
Upanishads  111, 113, 221, 224, 290

## V

Vedanta  9, 10, 22, 28, 94
vital body  110, 115, 137, 143, 168, 201, 223, 242, 243, 244, 258,
     260, 283, 294, 308, 348, 350, 363
V-organ  142, 143, 144

## W

W. E. Hill  56
working memory  128

## Z

Zen Koans  130

Made in the USA
Middletown, DE
26 June 2022